ELIZABETHAN MYTHOLOGIES

Studies in poetry, drama and music

ROBIN HEADLAM WELLS

Senior Lecturer in English
University of Hull

CAMBRIDGE
UNIVERSITY PRESS

Published by the Press Syndicate of the University of Cambridge
The Pitt Building, Trumpington Street, Cambridge CB2 IRP
40 West 20th Street, New York, NY 10011–4211, USA
10 Stamford Road, Oakleigh, Melbourne 3166, Australia

First published 1994

Printed in Great Britain at the University Press, Cambridge

A catalogue record for this book is available from the British Library

Library of Congress cataloguing in publication data
Wells, Robin Headlam.
Elizabethan mythologies : studies in poetry, drama, and music /
Robin Headlam Wells.
p.   cm.
Includes bibliographical references.
ISBN 0 521 43385 1
1. English literature – Early modern, 1500–1700 – History and criticism.
2. Music and literature – England – History – 16th century.
3. Music – England – 16th century – History and criticism.
4. English literature – Greek influences.
5. Mythology, Greek, in literature.
6. Symbolism in literature.
7. Music and mythology.
8. Symbolism in music.
I. Title.
PB428.M8W45   1994
820.9′15 – dc20   93–11944   CIP

ISBN 0 521 43385 1 hardback

Music examples set by Da Capo Music Ltd, Hedon, East Yorkshire *for Jenny*

Contents

ix

Illustrations

Preface

The essays that go to make up this book were written over a number of years in between work on other projects. During this period the world of Renaissance studies has been transformed by the advent of new approaches to historical scholarship. New Historicism and Cultural Materialism, as the American and the British versions of the new movement are known, owe much to the post-structuralist Marxism popularized by Louis Althusser and the revisionist historicism of his Sorbonne pupil Michel Foucault; they seek to locate Renaissance texts in contexts that are said to have been ignored or marginalized by traditional Renaissance scholarship. As Terence Hawkes puts it, 'the project involves ... reinserting [texts] into the cultural history of their own time ... and merging them back into the context of the circulating discourses from which "English" has prised them'.[1]

My own debt to the new post-structuralist historicism will be evident if I say that I recognize that Elizabethan preoccupation with the power of words and music is the score, to borrow a metaphor of Althusser's, of an essentially ideological concert. What is not clear to me is how traditional scholarship, in recovering the psychological, social, political and intellectual environment in which the Renaissance writer lived and worked, has managed to prise literature free from its cultural context. Because I do not share Hawkes' contempt for the traditional historical scholarship on which the new historicisms are so heavily dependent,[2] I shall not be setting out to expose 'the resounding failure of ... humanist criticism' to provide a theoretical account of itself;[3] nor do I intend to contribute to 'the current endeavour within radical criticism to contest and displace ... established interpretations of canonical literary works'.[4] In fact, I shall not even attempt to impose a single thesis on the heterogeneous materials I discuss. Though I am interested in the politics of art, I do not believe that the cause of criticism is best advanced by repeatedly putting the same questions: if you start from the premise that every text either colludes with or resists oppression (an approach that characterizes recent musical as well as literary criticism),[5] it will not be surprising if you tend to come up with some rather predictable conclusions. If I am able to offer new readings of some Elizabethan plays, songs and other cultural artefacts, these are probably best seen, not as radical correctives to the ineptitudes of my predecessors in the field of Renaissance ideas of music and musical harmony, but as tributes to the work of critics whose originality and scholarship I cannot hope to emulate. Chief among these I count G. L. Finney, S. K. Heninger, Jr, John Hollander, James Hutton, Kathi Meyer-Baer, Claude V. Palisca, Bruce Pattison, Leo Spitzer, John Stevens, D. P. Walker and Frances Yates, though of course there are many more. I list those in my notes.

Inevitably some important works have appeared while this book was in press. Among them Peggy Muñoz Simonds' *Myth, Emblem, and Music in Shakespeare's 'Cymbeline'* and Brian Vickers' *Appropriating Shakespeare* require mention for the bearing they have on two of my central concerns in the pages that follow, the first for its learned treatment of the Orpheus myth in the Renaissance, the second for its relentlessly sceptical interrogation of the philosophical and linguistic bases of modern literary theory. Had they appeared a year or two earlier both would have saved me much time.

Over the years I have been working intermittently on these essays I have learnt much from the discussions of historicism, traditional and otherwise, that I have had with Tom McAlindon. I owe him special thanks. Friendly acknowledgment is also due to James Booth, Andrew Gurr, Owen Knowles, John Milsom, Anthony Pratt, Anthony Rooley, György Szőnyi, Bruce Woodcock, and Rowland Wymer for helpful criticism and advice; to Graham Sadler and Shirley Thompson for generous assistance with musical analysis and transcription; to Poppy Holden for showing me, in the course of our recitals, that the belief of Renaissance humanists in the magical power of song was not misplaced; and to Phil Lourie for helping me to understand the iconography of the orpharion and other instruments he built for me. I am also grateful to my anonymous publisher's readers for saving me from many errors. Those that remain I attribute, not to the inscriptions of ideology, but to my own ignorance.

Acknowledgment of another kind is due to the British Academy for supporting my visit to the Huntington Library as an Exchange Fellow in Spring 1987, and to the Leverhulme Trust for generous assistance in meeting research and publication costs. I am grateful to all three institutions, and especially to the Huntington Library staff for their 'sweete semblaunt, friendly offices that bynde, / And all the complements of curtesie' (*Faerie Queene*, VI.x.23).

Chapter 1 first appeared in a different form in the *Huntington Library Quarterly*, chapters 4, 5, 6 and 8 in *Early Music*, and chapter 7 in *Music and Letters*. Chapter 2 is a substantially revised version of an article written in collaboration with Alison Birkinshaw and published in *Shakespeare Studies*. I am grateful to Oxford University Press and to the editors of these journals for permission to reprint articles in a revised form. For permission to reproduce material in their keeping I thank the Bodleian Library (illus. 2), The British Library (illus. 4, 28), Painton Cowen (illus. 7, 16), Groeningemuseum, Bruges (illus. 3), Keysersche Verlagsbuchhandlung (illus. 34), Librairie Larousse and Reed International Books (illus. 38), Phil Lourie (illus. 18, 22), Museo Nacional del Prado, Madrid and Bridgman Art Library (illus. 12), Museo del Tempio di Venere, Pompeii (illus. 33), Nationalbibliothek, Vienna (illus. 14), National Gallery, London (illus. 36), Princeton University Library (illus. 8), John Pringle (illus. 31, 32), Sadea editore, Florence (illus. 13), Fundación Colección Thyssen-Bornemisza, Madrid (illus. 35), Villa Farnese, Caprarola (illus. 5), Lawrence Witten (illus. 21).

Abbreviations

Periodicals and series

AM	Annales Musicologiques
BJRL	Bulletin of the John Rylands Library
CE	Cahiers Elisabethains
CI	Critical Inquiry
CJ	Cambridge Journal
CL	Comparative Literature
CLS	Comparative Literature Studies
CM	Classica et medievalia
CQ	Critical Quarterly
ECS	Eighteenth-Century Studies
EETS	Early English Text Society
ELH	Journal of English Literary History
ELR	English Literary Renaissance
EM	Early Music
EngM	English Miscellany
ES	English Studies
EStud	Essays and Studies
GSJ	Galpin Society Journal
HUCA	Hebrew Union College Annual
IRASM	International Review of the Aesthetics and Sociology of Music
JEGP	Journal of English and Germanic Philology
JMT	Journal of Music Theory
JWCI	Journal of the Warburg and Courtauld Institutes
Lib	The Library
LRB	London Review of Books
LSJ	Lute Society Journal
ML	Music and Letters
MLN	Modern Language Notes

MLQ   Modern Language Quarterly
MLR   Modern Language Review
MQ   Musical Quarterly
MR   Music Review
NLR   New Left Review
NQ   Notes and Queries
NYRB   New York Review of Books
OLR   Oxford Literary Review
PLMA   Proceedings of the London Musical Association
PMLA   Publications of the Modern Language Association of America
PRMA   Proceedings of the Royal Musical Association
PQ   Philological Quarterly
RenQ   Renaissance Quarterly
RES   Review of English Studies
Rhet   Rhetorica
RP   Romance Philology
RS   Renaissance Studies
SAQ   South Atlantic Quarterly
SE   Studies in English
SewR   Sewanee Review
ShS   Shakespeare Survey
Spec   Speculum
SP   Studies in Philology
SQ   Shakespeare Quarterly
SS   Sight and Sound
SStud Shakespeare Studies
StudR Studies in the Renaissance
TAPS   Transactions of the American Philosophical Society
TR   Texas Review
UR   University Review
WA   World Archaeology

Shakespeare's plays and poems

Ant.   Antony and Cleopatra
AYL   As You Like It
Err.   The Comedy of Errors
1H4   Henry IV, Part I
2H4   Henry IV, Part II
H5   Henry V

3H6	*Henry VI*, Part III
Lr.	*King Lear*
Mac.	*Macbeth*
Meas.	*Measure for Measure*
Mer.V.	*The Merchant of Venice*
MND	*A Midsummer Night's Dream*
Oth.	*Othello*
R2	*Richard II*
Sonn.	*Sonnets*
Troil.	*Troilus and Cressida*
Wint.	*The Winter's Tale*

Note: all quotations from Shakespeare are from *The Complete Works*, original spelling edn, ed. Stanley Wells and Gary Taylor (Oxford: Clarendon Press, 1986); all quotations from Spenser are from *The Poetical Works*, ed. J. C. Smith and E. de Selincourt, one-volume edn (Oxford University Press, 1912).

Introduction

There's not the smallest orbe which thou beholdst
But in his motion like an Angell sings,
Still quiring to the young eyde Cherubins;
Such harmonie is in immortall soules,
But whilst this muddy vesture of decay
Dooth grosly close it in, we cannot heare it.

(Merchant of Venice, v.i.60–5)

In this concert, one ideological State apparatus certainly has
the dominant role, although hardly any one lends an ear to its
music: it is so silent!

(Louis Althusser, 'Ideology and Ideological State Apparatuses')

ELIZABETHAN WORLD PICTURES

In a lecture dedicated to the memory of Lucien Goldmann,
Raymond Williams once admitted that he had spent years trying to
escape from that notorious *bête noire* with which every student of
English Literature has to do battle – the Elizabethan World
Picture. It may have been a fascinating thing in itself, said
Williams, but for him it often seemed to be more of a hindrance
than a help when it actually came to reading the drama of the
period.[1]

The Elizabethan World Picture is the title E. M. W. Tillyard gave to
a small book he published in 1943 as an offshoot of his influential
Shakespeare's History Plays. It refers to that remarkable gramarye of
post-medieval cosmological, political and ethical doctrine in which
every educated Elizabethan was supposed to believe without demur
or reservation. Fundamental to this world view is the idea of
harmony: individual psychology, family relations, politics – all were
evoked in musical metaphors; in fact it is a favourite maxim among
Renaissance writers that the world itself is made of music. It is these

I

ideas, their representation in literature and other cultural forms, and their political appropriation that are my subject.

For some decades after its publication *The Elizabethan World Picture* was popularly regarded as the authoritative intellectual history of the period. This was in spite of the fact that the book had already begun to be challenged by the early 1950s on the grounds of its schematic and reductive view of Elizabethan habits of thought.[2] Over the next thirty years the sense that Tillyard had related only part of a highly complicated narrative was confirmed as specialists working in the closely related fields of Elizabethan cosmology, politics, legal theory and poetics all contributed to the task of completing the story he had begun.[3] It has become clear from this expanded narrative that the later sixteenth century was a period characterized not so much by its unquestioning acceptance of a monolithic body of quasi-official doctrine as by its vigorous scepticism. What Tillyard took to be a unified world view commanding universal assent is perhaps better seen as a 'strategy of containment', to use Frederic Jameson's terms,[4] a device whose ability to provide Elizabethan society with an intellectually and emotionally satisfying account of itself depended on the degree to which it was capable of effacing that society's underlying contradictions. As one of a number of competing ideologies, the so-called Elizabethan World Picture can be more accurately designated by a term that Tillyard himself used to describe a contemporary body of specifically historiographical and political doctrine – the Tudor Myth. When it is apparent that Tillyard's narrative deals, not with history, but with myth, the reasons for its elegant simplicity become clear. As Roland Barthes puts it in his seminal *Mythologies*, 'myth acts economically: it abolishes the complexity of human acts, it gives them the simplicity of essences, it does away with all dialectics, without any going back beyond what is immediately visible, it organizes a world which is without contradictions'.[5] Though this is not the way he himself saw it, it is in fact just such a world that Tillyard evokes in *The Elizabethan World Picture*.

THE MUSICIAN-KING

That the Elizabethans were quite capable of deconstructing their own myths of order is evident from a poem like *Hero and Leander*. Marlowe's poem survives only as a fragment. It breaks off at a moment of extreme lyrical beauty when gods and mortals are apparently united in cosmic harmony. As the fated couple's first night of illicit love draws to its end Hero tries to hide herself, unhappy at the thought of a prying sun discovering her secret. But so dramatic is her transfiguration by the pleasures of 'this blessed night',[6] that her radiance, filling the room with light, deceives Hesperus into thinking that it is time to prepare Apollo's chariot. And so before dawn is actually due to break, 'ougly night' is banished, the sun rises and the world is filled with the sound of celestial music. As the climax, both of love's inevitable course, and also of Marlowe's narrative, the scene is nothing less than an epiphany, a visionary revelation of the glories of youthful passion. But as is usually the case with such moments of intense lyrical beauty in Marlowe, it is a deeply ironic scene. Though Marlowe died before he could complete the story, its tragic conclusion is anticipated in another tale of illicit love that he tells in *Hero and Leander*. This is the story of Mercury and Herse.[7]

The Mercury story is a myth-of-origin. It explains why it is that Fate will always be hostile to poets and lovers. Fresh from his defeat of Argus, the precocious young god is captivated by the unspoilt charms of a country maiden. Mercury knows well that 'Maids are not woon by brutish force and might, / But speeches full of pleasure and delight' (1.419–20) and deploys all his legendary rhetorical skills in his attempt to win her. Flattered though she is by such eloquent attentions, the shepherdess has enough presence of mind to impose a task on her illustrious lover as a price for submitting to his energetic charms. She demands that he steal a cup of nectar from the gods. Mercury is no innocent in the art of theft and audaciously helps himself from Jupiter's own cup. For his crime he is banished from heaven. However, Mercury is nothing if not enterprising and quickly plans his revenge: he persuades Cupid to intercede with the Destinies on his behalf. They agree; Saturn is reinstated on the throne that his son had usurped, and Mercury is readmitted to heaven. But this is not the end of the story. Angry at Mercury's subsequent ingratitude, the Destinies now revoke their decree and restore Jupiter, banishing Mercury once more from heaven. Such is Mercury's resource, however, that not even the cruel Destinies can suppress him for ever. But though they cannot prevent him gaining access to heaven's court, they still have the power to impose a curse on their disrespectful protégé. Their malediction is a mythological account of why writers will always be poor and at odds with authority:

> Yet as a punishment they added this,
> That he and *Povertie* should alwaies kis.
> And to this day is everie scholler poore,
> Grosse gold, from them runs headlong to the boore.
> Likewise the angrie sisters thus deluded,
> To venge themselves on *Hermes*, have concluded
> That *Midas* brood shall sit in Honors chaire,
> To which the *Muses* sonnes are only heire:
> And fruitfull wits that in aspiring are,
> Shall discontent run into regions farre;
> And few great lords in vertuous deeds shall joy,
> But be surpris'd with every garish toy.
> And still inrich the loftie servile clowne,
> Who with incroching guile, keepes learning downe.   (1.469–82)

Mercury is a complex figure. He is noted for his eloquence, and for his silence; he is a representative of order, and of trickery; he is a type of the probing intellect, and he is sexually precocious.[8] His ambivalent character is symbolic of the dual nature of the arts of which he is patron. As Marlowe portrays him – libidinous, plausible, thieving, disrespectful – he is an embodiment of everything that authority finds most threatening. The story of his affair with Herse and his provocation of Fate serves in part to prepare the way for the tragic end that, as we know from Musaeus, awaits Hero and Leander. But Marlowe's story is more than just a racy myth-of-origin accounting for the fact that the course of true love never did run smooth: it is also an ironic inversion of the familiar humanist myth of the birth of civilization.

As an exemplar of the art of eloquence, Mercury is traditionally linked in humanist mythology with those symbolic founders of civilization, Amphion, Arion, and Orpheus. According to Horace it was Mercury who first tamed man's savage nature when he gave him the power of speech.[9] The myth is well known to sixteenth-century readers.[10] The Preface to Thomas Wilson's *Arte of Rhetorique* (1560) embodies a representative version of it. Combining Christian theology with echoes of Ovid's account of the four ages of the world (*Metamorphoses*, 1.89–150), Wilson tells how fallen humanity was wooed from a state of nomadic barbarity by the civilizing power of eloquence. This is the reason, he says, why poets have represented Hercules as a figure of such great symbolic significance:

For his witte was so great, his tongue so eloquent, and his experience such, that no one man was able to withstande his reason, but euery one was rather driuen to doe that which he would, and to will that which he did: agreeing to his aduise both in word and worke in all that euer they were able. Neither can I see that men could haue beene brought by any other meanes, to liue together in fellowship of life, to maintaine Cities, to deale truely, and willingly obeye one an other, if men at the first had not by art and eloquence, [been] perswaded [of] that which they full oft found out by reason.[11]

In its broad outlines Wilson's version of the humanist myth of the birth of civilization is entirely conventional. Though it happens to be Hercules in this case who is cast in the role of symbolic civilizer of humanity, his name is interchangeable with those of Amphion, Arion, Orpheus, and of course Mercury himself, original inventor of the lyre. Characterized by Henryson in the *Testament of Creisseid* as 'Richt eloquent and full of rethorie, / With polite termis and delicious . . . Setting sangis and singand merilie',[12] Mercury is noted above all for his mastery of those arts that were regarded by Renaissance humanists as the very foundation of civilized life. Ben Jonson observes that 'Speech is the only benefit man hath to expresse his excellencie of mind above other creatures. It is the Instrument of Society.' Echoing Horace, he goes on to explain that this is the reason why 'Mercury, who is the President of Language, is called *Deorum hominumque interpres.*'[13]

Presidency of Language is an office whose holder enjoys powers of a prodigious kind. As Wilson insists, a man of eloquence is capable of persuading people to do whatever he wishes. However, the real mark of his power is not his ability to *force* people 'to yeeld in that which most standeth against their will',[14] but rather his skill in inducing them 'to *will* that which he did'. Social control, in other words, is achieved not only by coercion but, as Gramsci argues, by appropriating culture in such a way that people willingly consent to their domination.[15] The man of eloquence who, by introducing letters, persuades a barbarous nation to forsake its brutal practices and embrace the constraints of civilization is essentially a figure of authority. The truth contained in the myth is one that was understood perfectly well by the great sixteenth-century educators. In establishing a systematic programme of state education designed to equip a rising middle class for its new hegemonic role in the Tudor administration, men like Colet, Ascham and Mulcaster perceived very clearly the power that lay in mastery of rhetoric. Such is the force of affective language that a skilful orator might 'with a word ... winne Cities and whole Countries'.[16]

In addition to his mastery of the civilizing arts of poetry and song, Mercury is conventionally associated with authority and government through the caduceus that is his emblematic staff of office. A symbolic reminder of another of Mercury's exploits – his pacification of two fighting serpents – the caduceus is an emblem of peace, control, government, and ultimately monarchy itself.[17] In both his pagan and his Christian manifestations the musician-king is a key figure in the structure of Renaissance thought. His unique position is a function of the universal law of correspondence. In a classic account of this familiar principle Pierre de La Primaudaye explains in his enormously popular *French Academie* (1577; English trans. 1586) how elements, individuals, families, states all form part of a universal pattern of divinely instituted order:

As we see that in the body of this vniuersall frame, there is (as the Philosophers say) matter, forme, priuation, simplicitie, mixture, substaunce, quantitie, action and passion, and that the whole world being compounded of vnlike elementes, of earth, water, ayre and fire, is notwithstanding preserued by an Analogie and proportion, which they haue togither: and as we see in a mans body, head, hands, feete, eyes, nose, eares: in a house the husband, wife, children, master, seruantes: in a politike body, magistrates, nobles, common people, artificers; and that euery body mingled with heate, cold, drie and moyst, is preserued by the same reason of analogie and proportion which they haue togither: So is it in euery common-wealth well appointed and ordred, which consisting of many and sundry subiects, is maintained by their vnitie, being brought to be of one consent & wil, and to communicate their works, artes and exercises together for common benefit & profit.[18]

Since the order of the universe consisted in the harmonious reconciliation of opposing or discordant qualities,[19] it followed from the doctrine of correspondence that the same principles of harmony must obtain in any well-regulated state. Popularizing those Pythagorean ideas of world harmony that had been transmitted to the Middle Ages by the Church Fathers, La Primaudaye explains how the structure of the orderly society depends on musical principles:

A citie or ciuill company is nothing else but a multitude of men vnlike in estates or conditions, which communicate togither in one place their artes, occupations, workes and exercises, that they may liue the better, & are obedient to the same lawes and magistrates ... Of such a dissimilitude an harmonicall agreement ariseth by due proportion of one towards another in their diuers orders & estates, euen as the harmonie in musicke consisteth of vnequal voyces or sounds agreeing equally together.[20]

Because it was a widely accepted truth that 'all things that mooue within this generall globe are maintained by agreeing discords',[21] La Primaudaye's musical simile has the value not so much of a trope as of literal analogy: the principle that underlies the harmony of a consort of four dissimilar voices 'agreeing equally togither' is one and the same as that which integrates the harmonious community. The same rule of analogy applies equally to the individual. 'Looke vpon the frame, & workmanship of the whole worlde', writes John Case in a treatise entitled *The Praise of Mvsique*, 'whether there be not aboue, an harmony between the spheares, beneath a simbolisme between the elements. Looke vpon a man, whome the Philosophers termed a little world, whether the parts accord not one to the other by consent and vnity.'[22]

Deriving his authority from heaven and responsible for guarantee-ing on earth, through the agency of his paternal love for his subjects, that harmony which is the defining feature of the cosmos, the musician-king is, as Jonson says of Mercury, *deorum hominumque inter-pres*. Although Renaissance versions of the Arion/Orpheus/Mercury myth have many variants, their symbolic purpose is broadly similar. In allegorizing the story of the poet-musician who delights the world with his magically persuasive songs, and turning it into a fable about the preservation of social harmony, humanist poets and rhetoricians were transforming contemporary political reality into myth. When Ulysses delivers his portentous warnings about the catastrophic con-sequences of untuning the string of degree his patrician rhetoric is likely to persuade all but the most critical that these are authentic universal truths: to question 'primogenitie and due of birth / Prero-gatiue of age, crownes, scepters, lawrels' (*Troil.*, i.iii.106–7) is to defy nature herself. However, stripped of their cloak of mystifying lati-nisms, the same sentiments reveal their crudely partisan purpose. Stephen Gosson puts the case in rather blunter language:

If privat men be suffered to forsake their calling because they desire to walke gentlemen like in sattine & velvet, with a buckler at their heeles, pro-portion is so broken, unitie dissolved, harmony confounded, that the whole body must be dismembred, and the prince or heade cannot chuse but sicken.[23]

So much for the ladder of all high designs.

That *Hero and Leander* should have provoked such an aggressively moralistic response as Chapman's sequel is not really surprising. For in representing the poet-musician not as an authority figure dispensing laws to a recalcitrant humanity, but as a rebel who challenges a corrupt establishment, Marlowe is subverting one of the age's ruling ideas and exposing it for the political fable that it is. For all its delicious verbal beauties and its tender evocation of love's awakening, *Hero and Leander* is no sentimental romance. Although the fragment ends with an image of universal harmony, we have already been warned by Mercury's story that this apparent truce between man and fate is, like the dawn, a false one. If there is an underlying motif in this most Ovidian of Elizabethan epyllions, it is not harmony, but conflict – between youth and age; between passion and wisdom; between learning and wealth; between men and gods. The binary world it evokes is one in which authority, instead of uniting its subjects in loving concord, guarantees perpetual strife by 'keep[ing] learning downe' and ensuring 'That Midas brood shall sit in Honors chaire.'

THE POWER OF MYTH

The humanist myth of the birth of civilization through song has its origins in classical poetics. In Horace's allegorization of the Orpheus story (*Ars poetica*, 391–401) the Renaissance found a model that served as a basis for its own mythical account of the process by which authority persuades its subjects willingly to accept the rule of law. The chapters in part I of this book deal with three variations on the theme of the prince who restores harmony to a discordant society.

Governments have always used myth to sanction power. However, at the Reformation the Tudor administration was faced with an urgent need radically to reshape social attitudes. It is here that England witnessed the beginnings of that cult of regal quasi-divinity which is such a remarkable feature of the latter years of Elizabeth's reign.[24] Portraying the British as 'a chosen and peculiar people',[25] Elizabethan pamphleteers represent their queen as a semi-divine figure sent by God to fulfil the historic task of defeating popery and restoring the authentic primitive church.[26] By the last two decades of the sixteenth century it is not just pamphleteers but poets, dramatists, painters, and composers who contribute to the cult of Elizabeth.[27] The central document in this extraordinary body of propaganda is Spenser's *Faerie Queene*. As Stephen Greenblatt rightly says, Spenser is fascinated by power and does everything he can to link his own art with its symbolic and literal forms.[28] Taking on himself the office of epic recorder of his nation's providential role in world history, Spenser reveals, through a complex network of typological parallels linking past, present, and future, the processes by which God's purpose is about to be fulfilled in this, the latter end of time. Ironically, it is in the context of an increasingly militaristic international political environment – reflected in the wanton violence with which Astraea's deputy Talus suppresses rebellion – that Spenser depicts his patron as a 'Prince of peace from heauen blest' (IV.proem.4). In a world divided by religious conflict, only 'a God or godlike man' can restore harmony. Such a man was Orpheus, who

> when strife was growen
> Amongst those famous ympes of Greece, did take
> His siluer Harpe in hand, and shortly friends them make.   (IV.ii.1)

Although he does not compare himself explicitly with Orpheus, it is clear that Spenser is referring to his own poetic art when he defines Orpheus' 'musicke' as 'wise words with time concented' (IV.ii.2). Spenser's own medium is language. But appropriately enough for a poet who, like Gower, wanted his name to be associated with one of the classical exemplars of eloquence, his poem is full of music; in fact music is one of its key images, linking together all three levels of allegory – the tropological, the historical and the anagogical. In considering the political significance of these images in chapter 1 I shall focus on the Bower of Bliss, an episode that has probably attracted more critical attention than any other in Spenser's poem.

It is well known that St John's Revelation provides the symbolic framework for the apocalyptic elements in Spenser's political allegory. Despite the growing influence of the new political historiography exemplified by Machiavelli and Guicciardini,[29] the key to the meaning of political events for the great majority of sixteenth-century Protestants was still the Bible.[30] Drawing on contemporary interpretations of Revelation as a prophecy of the Protestant destruction of the Babylon-that-is-Rome, Spenser sets the drama of Christian life in the wider historical context of a battle between church and Antichrist. In doing so he both reflects and contributes to that aggressively nationalist mythology that is characteristic of England in the 1590s. Acrasia's seductive music stands not only for the temptations of the flesh, but also, historically, for the beguiling voice of religious dissent. Only if that siren music is ruthlessly silenced (sirens were a traditional figure for those heretical doctrines that threatened to undermine the church's authority) will God's chosen people be free to sing the triumphal New Song of an elect nation. The ferocity with which Guyon performs his task may be, as Greenblatt argues, a classic example of the way authority deals with supposedly demonic threats to established order.[31] Historically, though, it is a measure of the apocalyptic significance of his mission. As St John had prophesied, when Babylon fell its destruction would be marked by violence of cataclysmic proportions (18:21), so Gloriana's agent acts in a manner appropriate to his role as champion of God's chosen people against Antichrist; his violence is a sign of his predestined role in international affairs.

When Spenser implicitly compares his own art with that of Orpheus, the effect is to align himself with the authority Orpheus represents. The Christian counterpart of the musician-king who brings harmony to a discordant world through the magic of his songs is the Pauline New Man (Eph. 4:24). In patristic theology the New Man is he who sings not the old music of the pagan minstrels, but the New Song of Christ, the 'supreme musician of the world';[32] he is *Orpheus redivivus*. Reinterpreted by sixteenth-century reformers as a type of the elect, the New Man takes on a specifically political role as shaper of a new independent Christian state in which 'Gouernment, though high and low, and lower, / Put into parts, doth keepe in one consent, / Congreeing in a full and natural close, / Like Musicke' (*H5*, 1.ii.181–4). It is just such a role that Shakespeare's Prince Hal fashions for himself (see chapter 2). As Richard, in the first play of the tetralogy, appeals anachronistically to a theory of kingship that is essentially Tudor in its emphasis on the sacrosanctity even of tyrannical princes, so Hal cultivates the myth, promulgated by his sixteenth-century chroniclers, of the New Man who, having cast off his unregenerate self, becomes a 'true louer of the holy Church' (*H5*, 1.i.23). The Old Song – Falstaff is represented in both parts of *Henry IV* as an *aficionado* of the devil's music – must give way to the New. So successful is Hal's performance in his new role, and so adept is he in the art of political stage-management, that this doubt-ridden military adventurist is able to persuade his subjects that, like Spenser's Elizabeth, he is a 'Prince of peace from heauen blest'.

However, where Spenser is himself centrally involved in the cultivation of the myth of an elect nation, Shakespeare offers his audiences a critical view of the myth-making process.[33] The world of *Henry IV* is one in which not only the prince, but the rebel too, 'Deriues from heauen, his Quarrell, and his Cause' (*2H4*, i.i.206). By showing the way politicians manipulate myth in order to secure or maintain power, and by scrupulously refusing to privilege any one particular voice, these plays illustrate ideology in the making.[34] Their dramaturgical self-consciousness suggests that this effect is no less calculated than, let us say, Barthes' analyses of twentieth-century *petit-bourgeois* mythology. It has long been recognized that Shakespeare took a keen interest in the affective power of theatre, inviting audiences, by such devices as Bottom's amateur dramatics or Rosalind's play-acting, to reflect on the nature of dramatic illusion. Metadramatic self-commentary is a feature not only of the comedies, but of many of the histories and tragedies as well. Of all the plays there is none that is more self-conscious in the way it calls attention to its own dramatic devices than *The Tempest* (see chapter 3).

By the time Shakespeare wrote his last play, humanists had been debating the question of art's didactic function for some decades. Shakespeare now takes the traditional figure of the musician-king, adapts him, and weaves around him a story that is at once a parable about the art of politics and, at the same time, a reflection on the politics of art. In submitting to critical scrutiny the familiar humanist commonplaces concerning the meliorative potential of words and music, the play is in effect asking its audiences to distinguish between myth (in a Barthesian sense) and fiction, the one inviting absolute, the other conditional, assent.[35]

A 'TRUE SCIENCE OF HUMAN NATURE'

It is a commonplace of Renaissance thought that by harmonizing the discordant spirit, music can go some way towards repairing the defects of the Fall. The best-known contemporary expression of this idea is probably Lorenzo's speech *de laudibus musicae* in the fifth act of *The Merchant of Venice*. Lorenzo's encomium is justly celebrated for its lyrical beauty. Reminding his now docile pupil of the 'sweet

power of musique' and of how even beasts are susceptible to its
influence, he gives her a conventional interpretation of the Orpheus
story:

> therefore the Poet
> Did fain that Orpheus drew trees, stones, and floods,
> Since naught so stockish hard and full of rage,
> But musique for the time doth change his nature.   (v.i.79–82)

But not even Lorenzo's eloquence and the sentimental atmosphere
of the moonlit scene, augmented by the sounds of soft music, can
disguise the fact that the story he tells her is a political myth.
Orpheus is a lawgiver. Those who resist his authority are dissidents –
men who are, in Lorenzo's own words, 'fit for treasons, strategems,
and spoils' (v.i.85).

Shakespeare may be under no illusions about the political
potentialities of myth and the seductive charm of its melodies; but it
would be wrong to suppose, because Lorenzo tells Jessica that music
can apparently change our very nature ('for the time') that here is
evidence of a de-centred view of the self. On the contrary, if
Shakespeare seems to be undercutting the romantic elements in this
scene, it is not because he is hinting at a materialist view of the self,
but because he has a very clear sense of the innate and essential
limitations of human nature 'whilst this muddy vesture of decay /
Dooth grosly close it in'. The chapters in part II deal with some
unfamiliar expressions of the humanist belief in the transforming
power of music. In doing so they emphasize the essentialism of an
age whose view of 'man' is still firmly rooted in a humoral psychology that minimized educational and environmental influences. The
point would not be worth labouring if there were not a widespread,
but mistaken, assumption in recent criticism that the Renaissance
witnessed a radical challenge to the traditional belief that there is an
irreducible essence of human nature that is fundamentally the same
in all ages.

An axiomatic principle in post-structuralist Marxism is the artefactual nature of social reality. Modern social anthropology argues
that the self is a social structure. Analysis of the typified nature of
social interaction undermines common-sense assumptions about the
self as a consistent entity. Not only our general outlook or world
view, but our conception of ourselves is pre-defined for us by society,
and may undergo radical transformation as those external influ-

ences are modified. In the words of the American sociologist Peter Berger, 'society not only controls our movements, but shapes our identity, our thought and our emotions. The structures of society becomes the structures of our consciousness.'[36] This does not mean that human nature disappears altogether. Not even Marx, the father of modern sociology, would deny that there is an essential trans-historical human nature; indeed, his whole philosophy of history depends on the notion of a human *telos* that can be fully realized only when social conditions have been transformed. It means rather that human beings are shaped by society as much as they shape it.[37]

This dialectical view of man has been familiar enough to social scientists and literary critics since the 1930s.[38] But it did not acquire fashionable currency in literary critical circles until the 1960s, when Althusser and Foucault emphasized its political implications. Basing their materialist theory of ideology on a (widely disputed) anti-essentialist reading of Marx,[39] they stressed the repressive role of culture. For Foucault, power is not simply a question of the control exercised by those institutional structures that have always inter-ested political historians; it is something that is rooted in the total system of social networks.[40] To post-structuralist historicists, and Cultural Materialists in particular, Foucault's theory of power rela-tions seemed to offer an enabling key to Renaissance literature: if it could be shown that the major Renaissance writers had anticipated our own modern understanding of the artefactual nature of the self, surely this must force us to revise our view of their political phil-osophies. Such, at any rate, is the view taken by Jonathan Dollimore in *Radical Tragedy*.

Radical Tragedy has been a major influence in post-structuralist historicism, an influence comparable with that of Greenblatt's *Renaissance Self-Fashioning* in America. In a synoptic survey of the Western intellectual tradition Dollimore claims that a developing awareness among Renaissance intellectuals of the way the self is formed by ideology led to a brief period when essentialist views of human nature were rejected before once more gaining ascendancy in a new form with the Enlightenment. Among the English and continental writers whom he sees as exponents of the new anti-essentialism are Pico, More, Castiglione, Machiavelli, Montaigne, Bacon, Donne and Hobbes. This is a heterogeneous group of writers, but in all of them he sees evidence – based in some cases on an apparent misunderstanding of rather outdated secondary sources –

of a radical scepticism concerning traditional representations of
human nature. In Pico della Mirandola, for example, he believes
that we find a conception of the self that seems 'specifically modern'
in its recognition of the fluidity of man's being.[41] Dollimore is
quoting from Ernst Cassirer's discussion of Pico's celebrated *Oration
on the Dignity of Man*. At first sight it might seem strange to find
Cassirer, intellectually conservative celebrant of the metaphysical
subject, apparently attributing to Pico a materialist view of human
nature. However, if we turn to Cassirer's essay, we find that when he
speaks of Pico's 'specifically modern pathos of thought', what he is
actually referring to is not a deterministic theory of the self, but the
exact opposite. Cassirer's essay was first published in 1927; its thesis
reflects a long-since-discarded Burckhardtian view of Renaissance
man and his supposedly newly found sense of self-determination.
Cassirer believes that for Pico, man's supremacy in the natural
world consists precisely in his capacity for what Greenblatt calls
self-fashioning:

Man asserts his pre-eminence over all other beings ... and this pre-
eminence is based on the fact that man does not receive his being as
something finished but that he forms it by virtue of his free will. This
formation excludes the possibility of any determination from without, be it
'material' or 'spiritual'.[42]

The fact that man is, in a phrase that Dollimore quotes from Pico's
Oration, 'neither of heaven, nor of earth, neither mortal nor immortal',[43] does not mean, as Cassirer supposed, that he can literally
choose his own metaphysical nature.[44] It means rather, as countless
medieval and Renaissance writers argued, that, given his essentially
divided nature, fallen man is capable of developing either the
rational or the bestial side of his being. Fundamental to the whole
argument of the *Oration* is the twin proposition that man is uniquely
situated at the symbolic centre of the universe, and that the laws of
his own nature precisely mirror those of the macrocosm (see below,
chapter 5); it is an argument that provides little ground for claiming
that its author was in some way de-centring man, or that he
anticipated a materialist theory of human nature.

Similar objections may be made, more briefly, of the other writers
whom Dollimore cites as exemplars of the new anti-essentialism.
Castiglione may acknowledge that the courtier will probably have
to dissimulate in order to win his prince's favour; but he warns that,
in doing so, the courtier must never attempt to act a part that is

contrary to his own essential nature.[45] More may put a powerfully persuasive environmentalist argument into Hythloday's mouth; but it is this same genial 'dispenser of nonsense' who, in the final pages of *Utopia*, admits that pride is so deeply rooted in human nature that it 'can not be plucked out'.[46] Bacon may observe in his essay *Of Custom and Education* that 'Nature, nor the Engagement of Words, are not so forcible as Custome'; but in the companion essay, *Of Nature in Men* (which Dollimore omits to mention), he characteristically presents the other side of the argument: 'Nature is Often Hidden, Sometimes Ouercome, Seldome Extinguished.'[47] Donne may confess that 'this terme, the Law of Nature, is so variously and vnconstantly deliuer'd, as I confesse I read it abundant tymes, before I vnderstood it once';[48] but informing the Holy Sonnets (in which Dollimore sees evidence of a radical anti-essentialism) is a classic Calvinist recognition of the fact that all men, by their very nature, are unavoidably tainted with the corruption of original sin. Machiavelli may ignore the familiar question of providence's role in history for the far more immediate one of political survival; but underlying his cyclical theory of history is a sense that men are always and everywhere the same. Hobbes may proclaim his uncompromising materialism at the outset of the *Leviathan*; but it is with a discourse on 'the natural condition of mankind' that he prefaces his treatise. Even Montaigne, most sceptical of all debunkers of the idea of natural law, believes – at least until he changes his mind – that in the South American Indian he has at last found the true essence of primitive human nature not yet bastardized by the corrupting influence of civilization.

It was on the basis of certain trans-historical facts alone – facts that were rehearsed by writer after writer – that Renaissance humanists believed any 'true science of man'[49] could be founded. The phrase comes from a treatise called *Of Wisdome* (1601) by the influential sceptic (and close friend of Montaigne) Pierre Charron. Charron recognizes that man has a fatal propensity for concealing from himself those uncomfortable facts of human nature. He writes: 'man is extreamely counterfeited and disguised, not only man with man, but euery man with himselfe'. Nevertheless, true knowledge of our essential nature is the axiomatic foundation of any wise action. For Charron, as for Pico, 'the first lesson and instruction vnto wisdome ... is the knowledge of our selues and our humaine condition; for the first in euery thing is well to know the subiect, wherewith a man hath to do'.[50]

There is undoubtedly a new sense in Renaissance England of the fluidity of the self, and of the way social identity, in particular, is shaped by external forces. But it would be wrong to interpret this as evidence of a radical anti-essentialism. It is 'knowledge of our selues' – and certainly not any desire to challenge the notion of an irreducible human nature – that leads the more sceptical writers of the period to question the meliorism of a sentimental Neoplatonist like Shakespeare's Lorenzo. Chapter 4 below shows how poets and composers attempt to put into practice the belief, fundamental to every humanist's credo, that the combined effects of music and poetry can move the mind to virtue. By matching verbal schemes with analogous musical figures it was possible to construct a kind of rhetorical ladder and thus realize the Neoplatonist's dream of ascending the *scala naturae* and leaving behind the world of the senses. At least that was the theory. In practice, Elizabethan writers were generally suspicious of Neoplatonic theories of perfectibility. When Dowland sets his singer climbing the ladder of love that is supposed to lead to heaven, he quickly brings him back to earth with the reminder that such visions are no more than 'dreames, / Of a vaine desire'.[51]

If Elizabethans have reservations about the transforming power of words and music, it is because they recognize the inherent limitations of human nature. What enables them to define man's potentialities with such precision is the doctrine of correspondence. That the microcosm–macrocosm analogy formed the basis of most political, psychological and ethical thinking until well into the seventeenth century is well known and has been amply illustrated with reference to the drama of the period. Chapter 5 considers this familiar topic from an organological point of view. Because it was believed that the universe itself was like a vast musical instrument, it was natural enough that those principles of cosmic harmony should have been incorporated in the design of musical instruments. The lute in particular was regarded as symbolic of the harmony it expressed: its rounded belly was like the arch of the heavens, while its strings were like the tendons of God stretched across the cosmos. Reflecting, as they did, the harmony of a teleological universe, those same strings were commonly seen as a symbol of political concord or, if they happened to be broken, of discord. But it was the lute's intricately decorated sound hole, or rose, that expressed most precisely the *discordia concors* that was the key to personal, social and political harmony. Adapting the geometric figures that his instrument inherited from its Islamic origins, the Renaissance luthier created what is in effect a mandala that expressed in a single complex figure the nexus between microcosm and macrocosm.

To challenge the more sentimental forms of Neoplatonism is not to deny the persuasive power of song. Chapter 6 deals with an unusual iconographic expression of the Arion/Orpheus/Mercury myth. If the musician-king was a symbolic figure of great political significance, there was clearly much prestige to be won by identifying yourself with him. Thus we find poets and composers as diverse as Gower, Milan, Spenser and Dowland[52] inviting comparison between themselves and one or other of the legendary poet-musicians of antiquity. The instrument with which these mythical figures are associated is the lyre. But anything like an authentic reconstruction of the primitive lyre with its seven unstopped strings would have been incapable of articulating the harmonic accompaniments of the newly fashionable lute song, or air. And so, just at the time when the air was gaining popularity in England, a new instrument was invented. It was called the orpharion. The orpharion is a product of the Elizabethan cult of the antique; its name is a clear allusion to its imaginary provenance. By specifying the new instrument as an alternative form of accompaniment, lutenist song-writers arrogated to themselves something of the prestige of the musician-king of antiquity.

THE GAME OF LOVE

According to humanist myth, the state is like a family, united in loving concord by the offices of a paternal musician-king whose task is to harmonize the conflicting elements in society by his 'discreete and wholsome lessons vttered in harmonie and with delicious instruments'.[53] In reality the world of the Elizabethan courtier-poet was one of intrigue, scandal and fierce competition for advancement. The chapters in part III consider the social function of song in a world where the stock rhetorical formulas of the love lyric – supplications, pleas, complaints, acts of revenge – are often employed as metaphors for the hazardous game of social or political advancement.

No one reading a series of Elizabethan sonnets or listening to a representative selection of lute songs can fail to be struck by the number of times a speaker or a singer will go out of his way to insist on his sincerity. For many years it was supposed that when an Elizabethan poet made a point of announcing, usually in outrageously flamboyant language, his intention of eschewing rhetoric and delivering the round unvarnished tale of his heart, he probably had no other purpose in mind than some innocent fun with his audience. Post-structuralism has recently challenged this assumption.

In 1947 Rosemond Tuve offered what, at the time, looked like a definitive corrective to the Edwardian biographical approach to lyric poetry – an approach that still survived in much Renaissance criticism of the 1920s and 1930s. Tuve's exhaustive examination of contemporary poetic practice in the light of Renaissance theories of poetry gave rise in the following decades to a number of outstanding critical studies of Elizabethan poetry. Inspired by Tuve's historicism, scholars like Donald Guss and David Kalstone asked not how personal experience got transmuted into poetry, but how literary convention provided the Renaissance poet with the raw materials of his art.[54] The typical Renaissance lyric began to look less like a spontaneous overflow of powerful feelings than a space (to use Barthes' phrase) in which a variety of writings, none of them original, blend and clash. Underlying the new post-war historicism was a general consensus that Elizabethan poetry aspired to an affective rather than an expressive ideal. That consensus was to survive until the 1980s. In a volume in Terence Hawkes' influential 'New Accents' series Antony Easthope set out a revisionist theory of Renaissance poetics. Disregarding the work of Tuve and her followers, Easthope returned to what was, in effect, a new version of Edwardian naive realism, claiming that in the Renaissance we see poetry aiming for the first time 'to give transparent access to the represented'.[55]

Like Dollimore, Easthope subscribes to the theory of a bourgeois literary discourse whose project is the construction of unitary subjects. Easthope believes that the 'founding moment' of the new bourgeois *épistème* is not in the seventeenth century, as Dollimore argues, but in the 1580s and 1590s. ('It is well-known that [the transcendent subject] did not exist in the ancient world, nor in any developed form in the feudal period.'[56]) Where Tuve claimed that the Renaissance poet's conception of the mimetic function of poetry led him to stress the 'conceipt' without stressing the 'conceiver',[57] Easthope argues that it is the individual speaking voice that is emphasized in the Renaissance lyric. For him, reading a Shakespeare sonnet is rather like going to the pictures: 'Just as realist cinema uses its means of enunciation, a photographic image and recorded sound, to produce "real" people in a "real" story (the enounced), so the sonnet uses appropriately poetic means for a similar purpose.' The effect, says Easthope, is so realistic that you almost forget you are reading poetry and imagine that you are listening to Shakespeare himself talking to you.[58] However, given the self-reflexive concern of these sonnets with the affective potential of rhetorical language, it is something of a puzzle to understand how it is possible to read them without being aware of the fact that you are reading verse.

There is general agreement among post-structuralist historicists that the critic's job is to act not as a self-appointed public relations agent, but as a consumer watchdog scrutinizing the ideological wares the text is intent on selling us. But before you can run a consumer test or check for any aporias that might be lurking in the system, you have to know what functions the product is supposed to be able to perform. For it would be embarrassing, after stripping the device down to its subtext, to find that the maker (*poeta*) has already anticipated the apparent design-problem you have identified. Easthope argues that with poets like Sidney and Shakespeare 'recognition ... of the poem as constructed artifice is suppressed in favour of the poem as spontaneously generated'.[59] It is true that poet after poet in this period declares, in language of ever-increasing sophistication, that where other poets rehearse only hackneyed formulas, he alone speaks the plain and simple truth. But not for a moment does he expect his seemingly candid declarations of simplicity to be taken at face value. The mark of a successful poet is the artful concealing of art. 'Our Courtly Poet', writes Puttenham, '[must be] a dissembler ... in the subtilties of his arte: that is, when he is most artificiall, so to disguise and cloake it as it may not appeare, nor seeme to proceede from him by any studie or trade of rules, but to be his naturall: nor so euidently to be descried, as euery ladde that reades him shall say he is a good scholler.'[60] The essence of the poetic *sprezzatura* that Puttenham is describing here is the delicate balance it must strike between ostentation and concealment. No member of the elite for whom you are writing is going to be impressed by a display of talent so meretricious that 'euery ladde' can appreciate the work that has gone into it; on the other hand, though, there is no point in disguising your art so successfully that even the *cognoscenti* fail to recognize the difficulty of what you are doing. Fundamental to the success of a sophisticated courtly satire of this kind is a set of precise conventions to play with. One of those conventions was the pretence that, unlike your dull-witted predecessors, you are writing from the heart. Had a poet like Sidney, or Donne or the anonymous lyricist I discuss in chapter 7 known that in centuries to come his irony was going to misfire and that readers would actually take the absurd posturing of his persona at face value he might have recalled, with a profound sense of futility, the anxious prayer with which Chaucer sent his greatest poem into the world: 'Go, litel bok, go ... That thow be understonde, God I biseche!'[61] (Had he known that Foucault was going to assert that the concept 'literature' did not exist until the nineteenth century[62] he would probably have laughed.)

The proleptic declaration of candid simplicity is a rhetorical formula that has a long history going back through Chaucer, Persius and Ovid at least as far as Plato.[63] In rehearsing it poets may have been indulging in nothing more serious than a play of words. But there were compelling reasons why Elizabethan writers took a more than light-hearted interest in the art of self-concealment. Chapter 7 argues that in a society where life itself was, in Ralegh's punning words, 'a play of passion',[64] and the drama of sexual relationships, whether real or pretend, was played out on a public stage, a talent for artful dissimulation was not just a pleasing accomplishment; it was necessary for survival. By foregrounding conventional elements in their lyrics, Elizabethan song-writers distanced themselves from the sentiments they expressed, effectively discouraging the kind of biographical readings favoured by Edwardian criticism.

Few major Elizabethan artists illustrate better the pitfalls of biographical criticism than John Dowland (see chapter 8). Noted for his cheerful disposition, Dowland created for himself a persona that was the antithesis of his own temperament. In fact, through a conceit that he himself used for the title of one of his instrumental pieces – 'Semper Dowland semper dolens' – his name became virtually synonymous with melancholy. So moving are Dowland's anguished laments that commentators have been tempted to see them as expressions either of some as yet unidentified personal tragedy, or else of a profound religious sensibility. There is little evidence for either of these suppositions. The lyrics that Dowland chooses for his most serious vocal works are remarkable chiefly for their self-conscious use of stereotyped rhetorical formulas. They point to a provenance not in the recesses of a tortured psyche but in a thoroughly professional interest in the techniques of affective writing. Nor is the fact that Dowland deliberately cultivates a fashionable persona evidence of a recognition on his part of the fragmented or discontinuous nature of the self. For Dowland the melancholy song provided as effective and stylish a means of concealing the true self as did the mildly disreputable light air for Campion and Rosseter, or the Petrarchan sonnet sequence for Sidney or Barnfield. If the notion of giving 'transparent access to the represented' has any meaning at all for these poets and composers it is something to be played with, rather than embraced as a serious criterion of artistic endeavour. Theirs is a *scriptible* rather than a *lisible* art, as Barthes would put it.

If Renaissance humanists accord special prestige to the solo song with instrumental accompaniment, it is on account of its supposed origin in classical musical practice. The secret of Orpheus' magical songs was thought to lie in their unique combination of music and poetry. But if song can inspire a love of virtue, it is also capable of inciting passions of a less noble kind. As Shakespeare's Duke Vincentio remarks, 'Musick oft hath such a charme / To make bad, good; and good prouoake to harme' (*Meas.*, iv.i.14–15). Eloquence may be the key to social control; but by the same token it can also be used for seditious purposes, as those Puritans understood who sought to suppress anything that smacked of artifice. With its intrinsically ambivalent nature, song was a valuable strategic device for the serious competitor in the game of love. The social function of song is also the subject of chapter 9. *Twelfth Night* is a play about fashionable people. The world it portrays is that of the country house party. It is a cossetted, self-indulgent world of elegant and stylized games-playing. The major characters are all experienced and skilful players who know how to parry their opponents' moves without causing injury. The game they are playing is called Romantic Love. Part of the game's attraction is its exclusiveness; it can only be played by people who have the means to be idle in style and who can afford the food, the clothes and the music that are necessary in order to create the right atmosphere for passion to flourish in – even if it is only a pretend passion. Songs form an essential part of this world. They serve an important social function for the 'ydle shallowe things' who commission them; but they also embody in their transitory beauty the superficial charm of an aristocratic society threatened by the 'whirlegigge of time'.

PART I

Music, myth and politics

CHAPTER I

Spenser and the politics of music

> Renowned Prince, when all these tumults cease,
> Even in the calme, and Musicke of thy peace,
> If in thy grace thou deigne to favour us,
> And to the Muses be propitious,
> *Caesar* himselfe, Romes glorious wits among,
> Was not so highly, nor divinely sung.
>
> (Michael Drayton)

These words were written not to Queen Elizabeth, but to her successor James I. The hyperbole is typical of Renaissance panegyric. But the cloying cajolery as Drayton tries to strike a bargain with his prince sounds exactly like Spenser. 'Let her accept me as her faithfull thrall', he wrote in the guise of a Petrarchan lover supplicating a conventionally cruel mistress,

> Then would I decke her head with glorious bayes,
> and fill the world with her victorious prayse.[1]

Like Spenser, too, Drayton compares his prince with Caesar, hinting at the kind of typological relationship between Britain and the ancient world that was such a favourite device with Elizabethan panegyrists. It was in order to show that the British were a 'chosen and peculiar people'[2] marked out by providence for a special purpose that chroniclers, poets and dramatists invented fictional genealogies for both Elizabeth and James, tracing their ancestry back to its imagined origins in the legendary past. For Spenser, as for Drayton, the *pax musica* is a mythical construct. Embodied in the bland phrase 'Musicke of thy peace' is not simply that familiar neo-medieval image of domestic harmony beloved by James in which prince and subjects coexist like members of one family, but a political and theological ideal endorsed and ratified by the will of a Protestant heaven.

25

I

In a recent Marxist essay on Spenser, Simon Shepherd notes how modern Spenser criticism has typically concerned itself with 'all sorts of stuff about mythology, iconography, arcane philosophy, neo-platonism and numerology' and has apparently forgotten the fact that Spenser himself lived in 'a real world ... in which people have to eat, live, defend themselves, survive'.[3] A bracing appeal to common sense. However, even pre-structuralist Marxists, as well as non-Marxists, recognize the artefactual nature of the 'real' world of common sense. If we are to have any notion at all of what counts as real for the Elizabethans, and how their political realities differ from our own, we need to know something of the mythological materials on which their discourses draw. The key metaphor in most Elizabethan political treatises is musical harmony. In formulating their constitutional arguments, both apologists and critics of the crown appeal to the laws of a nature whose most essential features are 'harmonicall agreement' and 'due proportion'.[4] It is not surprising, therefore, that music, both earthly and divine, should feature prominently in the most important political poem of the period. It occurs at many of the key episodes in *The Faerie Queene* and almost invariably signals events or situations of special portent. Most complex in its use of musical symbolism is Acrasia's Bower of Bliss.

The Bower of Bliss is the culminating episode in a book whose object is to show, not just what temperance is like, but why it is a political imperative. It is because temperance is not merely a private virtue, but also 'necessary in every politicke government',[5] that the hero's instruction in Alma's castle takes the form of a history lesson (II.x). That the story which Guyon reads in Alma's chronicles is one that has its beginnings in Troy is doubly significant. By tracing the ancestry of the British people to its origins in the ancient world these chronicles serve in part to reveal the significance of the present as part of a divine historical plan; but they also teach a political lesson. The sack of Troy was the archetypal example of a state overthrown by lust. As Ralegh laconically puts it in his *History of the World*: 'All writers consent with *Homer*, that the rape of *Helen* by *Paris* the son of *Priamus*, was the cause of taking arms.'[6] If history is in one sense the record of man's attempts to control his 'natural' passions by means of the arts of civilization, then the lesson it teaches is the primacy of temperance among the civic virtues. The supreme test of Guyon's own temperance takes place in the Bower of Bliss. Tempted by the siren voice of nature to abandon his mission, he is in danger of jeopardizing not only his own humanity, but also the regime he serves. The allegorical setting for this epic psychomachia is a neo-medieval garden of love where the music of the flesh competes with the voice of reason for the hero's soul.

Even before Guyon reaches Acrasia's magic island his ears are assailed, like those of Odysseus, by the 'rare melody' of erotic temptation (II.xii.31–2). And as the mermaids sing to him of a life free from 'troublous toyle' the sea and the winds provide a natural accompaniment to their beguiling song:

> With that the rolling sea resounding soft,
> In his big base them fitly answered,
> And on the rocke the waues breaking aloft,
> A solemne Meane vnto them measured,
> The whiles sweet *Zephirus* lowd whisteled
> His treble, a straunge kind of harmony;
> Which *Guyons* senses softly tickeled,
> That he the boateman bad row easily,
> And let him heare some part of their rare melody.

Apart from its extreme beauty, the most significant thing about this stanza is the fact that nature is in such obvious sympathy with the artful mermaids and their 'sweet skill in wonted melody' (31).

The meaning of the relationship between nature and art in *The Faerie Queene* has been the subject of a lengthy critical debate. In 1936 C. S. Lewis established the terms of the debate in a seminal analysis of the Bower of Bliss. Lewis argued that in contrast with the natural virtue of the Garden of Adonis, the patently evil Bower was characterized essentially by its artificiality: 'the one is artifice, sterility, death: the other, nature, fecundity, life'.[7] Lewis' analysis of these two episodes has been extraordinarily influential. A quarter of a century later John Hollander claimed in his important *Untuning of the Sky* that an account of the musical elements in the Bower of Bliss 'bears out C. S. Lewis' contention that it is the very artificiality of the Bower of Bliss (as opposed to the *natural* beauty of the Garden of Adonis, where, incidentally, there is no music at all), that signifies its role as the evil paradise'.[8] In another influential book A. Bartlett Giamatti argued that Lewis' reading was 'undeniable'. 'Art', he says, 'tries to undermine and corrupt nature, just as Acrasia's principle of sexual indulgence undermines and corrupts the natural instincts of man.'[9] The problem with such an interpretation is that nature, instead of being set in antithesis to the artificial elements of the island appears to mingle with them.

When Guyon arrives at Acrasia's Bower he is met with a bewitching combination of natural and artificial sounds:

> Eftsoones they heard a most melodious sound,
>   Of all that mote delight a daintie eare,
>   Such as attonce might not on liuing ground,
>   Save in this Paradise, be heard elsewhere:
>   Right hard it was, for wight, which did it heare,
>   To read, what manner musicke that mote bee:
>   For all that pleasing is to liuing eare,
>   Was there consorted in one harmonee,
> Birdes, voyces, instruments, windes, waters, all agree.
>
> The joyous birdes shrouded in chearefull shade,
>   Their notes unto the voyce attempred sweet;
>   Th'Angelicall soft trembling voyces made
>   To th'instruments divine respondence meet:
>   The siluer sounding instruments did meet
>   With the base murmure of the waters fall:
>   The waters fall with difference discreet,
>   Now soft, now loud, unto the wind did call:
> The gentle warbling wind low answered to all.   (II.xii.70–1)

Once again, the striking thing about Spenser's description of the Bower's magical 'sounds and sweet airs' is his emphasis on the co-operative alliance between natural and artificial forms of music. The motif is repeated once more as Guyon discovers Acrasia entertaining her newest lover. While Verdant sleeps after 'long wanton ioyes' a disembodied voice sings of the pleasures of love, and the ephemerality of youth and beauty. When this seductively beautiful, and notably artificial, *carmen amatorium* is over the birds break into fresh song as if endorsing the singer's sentiments:

> He ceast, and then gan all the quire of birdes
>   Their diuerse notes t'attune vnto his lay,
>   As in approuance of his pleasing words.   (II.xii.76)

Whatever the relationship is between art and nature, it is certainly not true to describe it as some kind of battle between natural virtue and the vices of artifice. As Spenser himself says, 'Birdes, voyces, instruments, windes, waters, all agree.'

Other critics have suggested that the key to the significance of the Bower lies, not in a simple antithesis between nature and art, but in some sort of 'competitive alliance',[10] 'improper rivalry'[11] or 'war'[12] between the two. On the face of it this would seem a promising line of interpretation. It was, of course, axiomatic that the true function of art was to repair the defects of our fallen nature so that, reversing the terms of C. S. Lewis' antinomy, the whole of history could in one sense be regarded as a struggle between natural barbarity and civilized order. How could mankind 'have been brought by any other meanes, to live together in fellowship of life, to maintaine Cities, to deal truely, and willingly obeye one an other', asks Thomas Wilson, 'if men at the first had not by art ... [been] persuaded [of] that which they full oft found out by reason'.[13] Spenser seems to hint at such a relationship between art and nature when he tells us that 'nature had for wantonesse ensude [imitated] / Art, and that Art at nature did repine' (II.xii.59). But, if the relationship is judged by its effects, it would appear to be more in the nature of a conspiracy than a feud. Stanza 59 continues:

> Each did the others worke more beautifie;
> So diff'ring both in willes, agreed in fine:
> This Gardin to adorne with all varietie.

However, if art and nature are clearly in alliance, it is not easy to see how Ruth Nevo is able to claim that the music of Acrasia's Bower is 'clearly praiseworthy for its combination or collaboration of Nature (winds, waters, etc.) with Art (voices, instruments, etc.), the result being a consort "in one harmonie [of] all that pleasing is to living eare"'.[14] If anything the reverse is the case: it is precisely the combination of natural beauty and affective song that is so fatally alluring to Acrasia's victims.

It is true that Spenser often uses music to symbolize states of moral and spiritual harmony. The betrothal ceremonies in Books I and IV are signal examples. As Una and the Redcrosse Knight pledge themselves to marriage, an unseen voice sings of heavenly love (I.xii.38–9). *Musica mundana* also accompanies the wedding of the Thames and the Medway in Book IV (xi.23). Divine endorsement of the forms of human government is similarly implied by the *angeletti* carolling 'heauenly things' who surround the regal figure of Mercilla in Book V (ix.28–9).

Natural music serves a similar symbolic function in *The Faerie*

Queene. When Belphoebe, whose voice sounds like 'heauenly musicke' (ii.iii.24), rescues the bleeding Timias in Book iii she takes him to her 'bowre of blis' (iii.v.35) to cure his wounds. Belphoebe's bower is like an 'earthly Paradize' in which 'the birds song [sang] many a louely lay / Of gods high prayse, and of their loues sweet teene' (40). Natural music is also a feature of that other earthly paradise in Book iii, the Garden of Adonis. Among the fruits and blossoms of this *locus amoenus* are 'ioyous birdes' who 'their true loues without suspition tell abrode' (iii.vi.42). Natural music is again identified with events of mystical import in Book vi, where birdsong, together with trees, waters and the perfume of flowers is evidence of 'natures skill' (vi.x.5) in devising Venus' pleasance on Mount Acidale (x.5ff).

In all these incidents music – both celestial and natural – is a symbolic intimation of harmony established between God and man. However, music, and birdsong in particular, has an alternative and more sinister function in *The Faerie Queene*. In the very first incident in the poem the sound of singing birds seems to signify not so much a state of spiritual harmony as the dangers of allowing yourself to be guided by the senses. As the Redcrosse Knight and Una enter the wandering wood in canto i they are

> with pleasure forward led,
> Ioying to heare the birdes sweete harmony,
> Which therein shrouded from the tempest dred,
> Seemd in their song to scorne the cruell sky.   (i.i.8)

If there is a symbolic link in this stanza between birdsong and the pleasures of the senses, those pleasures are apparently of a quite innocent nature. Less innocent is the context in which the Redcrosse Knight is next entertained by the 'sweet musicke' of birds. Heeding the transparent warnings of the House of Pride, he flees the castle, only to be trapped by temptation of a more insidious kind. The setting for his erotic reconciliation with Duessa at the beginning of canto vii is a *locus amoenus* 'Wherein the cherefull birds of sundry kind / Do chaunt sweet musick, to delight his mind' (i.vii.3). This time indulgence in the pleasures of the senses immediately places the Knight in mortal danger, for it is while he is thus 'carelesse of his health, and of his fame' (7) that he is taken prisoner by Orgoglio. A *locus amoenus* also provides the setting for erotic temptation in Book ii. Like Belphoebe's 'bowre of blis', Phaedria's garden is an earthly paradise, a 'chosen plot of fertile land' (II.vi.12) in which trees, flowers, perfumes and birdsong combine to delight the senses. But now the potential danger in nature's seductive beauty is clearly spelled out: 'trees, braunches, birds, and songs were framed fit, / For to allure fraile mind to carelesse ease' (13). Birdsong is again explicitly identified with sensuality in Castle Joyeous. While the patrons of this mock-classical seraglio with its many beds arranged in 'the antique worldes guize' are 'swimming deepe in sensuall desires' (III.i.39), their revels are accompanied by a kind of natural consort consisting of *musica instrumentalis* mingled with the song of birds:

> And all the while sweet Musicke did diuide
> Her loose notes with Lydian harmony;
> and all the while sweet birdes thereto applide
> Their daintie layes and dulcet melody,
> Ay caroling of loue and jollity,
> That wonder was to heare their trim consort.   (III.i.40)

Innocent as birdsong may be in Belphoebe's garden, it clearly serves a symbolic function of a very different kind in these two latter episodes. But it is in Acrasia's Bower of Bliss that natural music plays its most insistently seductive role. With its fountains, trees, flowers, perfumes and music, Acrasia's garden incorporates all those elements that characterized not only Phaedria's 'nest' of love, but also Belphoebe's chaste 'bowre of blis'.

We are first introduced to the Bower in canto v, when Atin discovers the lascivious Cymochles disporting himself 'Amidst a flocke of Damzels fresh and gay'. As they indulge their 'wanton follies' natural music acts as a stimulant to their pleasures:

> the mery birds of every sort
> Chaunted alowd their chearefull harmonie:
> And made emongst themselves a sweet consort,
> That quickned the dull spright with musicall comfort. (II.v.31)

It is the same 'ioyous birdes' that greet Guyon on his arrival at the Bower. Like the birds in Phaedria's garden, their function is 'to allure fraile mind to carelesse ease'.

II

Music performs a dual function in *The Faerie Queene*. Although in some cases it symbolizes a condition of moral and spiritual harmony, it is most commonly used to signify the dangers of sensual indulgence. Traditionally understood, by a figure of synecdoche, to stand for the civilizing power of the arts in general, music, like any other art form, was susceptible of abuse; indeed, it had been a favourite target for Puritan attack in the sixteenth century. In the episodes I have cited we see both song and instrumental music apparently realizing the worst fears of the ascetic moralist and inflaming the passions rather than allaying them. However, it is not only man-made music that performs this corrupting role: nature appears at times to amplify the erotic propensities already excited by human artifice. That natural music should be represented in this ambivalent way is hardly remarkable. The Bower of Bliss is rich in self-conscious literary echoes, and in every one of Spenser's major literary sources for the incident music is portrayed in a similarly ambiguous fashion.

The most direct model for Acrasia's Bower in Armida's enchanted garden in Books 15 and 16 of *Gerusalemme Liberata*. It is well known that Spenser bases many of the details of canto xii on Tasso's narrative.[15] Like Acrasia's Bower, Armida's garden is a *locus amoenus* in which nature and art are so skilfully intermingled as to seem indistinguishable:

> So with the rude the polish'd mingled was
> That natural seem'd all, and ev'ry Part;
> *Nature* would craft in counterfeiting pass,
> And imitate her Imitator, Art. (XVI.x)[16]

As in Acrasia's garden, the music of winds, waters and birds forms a natural consort:

> The joyous Birds, hid under Green-wood Shade,
> Sung merry Notes on ev'ry Branch and Bough
> The Wind, that in the Leaves and Waters play'd,
> With Murmurs sweet now sung, and whistled now; (XVI.xii)

And as the 'false enticing pleasure' of the rose song (xiv–xv) concludes its frank invitation to venery, so a choir of birds responds, like Spenser's natural chorus, as if 'approving all she spake' (xvi).

In composing the Bower of Bliss Spenser drew also on Ariosto's description of Alcina's garden in the sixth and seventh books of the *Orlando Furioso*. Here again, birdsong, together with the trees, flowers, fountains and perfumed winds that are standard features of the literary garden of love, serves a maleficent purpose. For Alcina, like Acrasia, is a witch who turns her lovers into monsters when she has satisfied her lust.

The parallels between Alcina's and, more particularly, Armida's gardens and the Bower of Bliss make it clear that while Spenser is attempting, as he admits to Gabriel Harvey, to 'overgo' Ariosto's and Tasso's examples,[17] his understanding of the art/nature relationship is essentially theirs. *Orlando Furioso* and *Gerusalemme Liberata* are Spenser's most important narrative sources for the Bower of Bliss. But the symbolic garden is such a typical feature of late medieval love poetry that all three poets would undoubtedly have been familiar with at least some of the same examples. In Guillaume de Lorris' enormously influential *Roman de la Rose* bird-song is an important feature of the garden of the rose; indeed Guillaume spends some thirty lines cataloguing the various kinds of birds that inhabit his 'paradys erthly' (648)[18] and describing their song. Like Spenser's birds they sing in consort; but the most important thing about them is their moral ambivalence. For although Guillaume compares their 'blisful . . . swete and pitous song' (496–7) to that of angels, he also likens them to mermaids or sirens. 'These briddes', he says,

> They songe her songe as faire and wel
> As angels don espirituel.
> And trusteth wel, whan I hem herde,
> Full lustily and wel I ferde;
> For never yitt sich melodye
> Was herd of man that myghte dye.
> Sich swete song was hem among
> That we thought it no briddis song,
> But it was wondir lyk to be
> Song of mermaydens of the see,
> That, for her syngyng is so clere,
> Though we mermaydens clepe hem here
> In English, as is oure usaunce,
> Men clepe hem sereyns in Fraunce.   (670–84)

Part bird and part woman,[19] sirens had been traditionally interpreted as the lure of the flesh tempting the faithful to abandon the ship of the church. (The mast to which Odysseus had himself bound was taken to represent the cross; only by clinging to its protection could the faithful escape the seduction of the senses.)[20] Guillaume's comparison of the birds in the rose garden to sirens is appropriate because, for all its angelic beauty, theirs is the song of the flesh rather than the spirit. The same is true of the songs in Boccaccio's '*giardino amoroso*' in the third book of the *Teseida*. Although her voice is like an angel's (III.x), Emilia is in fact no goddess, as Arcita believes, but a mortal, singing, like the birds themselves, '*amorose canzon*' (viii),[21] songs whose effect is in both cases – human and avian – to inflame the passions of the listeners rather than to inspire religious thoughts.

The *Teseida* is one of Chaucer's major sources, not only for the *Knight's Tale*, but also for the garden of love in the *Parlement of Foules*, which Spenser in his turn imitates in the first canto of *The Faerie Queene*. Although the characters of the main contenders in Chaucer's avian debate are carefully delineated, the birds who sing in the garden of love that forms the induction to the *Parlement* are not identified. Their function is emblematic. As they sing 'with voys of aungel in here armonye' (191)[22] they symbolize the seductive beauty of a fallen nature. Like Tasso and Spenser after him, Chaucer creates an image of 'ravyshyng swetnesse' as birds, musical instruments and winds form a symphony of natural and artificial harmonies:

> Of instruments of strenges in acord
> Herde I so pleye a ravyshyng swetnesse,
> That God, that makere is of al and lord,
> Ne herde nevere beter, as I gesse.
> Therwith a wynd, unnethe it myghte be lesse,
> Made in the leves grene a noyse softe
> Acordaunt to the foules song alofte.   (197–203)

But once again an image of natural beauty is qualified by hints of corruption, for passing their time in the garden of love are not only 'Delyt', 'Gentilesse', 'Beute' and 'Youthe', but also 'Foolhardynesse', 'Flaterye', 'Desyr', 'Messagerye' and 'Meede' (224–8).

In each of these examples birdsong is one element of an imaginative complex whose purpose is to establish a symbolic contrast between divine and earthly love. Inherited from the ancient world as a rhetorical *topos*,[23] the *locus amoenus* is typically used by medieval poets to represent either a celestial paradise, or a false paradise of earthly delights. In either form its main features tend to be highly stereotyped; they derive partly from classical tradition and partly from patristic readings of the Song of Solomon as an allegory of the marriage between Christ and His Church. The phrases 'My sister my spouse is as a garden inclosed, as a spring shut vp, and a fountaine sealed vp' (Song of Sol., 4:12)[24] were interpreted as a symbolic prefiguration of the Virgin Mary in her role of mystical bride of Christ; by the later Middle Ages these elements had become typical features of the paradisal garden. There is no better illustration of the medieval commonplace that prelapsarian virtues become transformed in a fallen world into vices with which they are superficially identical than the garden of earthly pleasures. Acrasia's Bower of Bliss is a good example of how this familiar symbol depends on parody to make its point. Unlike the true paradisal garden, Acrasia's Bower is 'enclosed round about' not with an impregnable wall, but with a fence 'but weake and thin; (II.xii.43); its gate is not locked fast, but is 'wrought of substaunce light, / Rather for pleasure, then for battery or fight' (43); its well is not 'a spring shut vp, and a fountaine sealed vp', but an overflowing 'flood' that provides the scene for a display of the most blatant eroticism (60–8).

Like the other features of the earthly garden of pleasures, birdsong is a corruption of a divine principle. In the Garden of Eden birds sang only their Creator's praises.[25] The thirteenth-century Spanish poet Gonzalo de Berceo tells how, reclining in a paradisal garden ('prado egual de paraiso') shaded with trees and perfumed by flowers, he listens to the voices of birds – some taking the diapente, some the diapason – as they sing in perfect harmony their songs of devotion ('canto leales').[26] Berceo's garden is an allegory; his idealized birds represent the company of saints and martyrs offering praises to the Blessed Virgin. A late example of the medieval literary bird-chorus is the mid-sixteenth-century *Harmony of Birds*. Like Berceo's *Milagros*, this anonymous poem begins in a traditional shaded bower. Here the poet discovers a congregation of birds

> as thycke
> As sterres in the skye,
> Praisyng our Lorde
> Without discorde,
> With goodly armony.[27]

In celebrating the divine love that is the source of universal harmony, these poems draw on the stylized conventions of the uncorrupted garden of love. But if the birds in the Garden of Eden had not yet learnt to sing with double voice, their counterparts in a fallen world cannot always be relied on to justify their innocent appearance. In the virtuous their song may inspire devotional thought; but more often it excites erotic impulses, as the eighth song from *Astrophil and Stella* shows with such witty pathos. The scene of

Astrophil's unintentionally comic attempt to seduce Stella is well chosen, for in all its features it is a perfect neo-medieval garden of love: a shaded grove with trees, flowers, perfumes and birdsong. As he pleads with her to accept his service, Astrophil appeals to all these, and especially the birds, in support of his supplication:

> Never season was more fit,
> Never roome more apt for it;
> Smiling ayre alowes my reason,
> These birds sing: 'Now use the season.'
>
> This small wind which so sweete is,
> See how it the leaves doth kisse,
> Ech tree in his best attiring,
> Sense of love to love inspiring.[28]

It is because Astrophil's world, no less than the world of Guillaume's or Chaucer's dreamers, is one in which all things below the sphere of the moon have been contaminated by the fall that nature's music accords so harmoniously with the lover's own erotic desires. This too is why not only birds, but also the sea and the winds appear to endorse the arguments of temptresses like Armida and Acrasia.

Tasso's and Spenser's richly evocative image of a universe in which all natural phenomena contribute to a 'straunge kind of harmony' is a variation on a familiar theme in medieval literature. In the twelfth century Honorious of Autun compares the universe to a musical instrument:

The supreme artisan made the universe like a great zither upon which he placed strings to yield a variety of sounds ... A harmonious chord is sounded by spirit and body, angel and devil, heaven and hell, fire and water, air and earth, sweet and bitter, soft and hard, and so all things are harmonized.[29]

A classic Renaissance expression of the idea that, as Donne puts it, 'God made this whole world in such an uniformity, such a correspondency, such a concinnity of parts, as that it was an Instrument, perfectly in tune'[30] is contained in some lines by George Wither:

> From the *Earth's* vast hollow woombe,
> *Musick's* deepest BASE shall come.
> Seas, and Flouds, from Shore to Shore,
> Shall the COUNTER-TENOUR roare.
> To this Consort (when we sing)
> Whistling Winds, your DESCANT bring:

Which may beare the sound above,
Where the Orbe of Fire doth move;
And so climbe, from Spheare to Spheare,
Till our Song Th'ALMIGHTY heare.[31]

The belief that the created world, being based on number and proportion, was, in its original unfallen state, a visible and audible embodiment of divine harmony goes back to Pythagoras (see chapter 5). But in describing a world in which human voices praising their creator harmonize with the earth's natural music Wither is probably thinking of St John's Revelation:

And I heard a voyce from heauen, as the sounde of manie waters, & as the sound of a great thunder: & I heard the voyce of harpers harping with their harpes. And they sung as it were a newe song before the throne. (14:2–3)

The 'newe song' is the song of the spirit as opposed to the flesh. If, according to St Paul, the 'old man' signifies the un-regenerate self, and the 'new man' the penitent who has cast off the sins of the old Adam (Eph. 4:22), then the 'new song' mentioned by St John as he echoes the Psalmist (33:3; 40:3; 96:1; 98:1) and Isaiah (42:10) may be interpreted as a life dedicated to Christian piety, and the 'old song' as one of cupidity. The fatal ease with which lovers are capable of mistaking the one song for the other had been traditionally represented in Christian interpretations of the sirens singing to Odysseus. John Lydgate makes the same point by different means in a pair of bird poems. One is entitled 'The floure of Curtesye', the other 'A Seying of the Nightingale'.[32] Both poems begin with bird-song, a 'hevenly comfortable song' in one case, an 'An hevenly complyne with sugred ermonye' in the other. But, despite the fact that both songs are described as 'hevenly', only one of them is actually a song of spiritual devotion; the other is the familiar 'old song'. For what the poet-lover is really hearing as he listens to the sound of the birds' mating calls is the voice of his own natural desires.

It is sometimes suggested that the ambiguities of the Bower of Bliss are an unconscious reflection of Spenser's own suppressed sexuality.[33] From the way he writes about it, it seems likely that he experienced the conflict between conscience and desire as keenly as any sixteenth-century Protestant. However, in the light of the tradition of Christian symbolism I have been describing, it seems likely that the subtle confusions of Acrasia's Bower with its delicious

symphonies of natural and articial sounds owe as much to conscious
artistry as to incompletely sublimated concupiscence. To recognize
that danger of some kind is portended by the cacophonous cries of
the owls, night ravens, bats and other 'prophets of sad destiny' that
menace Guyon's boat in stanzas 35–7 requires no great powers of
moral perception on the hero's part; it was, after all, just such
'vncleane and hateful byrdes' that descended on Babylon when the
city fell (Rev. 18:2). What is much more difficult is to recognize evil
when it is subtly disguised as innocence. If the 'ioyeous birdes' in the
Bower of Bliss seem indistinguishable from those in the Garden of
Adonis – the same epithet is used in both episodes (II.xii.71; III.vi.42)
– this is because to the lover the old song sounds so much like the
new. Small wonder that Sidney's Astrophil, desperately trying to
disentangle desire from true love, cries 'I / One from the other
scarcely can descrie' (72). As Spenser himself remarks when the
Redcrosse Knight, his mind delighted by the 'sweet musick' of
'cherefull birds', begins to succumb to Duessa's sensual charms:

> What man so wise, what earthly wit so ware,
>   As to descry the crafty cunning traine,
>   By which deceipt doth maske in visour faire,
>   And cast her colours dyed deepe in graine,
>   To seeme like Truth, whose shape she well can faine . . .? (I.vii.i)

IV

The Bower of Bliss draws on a long and familiar tradition of
Christian symbolism in which music and birdsong serve to articulate
a dualistic conception of human nature. Three centuries before Pico
della Mirandola's celebrated and frequently quoted 'Oration on the
Dignity of Man' (1486), Alain de Lille had written in the *De planctu
Naturae* (c. 1160–5) of the struggle between passion and reason, the
one enabling 'man to hold converse with angels, the other driv[ing]
him to wanton with brute beasts'.[34] It is from Alain that Spenser's
Genius with his 'double nature' (III.vi.31) is in part descended.[35] In
his struggle for virtue man may be either assisted or hindered by
music, according to whether it allays or excites the passions. It is this
dualistic view of human nature and its susceptibility to the arts that
forms the basis of Spenser's tropological allegory.

But in this period moral concerns can seldom be disentangled
from their wider ramifications, as Stephen Greenblatt points out in a

New Historicist essay on the Bower of Bliss.[36] Greenblatt finds an aporia at the heart of Spenser's allegory. In the climactic episode of Book II we see the hero acting with a destructive violence that seems paradoxically to negate that very ideal of *mezzura* of which he is supposed to be champion. Yet for all his violence, he does not actually destroy his adversary, but instead ties her up in chains of adamant in order 'to keepe her safe and sound' (II.xii.82). An explanation of this paradox lies in the dynamics of power. As Nietzsche observed long before Foucault made the 'other' a fashionable concept, authoritarian governments have more need of enemies than friends.[37] Acrasia is Guyon's demonic other. He depends on her because she establishes his identity as a representative of authority. Guyon cannot kill Acrasia, Greenblatt argues, because if she ceased to exist as a constant threat to civility, the particular form of power he embodies would also cease to exist.[38]

In order to show how *The Faerie Queene* forms part of 'the texture of a particular pattern of life' Greenblatt draws a number of parallels with other contemporary narratives and events. He calls this strategy 'cultural poetics'. As it brings apparently unrelated areas of experience into startling juxtaposition, cultural poetics is highly effective as a way of defamiliarizing the period and forcing the reader to view it with fresh eyes. But its historical interest is of a strictly limited kind. Greenblatt's parallels, or 'reiterations', confirm what his analysis of the Bower of Bliss has suggested, namely, that authority will typically produce its other as a way of justifying its own exercise of power. This phenomenon is not unique to the sixteenth century. As Greenblatt himself remarks, it is something that is 'common to us all'.[39]

Although New Historicism, like Cultural Materialism, is committed to the theory that human nature is discursively produced, in practice it tends to ignore those contingencies and particularities that make the past another country, focusing instead on certain trans-historical cultural paradigms, especially those that reveal the social mechanisms of power. Unlike the New Historicist, the 'old' historian of culture is interested not so much in 'general and transcendental truths which will always be the same'[40] as in those aspects of the past that are alien.[41] Guyons' violent silencing of Acrasia's music may be a classic instance of authority producing its other. But historically it has a more specific meaning, one that is unique to the Reformation and its particular discourses. In addition to its tropological dimension, *The Faeire Queene* is also a self-proclaimed political poem conceived, like Virgil's *Aeneid*, as a celebration through myth and prophecy of a national ideal. The silencing of Acrasia's music forms an essential part of that political meaning.

v

Some years ago A. C. Hamilton drew attention to the close parallels between the symbolic climax of Book II and the corresponding events in Book I.[42] As Guyon must destroy Acrasia's corrupt garden in order to cast off the old unregenerate man, so the Redcrosse Knight's battle against evil takes place in a desecrated Eden, a 'blessed sted' in which 'all good things did grow, / And freely sprong out of the fruit-full ground, / As incorrupted Nature did them sow / Till that dread Dragon all did ouerthrow' (I.xi.46–7). And just as Acrasia's victories are crowned with the triumphal song of birds, so Una's betrothal to the Redcrosse Knight is marked by music; in this case, however, not the music of the flesh, but a 'new song' that elicits echoes of divine approval. It is well known that in terms of the poem's *sensus allegoricus* Una's marriage is a figure for the Tudor union of church and state, and, more precisely, for the idea of Elizabeth's 'marriage' to Christ[43] and to her people.[44] In his commentary on Book I John Upton noted that Spenser's account of the music at Una's wedding was an allusion to the song of the marriage of the Lamb in the nineteenth chapter of Revelation:[45]

And I heard like a voyce of a great multitude, and as the voyce of manie waters, and as the voyce of strong thondrings, saying, Halleluiah: for our Lord God almightie hath reigned. Let us be glad and reioyce, and give glorie to him: for the marriage of the Lambe is come, and his wife hathe made her selfe readie. (19:6–7)

In prophesying the bond between the Messiah and his community St John is here drawing on a well-recognized Old Testament tradition of representing the union between God and his chosen people in the figure of a marriage.[46] It is that bond, purchased with the Messiah's blood, that is the subject of the 'new song' in St John's fifth chapter:

And they sung a new song, saying, Thou art worthie to take the Boke, and to open the seales thereof, because thou wast killed, and hast redemed vs to God by thy blood.(9)

With the religious upheavals of the sixteenth century St John's prophecy took on a very specific meaning. Identification of the Pope with the Antichrist of Revelation had been made as early as 1378 by Wyclif after the Great Schism; by the second decade of the sixteenth century commentaries that interpreted the drama of the apocalypse as a prophecy of the war between Protestantism and popery were legion: 'in Tudor England a whole *genre* of tracts, treatises and sermons was devoted to proving that the papacy was the Antichrist prophesied in Scripture'.[47] Interpreting Revelation as an allegory of the Protestant Reformation, Henry Bullinger wrote in his highly influential *Hundred Sermons upon the Apocalipse*, 'The sume of all is this: the old and new Rome, the Empire and Popish kyngdome, which is the kyngdome of Antichrist shall perish.'[48] As the drama of the apocalypse is politicized, so the new song comes to be seen as a figure not simply for spiritual renewal, but for the restoration of the true Catholic Church. In his commentary on Revelation Bullinger interprets the voice from heaven like the sound of many waters (14:2) as the voice of the reformed church: 'we understand ... hereby, that the Church shall be populous, and speaking ... for the Church getteth from heaven power to preach and shew forth the gospell'. In the same passage he argues that the new song (14:3) is the song of the elect: 'For no man could learne that same song, save the electe' (fol. 201ᵛ).

Spenser draws extensively on contemporary political readings of St John in the first two books of *The Faerie Queene*. While the character of Una is based on a conflation of the Bride of the Lamb (21:9) and the Woman clothed with the Sun (12:1), her antithesis, Acrasia, is modelled in part on the Great Whore of chapter seventeen. The gloss to the Geneva Bible explains that the Woman clothed with the Sun who is threatened by a dragon signifies 'how ye Church which is compassed about with Jesus Christ the Sonne of righteousnes, is persecuted of Antichrist', while the Great Whore represents the papacy: 'This woman is the Antichrist, that is, the Pope with the whole bodie of his filthie creatures' (fol. 120).

This ready-made allegory of the Protestant Reformation provided Spenser with a richly evocative vehicle for his nationalistic message. For contemporary readers used to hearing Elizabeth lauded as a virgin begotten of the Lord, espoused to God's only Son to rule over Sion, it did not require an impossible leap of the imagination to identify their own defender of the faith with the 'royall virgin' of

Book 1 (ii.7; iii.5; viii.26). If the celestial music of Una's wedding feast signifies divine authorization of Elizabeth's rule and a recognition that the British were a people chosen by God for a historic purpose, then the corresponding music in Acrasia's Bower may be read as the siren voice of religious dissent threatening the integrity of the body politic. The sirens who lured the sailor from the safety of his ship with their songs of enchantment were a traditional figure for those heretical doctrines that threatened to undermine the authority of the church.[49] This traditional equation of enchantment with heresy now acquires a specifically Protestant meaning. As Bullinger explains in his commentary on St John, the wickedness of the Great Whore signifies 'corruption through inchauntment. Whereby is signified seducing by corrupte and wicked doctrine . . . Therefore God punisheth the corruption of doctrine, and crueltie of the Romishe Church practised agaynst the Saints of God' (fol. 255). Bullinger's identification of the Great Whore with the papacy is typical of the mainstream of Elizabethan commentaries on the Apocalypse. As one historian puts it: 'There was not a bishop nor superior ecclesiastic in the reformed church to whom the Pope was not in very truth the Antichrist.'[50] But it was not until after 1588 that Elizabethan apocalyptic thought began to acquire an aggressively nationalistic tone.[51] In 1596 George Gifford argued that the servants of God must 'seeke revenge even to the full upon this Romish whore, for all the evill which she hath wrought vnto the Church'.[52] In fact, says Gifford, in proportion as her 'daintie and delicate pleasures' have seduced the faithful, so must her punishment be unsparing.[53] Even more violent in its anticipation of militaristic vengeance is Arthur Dent's *The ruine of Rome*. Dent prophesies that the forces of Catholic Europe will suffer a catastrophic defeat and that 'the foules of the aire shall come to their great supper' and feed on the slaughtered armies.[54] In such a militant political environment Guyon's violent treatment of Acrasia and her subversive arts has a very precise historical meaning, one that Greenblatt's deconstructive reading, for all its subtleties, only obscures. Set in the mythical past of England's faeryland, Guyon's actions are prophetic of the final destruction of the seat of all heresy. As St John prophesies how the great city of Babylon, plagued by birds of ill-omen, shall be obliterated in a débâcle of violent destruction (18:21), so Guyon, forewarned by the evil 'prophets of destiny' that flock about his boat, is shown acting with a prefigurative 'rigour pittilesse' as he destroys Acrasia's 'pleasant bowres and Pallace brave' (83).

It would be wrong to assume that every incident in *The Faerie Queene* can be interpreted in terms of the four-fold theory of allegory that Spenser inherited from the Middle Ages. However, in a period when political writers continued, almost without exception, to base their arguments on analogical premises, it is inevitable that events in the personal domain will have social and political ramifications. Insofar as it was capable of allaying the passions, music was held to be morally beneficial. 'Great profit from it flows', writes Francis Davison,

> for why? it raiseth
> The mind o'erwhelmed with rude passions' might;
> When against reason passions fond rebel,
> Music doth that confirm, and those expel.[55]

It is this meliorative function of art that Acrasia's music has perverted. But according to the analogical argument, the individual is 'an abstract or briefe Storie of the Universal'.[56] As Spenser himself reminds us in his allegory of the House of Alma, the rebellious forces that threaten the body natural are one and the same as the dissident elements that seek to destroy the 'harmonicall agreement' of the body politic. The Bower of Bliss works primarily on the level of tropological allegory. But like Langland before him, Spenser sets the drama of Christian life in the wider context of an apocalyptic battle between church and Antichrist. In doing so he employs the same symbolic antithesis between St John's two cities with which Langland prefaces *Piers Plowman*, but now with that specifically Protestant interpretation that had become ubiquitous since John Bale's *Image of both churches* (1550) established a framework for Elizabethan apocalyptic thought.[57] As Book I culminates with a vision of the New Jerusalem, so Book II concludes with that favourite Elizabethan and Jacobean image of political corruption exposed – the destruction of Babylon.[58] A symbol of the temptations that jeopardize the rule of reason, Acrasia's music of the flesh is at the same time a threat to the triumphal 'new song' of an imperialist state.

CHAPTER 2

Falstaff, Prince Hal and the New Song

Take hede therefore that ye walke circumspectly, not as fooles,
but as wise, / Redeming the time: for the dayes are evil ...
Speaking unto your selves in psalmes, and hymnes, and spiritual songs.

(St Paul, Eph. 5:15–19)

SIR IOHN: Go thy waies old Iacke, die when thou wilt ... A bad
world I say. I would I were a weauer; I could sing psalms, or
any thing.

(*1H4*, II.iv.119–27)

The rejection of Falstaff is painful. Shakespeare's fat knight may
have a long theatrical ancestry as a vice figure,[1] but to the theatre-
goer he is plump Jack, the lovable rascal who is cruelly rejected by a
man who has no scruples about using others for his own ends. To
argue, with Dover Wilson, that the rejection of Falstaff stops being
painful once we recognize his symbolic significance[2] is not just bad
psychology, it obscures one of the essential points to emerge from the
two *Henry IV* plays, namely, that in a corrupt and treacherous world
the successful prince must be prepared to play the Machiavel and
employ what the great Flemish humanist Justus Lipsius contradicto-
rily calls a 'certaine honest and laudable deceipt' in order to safe-
guard his rule.[3] A commonplace of sixteenth-century political
thought, this is also a widely accepted modern critical view of the
plays.[4] It is now generally agreed that the world of *Henry IV* is one in
which authority depends for survival more on political acumen than
on divine protection. In that world both winners and losers exploit
myth for their own advantage. The myth to which Richard anachronistically appeals in such histrionic terms is the myth of the
sacrosanctity of kings and their accountability to God alone – not a
medieval doctrine, but an exaggerated version of a Tudor policy.
Like Richard, Hal too is an actor who exploits the dramatic

44

potential of myth for political purposes. But Hal is more than just an accomplished performer: he is also a shrewd and calculating actor-manager who chooses his company with care. The play he stages is a new variation on an old favourite – the reformed prodigal.[5] Chief supporting actor in this skilfully directed drama of kingship and power is Falstaff. But for Hal he is no mere 'pastime to be dismissed in due course', as C. L. Barber suggests,[6] but an indispensably dispensable part of the plot.

I

In claiming that members of an Elizabethan audience would no more think of protesting at the rejection of Falstaff than their ancestors would have thought of protesting against the summoning of Vice at the end of a morality play,[7] Dover Wilson resolves the discords of Shakespeare's text in a concluding vision of 'decency, order and justice'.[8] Shakespeare sends us home happy, says Wilson, in the knowledge that the 'generosity, magnanimity, respect for law, and selfless devotion to duty which comprise the traditional ideals of our public service' have been upheld by the mirror of all Christian kings.[9] It is true that in the sequel Exeter evokes a prospective image of the various parts of the new body politic 'Congreeing in a full and natural close, / Like Musicke' (*H5*, I.ii.182–3). But *Henry IV* offers no such harmonious closure. On the contrary, we are left with the uncomfortable sense that respect for the law is in some way linked with duplicity and that a reputation for magnanimity has been bought with cunning. Moreover, the political problems broached in the first play of the tetralogy remain conspicuously unresolved. These plays present us not with a piece of Elizabethan propaganda endorsing a theory of absolute obedience but with a dramatic representation of an essentially intractable problem.

It has long been recognized that the 'official' version of Eliza-bethan political doctrine set out by Tillyard in *Shakespeare's History Play* represents only one side of a vigorous contemporary debate.[10] It is a debate that begins with the Tudor attempt to change traditional thinking on the question of the nature of royal authority. Although medieval political theorists strongly deprecated rebellion, they con-ceded that a king who violated his coronation oath could no longer expect obedience from his subjects. In his treatise on kingship (*De regno*) St Thomas Aquinas argues that, while it may be more expedient for subjects to tolerate a mild form of tyranny than to rebel, deposition of tyrannical rulers is justifiable in extreme cases: 'It must not be thought that [the] multitude is acting unfaithfully in deposing the tyrant, even though it had previously subjected itself to him in perpetuity, because he himself has deserved that the coven-ant with his subjects should not be kept, since, in ruling the multi-tude, he did not act faithfully as the office of a king demands.'[11] Contemporary reactions to Richard's increasingly tyrannical rule show that his deposition was regarded by many as a legally justifi-able act.[12] In England it was only with the Reformation that the traditional belief in the rights of subjects to resist unjust authority was replaced by an officially promoted doctrine of non-resistance.

The revolution of 1533–4 had been carried out with the full co-operation of parliament, and the crown was in fact subject to strict constitutional limits. But having rebelled against established authority itself, the Tudor monarchy had to protect itself both against domestic dissatisfaction and the very real threat of retalia-tory invasion from Catholic Europe. This it did by emphasizing the sacrosanctity of the crown: 'To save the Royal Supremacy, a cult of royal authority had of necessity to be set up, and the king's person suffused with a glow of divinity.'[13] When in 1533 the Pope absolved Henry VIII's subjects of any debt of obedience to their king, government pamphleteers countered the bull of excommunication by stressing the religious sin of rebellion against God's anointed vicegerent. Government response was the same when Elizabeth was excommunicated in 1570. 'I do declare unto you', thundered the homily *Against Disobedience and Wilful Rebellion*, 'what an abominable sinne agaynst God and man rebellion is, and howe dreadfullye the wrath of god is kyndled and inflamed agaynst all rebels, and what horrible plagues, punyshmentes, & deathes, and finally eternall damnation doth hang over theyr heades.'[14] That the state's publicly proclaimed doctrine of non-resistance received such widespread acceptance is a measure of the success of the revolution. However, that is not to say that government propaganda went unchallenged. From the 1530s onwards a steady stream of dissident writers had reasserted the medieval belief in the principle of responsible tyranni-cide. In 1594, the year before *Richard II* is generally thought to have been first performed, the Jesuit exile Robert Parsons argued that kings may justifiably be removed 'if they fulfil not the lawes and conditions, by which and for which, their dignity was given them' provided that 'it is done uppon just and urgent causes and by publique authority of the whole body'.[15]

However, more significant (because more truly representative of popular opinion) than the polarized positions represented by the offical homilies on the one hand, and by radicals like Parsons on the other, are the views expressed by middle-of-the-road conservative writers. Early in Elizabeth's reign William Baldwin considers the question of obedience in terms which are interesting chiefly for their ambivalence. In an editorial address to the reader in his 1563 issue of *The Mirror for Magistrates* Baldwin writes:

Whatsoever man, woman, or childe, is by the consente of the whole realme established in the royall seat, so it have not bene injuriously procured by rigour of sword and open force, but quietlye by title, eyther of enherytance, succession, lawful bequest, common consent, or election, is undoubtedlye chosen by God to be his deputie; and whosoever resisteth anye such, resisteth agaynst God him selfe, and is a ranke traytor and rebele.[16]

At first glance it would appear that, as he brands all dissidents as 'rank traitors', Baldwin is simply rehearsing the government line on obedience. However, closer reading makes it clear that his carefully qualified definition of kingship allows for precisely the sort of situation in which Bolingbroke acquired the title.[17] In effect Baldwin is telling us both that rebellion is invariably wrong, and also that a successful usurper who has the consent of the people must be obeyed. The conundrum is unresolved. A similarly studied ambiguity can be seen in the way Elizabeth's own Privy Councillor Sir Thomas Smith defines a king as one 'who by succession or election commeth with the good will of the people to that governement'. Addressing the question of whether subjects have a right to resist tyranny, Smith refuses to condemn rebellion unequivocally, concluding lamely that on the whole it is better not to tamper with the status quo:

When the common wealth is evill governed by an evill ruler and unjust . . . if the lawes be made, as most like they be always to maintaine that estate: the question remaineth whether the obedience of them be just, and the disobedience wrong: the profit and conservation of that estate right and justice, or the dissolution: and whether a good and upright man, and lover of his countrie ought to maintaine and obey them, or seeke be all means to dissolve and abolish them . . . Certaine it is that it is always a doubtfull and hasardous matter to meddle with the chaunging of the lawes and government, or to disobey the orders of the rule of government, which a man doth finde alreadie established.[18]

From the equivocations of these essentially conservative writers as they confront the problems of kingship and authority in a post-Reformation state it is clear that moderate Elizabethan political opinion was remarkable not for its uncritical subservience to official government policy, but for its scepticism. What the modern reader of a representative selection of political pamphlets from the 1580s and 1590s encounters is something far removed from that monolithic structure of quasi-absolutist doctrine which Tillyard represented as constituting 'orthodox' Elizabethan political doctrine. As J. E. Phillips pointed out four years before Tillyard published *Shakespeare's History Plays*: 'In learned treatises and popular pamphlets alike ... a variety of theories and attitudes were developed concerning such individual political problems as the authority of the king, the function of law, the duties of subjects and the right of rebellion.'[19] It is that debate to which the second tetralogy contributes and of which it forms a part.

In the plays themselves we discover that the issues that Tillyard characterized as 'so simple that there is not much to do beyond stating the obvious and trying to make it emphatic'[20] turn out to be impossibly controverted. Instead of a clear-cut case of illegal usurpation by an unprincipled opportunist leading ineluctably to divine retaliation, we find an imbroglio of claims and counter-claims. The more Richard affirms the sanctity of his princely office, the less does he appear justified – by reason of his own tyrannical behaviour – in claiming its protection; the more a conservative old guard (Gaunt) insists on the principle of passive obedience, the less viable do such idealist policies seem as a solution to the problems of a real world. The effects of the Pandora's box of troubles opened by Richard's deposition are felt throughout the second tetralogy and, retrospectively, the first. A measure of their irresolvable complexity is the predicament faced by York, the man who proclaims the indisputable wickedness of rebellion against a hereditary monarch, only to insist with equal conviction on absolute obedience to his usurper. Confronted by the act of resistance that Richard's own flouting of the principle of hereditary succession has provoked, York admits that his dilemma is intractable:

>   both are my kinsmen.
> Tone is my soueraigne, whom both my oath
> And duety bids defend; tother againe
> Is my kinsman, whom the King hath wrongd,
> Whom conscience, and my kinred bids to right.   (*R2*, II.ii.111–15)

When the claims of the rival contenders in this drama of state power appear to cancel each other out with such diagrammatic symmetry and when no single voice of authority is clearly privileged, Leonard Tennenhouse's assertion that Shakespeare is 'using his drama to authorize political authority'[21] would seem to be a difficult one to sustain. It is true that Richard's prophecies of future civil strife prove to be accurate. But there is no evidence that these events are the work of an avenging providence. As Warwick tells Henry, further rebellion might have been predicted on purely empirical grounds (*2H4*, III.i.80–92). Any sense of tragic or heroic action in these plays is repeatedly undercut by buffoonery and treachery. For all Hotspur's winningly ingenuous idealism, it is in reality a sense of personal grievance and injured pride for which the Percys are fighting. As religious principles are forgotten in the dog-eat-dog world of civil war, where rebels and counter-rebels are seemingly little better than highwaymen holding honest citizens to ransom, and honour becomes a 'mere scutcheon', both sides are equally guilty of 'vnkind vsage, daungerous [i.e. menacing] countenance, / And violation of all faith and troth' (*1H4*, v.i.69–70). In this 'distempered' world of muddle, corruption and betrayal one fact emerges with great clarity, namely, that once the talismanic mystique of kingship has been lost or destroyed, national politics quickly degenerates into a brutally unheroic form of tragi-comedy. What had safeguarded Richard was not heaven's protection, but a myth. But myths can only exercise their power if people believe in them. With the failure of his father's plan to rehabilitate his name by making a pilgrimage to the Holy Land, the task of restoring popular belief in the sanctity of kingship falls to Hal. As A. D. Nuttall puts it, his job is to 'make the crown real again'.[22] It is Hal's willingness to employ the tactics of *realpolitik* in the realization of that project which is the mark of his success as a ruler. In the country of the deceitful it is the sharp-eyed man who is king.

II

Whatever its shortcomings may be, *The Fortunes of Falstaff* is a brilliant essay in historical criticism. In his discussion of 'The Falstaff Myth' Dover Wilson points out that it is Hal who associates Falstaff in turn with the Devil of the miracle play, the Vice of the morality and the Riot of the interlude.[23] Later critics have shown how this symbolic identification with a conventional image of corruption is amplified by biblical allusion: Falstaff is associated with the unregenerate man 'which is corrupt through the deceivable lustes', whom St Paul urges the Christian to cast off in order that he may 'put on the new man, which after God is created in right-eousness, and true holines' (Eph. 4:22–4).[24] What has not been noticed is that Falstaff's identification with the Pauline Old Man is confirmed in a remarkably precise way by the music with which he is associated. This musical theme is a crucial element in the political myth that Hal so astutely fosters. However, in discussing the sig-nificance of Falstaff's musical tastes I want to emphasize that the man is no less human for being a symbol.

It is well known that Shakespeare used the symbolic associations of certain musical instruments as a means of expressing character and theme.[25] In the stories of Apollo's contests with Pan and with Marsyas (Ovid, *Metamorphoses* XI and VI) mythographers saw a symbolic distinction between Apollonian stringed instruments and Dionysian wind instruments.[26] It was in this mythological conflict between order, temperance and harmony on the one hand, and the libidinous affections on the other that Giambattista Vico rightly saw a representation of the political struggle between civilization and barbarism.[27] The familiar medieval image of the devil with his horns and cloven goat's hooves derives from Pan. It is scarcely surprising, therefore, that the Pan-like Falstaff's musical predilections should be of a distinctly Dionysian character. Identified in both plays with 'ryot and dishonour' (*1H4*, I.i.85), he is associated with the kind of musical instruments appropriate to a 'tutor and feeder of . . . riots' (*2H4*, v.v.63). The gluttony and lechery that he inherits from the Vice figure of the morality interludes are suggested by references to two instruments in particular. In the following exchange from the scene in which Falstaff makes his first appearance, he is identified with the bagpipe:

SIR IOHN: Zbloud, I am as melancholy as a gyb Cat or a lugd beare.
PRINCE: Or an old lyon, or a louers Lute.
SIR IOHN: Yea, or the drone of a Lincolnshire bagpipe.
PRINCE: What saiest thou to a Hare, or the malancholy of Mooreditch?

(*1H4*, I.ii.71–4)

In the Middle Ages the bagpipe was closely associated with the pleasures of the flesh. Having been banished, after the thirteenth century, to the lower social orders,[28] it began to assume a wide role in the social life of rustic Europe and provided music for most social

1. Hercules facing the choice between Virtue and Vice. Music (a lute) is symbolically placed midway between the two figures. George Wither, *A Collection of Emblemes* (London, 1635), Book I, no. 22

gatherings. Its *obbligato* function in country festivals is graphically represented in European painting, notably in the work of Bosch and Bruegel, where it frequently appears as a symbol of gluttony and lechery.[29] However, it is the bagpipe's association with the tavern, symbolic abode of the devil, which is of most interest in the present context. Bosch, in the right-hand wing of *The Garden of Earthly*

2.   Music as a symbol of profane love. Fifteenth-century manuscript illustration
of a French translation of Boccaccio's *Il Filostrato*. Bodleian Library, Douce Ms
33¹, 43ᵛ

Delights, and Bruegel in the *The Peasant Dance*, both identify the
bagpipe symbolically with the inn. Indeed, in Bosch's painting a
bagpipe actually forms the sign of the infernal tavern. That the
bibulous Falstaff should be compared, among other 'vnsauory
similes', to 'a Lincolnshire bagpipe' is not inappropriate.

Nor is it very surprising that Hal should compare him with 'a
louers Lute'. Although the lute, as a stringed instrument, conventionally carries Apollonian associations, its symbolism is more
complex than that of the bagpipe. Its ambivalence as a symbol of
love is perhaps best illustrated in a pair of devices from George
Wither's *Collection of Emblemes, Ancient and Moderne*. An emblem from
the second book of Wither's collection shows the figure of Cupid
holding a lute. The legend tells us that '*Love's* a good *Musician*; and,
will show / How, every faithfull *Lover* may be so'. However, in an
emblem from Book 1 depicting the choice of Hercules the lute is
symbolically placed midway between Virtue and Vice, suggesting
that it may be used to promote either wisdom or else all that 'the

wanton *Flesh* desires to have' (illus.1).[30]   As a symbol of concupiscence the lute is commonly found in medieval paintings, both as a typical feature of the stylized *hortus amoenus* and in more naturalistic contexts. An example of the latter may be seen in a manuscript illustration to a fifteenth-century French translation of Boccaccio's *Il Filostrato* (illus. 2). In a scene in which Pandarus is shown tiptoeing towards the sleeping Cressida, a lute is prominently displayed on the *credenza* (see illus. 6). In this apparently quite naturalistic detail is neatly encapsulated the central theme of the story, at least as Boccaccio's translator saw it. In abetting the cause of profane love, music has been perverted from its true function as the inducer of virtue. Renaissance artists frequently place lutes in the hands not only of angels and *putti*, but also of courtesans. But it is again in the work of Bosch that the lute receives its most explicit treatment as a symbolic parody of virtue. In *The Last Judgment* Bosch juxtaposes a lute and a bagpipe to symbolize the discords of hell. Beside these instruments is a gigantic harp on whose strings a sinner has been hung. Here Bosch is alluding to the tradition of representing David's harp as a symbolic type of the cross upon which are stretched the sinews of Christ, the musician of the world (illus. 3).[31]

Unlike the bagpipe, which is generally associated with lechery and gluttony in this period, the lute's significance as a symbol of vice depends essentially on the idea of parody. Characteristic of evil is its propensity for mocking and perverting the true forms of virtue – something at which Falstaff is notably adept. Thus, although the iconography of the 'louers Lute' to which Hal compares the melancholy Falstaff may be arcane, its meaning in this context is clear enough. This is plainly no symbol of virtue. For undoubtedly the sound that Falstaff is used to hearing in the Eastcheap tavern is not an angelic chorus choiring to young-eyed cherubim, but the lascivious pleasing of a lute. Indeed, Falstaff makes it quite clear where his own preferences lie when he asks Bardolph: 'come sing me a bawdie song, make me merry' (*1H4*, III.iii.12).

In Part II Falstaff is consistently linked with the music of the tavern. What may escape the reader who has no opportunity of seeing the play in production is simply the amount of music it contains. In Act II, scene iv, for example, music forms an accompaniment to much of the action. Though the reader may note the Page's cue, 'The musique is come sir' (*2H4*, II.iv.216), he cannot be expected to remember, while he is attending to the multiple ironies

3.   The discords of hell. Hieronymus Bosch, *The Last Judgment* (detail)

of this complex gulling scene, that Sneak's 'noise' is still going on. Falstaff makes his entry in this scene singing two lines of a ballad: 'When Arthur first in court . . . / And was a worthy king' (II.iv.33, 35). He also threatens, later in the play, to publicize his 'defeat' of Colville in 'a particular ballad ... with mine owne picture on the top on't (Coluile kissing my foote)' (IV.iii.45–6). Falstaff's companions share his musical tastes. Pistol quotes from two ballads (II.iv.187–9, v.iii.139); Falstaff associates Justice Shallow with a hautboy and tells how he 'sung those tunes to the overscutch'd huswifes that he heard the carmen whistle, and sware they were his fancies or his good-nights' (III.ii.305–6); and Silence in Act v, scene iii, sings six ballad snatches.

Falstaff's association with tavern music underscores the link that Hal makes between him and the devil: 'there is a diuell haunts thee in the likenesse of an olde fat man' (*1H4*, II.iv.431–2). It has been pointed out, moreover, that music was a general characteristic of the Vice figure and his associates. J. R. Moore notes that in the morality plays

angels are never singers, as they were so commonly in the miracle plays. In the moralities before 1500 or shortly after the beginning of the new century, the holy characters and the repentant sinners sing in Latin, usually verses from the Vulgate ... But in the moralities of this period the vernacular song is regarded as a lure of the flesh and the devil. It is to be sung in taverns or in idle company elsewhere and it is intimately associated with music and dancing.[32]

Music, dance and lewd songs are associated with the vice characters in *Mankind* (*c.* 1465), *The Trial of Treasure* (1567), the *Interlude of the Four Elements* (1520?) and the *Interlude of Youth* (*c.* 1557), and with Lucifer himself in *Wisdom* (*c.* 1460). Like the evil characters of these plays, Falstaff and his companions are connoisseurs of the devil's music. But Falstaff's remark, 'a bad world I say, I would I were a weauer. I could sing psalmes or any thing' (*1H4*, II.iv.125–6) and his excuse to the Lord Chief Justice for the loss of his voice: 'I haue lost it with hallowing, and singing of Anthems' (*2H4*, I.ii.178) are more than simply witty pervasions of the truth. They form a part of an extensive network of biblical allusion that serves to identify Falstaff not simply with the theatrical Vice figure, but with the unregenerate man of St Paul's Epistle to the Ephesians.

III

The many allusions to St Paul in both parts of *Henry IV* have been well documented. Warwick's prediction that 'the Prince will, in the perfectness of time, / Cast off his followers' (*2H4*, IV.iv.745–75) and Hal's own words 'I know thee not, old man ... I have turn'd away my former self' (*2H4*, v.v.48–59) acquire particular significance in the light of St Paul's injunction to the Ephesians to cast off the Old Man and put on the new. Set against this pattern of biblical allusion, Falstaff's taste in bawdy tavern music may be seen not only as the wonderfully effective stage realism that it is, but also as an essential part of the play's symbolic structure. In this context Falstaff's two hypocritical references to church music, quoted above, sound very much like a witty parody of St Paul:

Take hede therefore that ye walke circumspectly, not as fooles, but as wise,

Redeeming the time: for the dayes are evil . . .

Speaking unto your selves in psalmes, and hymnes, and spiritual songs, singing and making melodie to the Lord in your hearts. (Eph. 5:15–16, 19)

The association of the Old Man with the Old Song was a commonplace of medieval theology, and Falstaff is consistently linked with the sort of music that would have characterized the song of the unregenerate man.

The Old Song was the antithesis of that spoken of in Psalm 40, verse 3:

And he hathe put in my mouth a new song of praise unto our God: manie shal se it and feare, and shal trust in the Lord.

And in Revelation, chapter 5, verse 9:

And they sung a new song, saying, Thou art worthie to take the Boke, and to open the seales thereof, because thou wast killed, and hast redemed us to God by thy blood out of everie kinred, and tongue, and people, and nation.

And chapter 14, verse 3:

And they sung as it were a newe song before the throne, and before the foure beasts, and the Elders, and no man colde learne that song, but the hundreth, fortie and four thousand, which were boght from the earth.

The Old Song was the music of the unenlightened, the melody of the flesh rather than of the spirit.

In the second century, Clement of Alexandria identified the New Song with the Word of God and thus with Christ, and contrasted it with the old music of the pagan minstrels who were supposed to have charmed beasts with their music. For Clement the 'heavenly word', that is, Christ, sings the 'new music, with its eternal strain that bears the name of God. This is the new song, the song of Moses.' The power of the New Song is such that, like Orpheus' music, it has made men out of stones and men out of wild beasts. They who were otherwise dead, who had no share in the real and true life, revived when they but heard the song. Furthermore, it is this which composed the entire creation into melodious order, and tuned into concert the discord of the elements, that the whole universe might be in harmony with it.[33]

Inevitably, the New Song that Clement speaks of is identified with the true music of David, which puts demons to flight and healed Saul.

A century later St Victorinus, Bishop of Petau, implicitly identified the New Song with the enlightened New Man:

'Twenty-four elders and four living creatures, having harps and phials, and singing a new song.' The proclamation of the Old Testament associated with the New, points out the Christian people singing a new song, that is, bearing their confession publicly. It is a new thing that the Son of God should become man ... It is a new thing to give remission of sins to men. It is a new thing for men to be sealed with the Holy Spirit.[34]

St Augustine (345–430), whose sermons were used throughout the Middle Ages, explicitly identified the Old Man with the Old Song, and the New Man with the New Song. In a number of sermons, he effectively collates St Paul's epistle to the Ephesians, chapter 4, verses 22–4, with Psalm 40, verse 3. In one sermon he says that the Old Man may become New and sing the New Song by following the dictates of St Paul.[35]

Falstaff's identification with the Old Song is suggested not only by his ironic talk of singing psalms, but also by the instruments he is associated with, for the Old and the New Songs were consistently characterized in terms of the traditional opposition between wind and stringed instruments. In an emblem designed to illustrate the ennobling powers of music Wither speaks of 'Faith new-songs' as the music of strings:

> Wee should in *Voice*, in *Hand*, and *Heart*, agree:
> And, sing out, *Faiths* new-songs, with full concent,
> Vnto the *Lawes*, ten-stringed *Instrument*.[36]

The source for Wither's 'ten-stringed instrument' and its identification with the Decalogue is Psalm 144:

I wil sing a newe song unto thee, o God, and sing unto thee upon a viole, and an instrument of ten strings. (Ps. 144:9)

The New Song is similarly identified with string music in St John's Revelation. The four-and-twenty elders who worship the lamb have

> everie one harpes and golden viales full of odours,
> which are the prayers of the Saintes,
> And they sung a new song.   (Rev. 5:8–9)

Medieval manuscripts depicting the Old and the New Songs make use of the traditional antithesis of wind and string instruments to illustrate their texts. D. W. Robertson has shown that the New Song is most frequently depicted as the music of David's harp, while the music of the flesh is represented by the bagpipe.[37] Falstaff's own musical inclinations are nicely consistent with this tradition.

IV

Falstaff's association with the music of the devil confirms the role of *vetus homo* in which Hal has cast him. Attractive as we may find him as a comic character, we cannot deny that he possesses all the vices castigated by St Paul: lasciviousness, gluttony, drunkenness, mendacity, self-deception. However, to say that he is a symbolic embodiment of the unregenerate man would not be entirely true. St Paul's letter is an allegory: the Old Man signifies human nature in its corrupt and fallen state; the New Man represents the individual who has been reborn through sanctifying grace. Patently, there is only a very limited sense in which this trope can be applied to *Henry IV*. Unlike St Paul's Epistle, the play is not, as Danby implies, an allegorical psychomachia.[38] Falstaff cannot be said to represent the wild, untamed aspect of Hal's nature when it is made clear as early as the second scene of Part I that the prince's apparent profligacy is part of an astute political stratagem. 'My reformation', says Hal in his first soliloquy,

> glittring ore my fault,
> Shal shew more goodly, and attract more eyes
> Then that which hath no foile to set it off.
> Ile so offend to make offence a skill,
> Redeeming time when men thinke least I will.
>   (*1H4*, I.ii.206–10)

We cannot truly say that Hal has cast off the Old Man within himself when his appearance of degeneracy was a political gambit designed to enhance his reputation. It is Hal himself who, in rejecting his followers and renouncing the world of the tavern, turns an act of political expediency into allegory. The fact that what he is claiming is not strictly true does not lessen its impact for his stage audience. In spurning the Old Man and assuming the 'new and gorgeous garment, Maiesty' (*2H4*, v.ii.44), Hal is not so much reforming his own life as symbolically casting himself in the public role of New Man.

Of Hal's skill as a performer there is no question. The Gadshill robbery; the acting out of the king's displeasure with his profligate son; the gulling of Falstaff at dinner – all these testify to an actor's natural talent for deception. But to suggest, as Graham Holderness does in what is otherwise one of the best recent discussions of *Henry IV*, that Hal's public declaration of his reformation represents a renunciation of the world of theatrical illusion[39] as he confronts the reality of duty is to misunderstand not only the prince's own nature, but that of the occasion itself. More than his other performances, this is essentially a piece of theatre which depends on the presence of a stage audience for its effect. Now, however, Hal can deploy the whole panoply of stage pageantry in support of his new role. In contrast with the disorder and confusion of act v, scene iv as Doll Tearsheet and Mistress Quickly are carried off shrieking and cursing by the beadle's men, the final scene is marked by its formality. The strewers lay their rushes; the trumpets sound; and the new king, bearing the symbols of his office and attended by his train, makes his coronation entry. The forms of Elizabethan pageantry which this scene so clearly reflects had been established by customs. Triumphal arches, formal orations, complimentary verses, songs, tableaux, masques and other emblematic displays of power all served to present an image of the perfect prince appointed by heaven to rule a chosen people.[40]

An important element in royal pageantry was the apparently spontaneous interruption, as for example when Elizabeth would 'chance' to meet one of the Wild Men who apparently thronged the English countryside. A glimpse of his sovereign is enough instantly to tame the Wild Man and turn his savagery to civility.[41] Falstaff's supplication of his king has the appearance of just such a calculatedly spontaneous interruption; indeed so far as he is concerned it probably is. But for Hal it provides the opportunity for a piece of quick-thinking improvisation on a theme that has already been plotted. Essential to the success of his scheme is a symbolic opponent. To establish himself in the public mind as the New Man he needs a symbolic embodiment of vice which he can be seen to reject. Having cast Falstaff firmly in the role of *vetus homo* Hal now capitalizes on a potentially embarrassing situation as he stages an emblematic enactment of his own reformation. 'Presume not that I am the thing I was', he tells Falstaff, and then, turning to his audience, continues 'For God doth know, *so shall the world perceiue*, / That I haue turnd away my former selfe' (v.v.57–9, my italics). What the world actually does perceive is of course partly a matter of what it wants to perceive and partly what it is encouraged to perceive. In the aftermath of a period of unprecedented social conflict one thing it desperately wanted to see was a heroic prince capable of leading England out of the turmoil of the last two reigns. A measure of Hal's success in persuading the world that he is just such a man can be seen in the Archbishop of Canterbury's account of his wondrous reformation in the first scene of *Henry V*:

> The breath no sooner left his Fathers body,
> But that his wildnesse, mortify'd in him,
> Seem'd to dye too: yea, at that very moment,
> Consideration like an Angell came,
> And whipt th'offending *Adam* out of him;
> Leauing his body as a Paradise,
> T'inuelop and containe Celestiall Spirits.   (1.i.25–31)[42]

In the archbishop's portentous rhetoric, with its echoes of the language of the baptism service, we see myth in the making. The new king has already become the subject of legend.

The allegorical conflict between the music of civilization and the siren voice of barbarism is a well-rehearsed *topos* in this period; indeed, the joco-serious struggle between Falstaff and Hal, the one with his incorrigibly Dionysian musical tastes, the other self-consciously identifying himself with the sun (*1H4*, 1.ii.201) inevitably recalls the contest between Pan and the youthful Apollo. But for an Elizabethan audience the reformed prince who is seen publicly to cast out his satanic other would have a more precise significance. As I have shown in chapter 1, the New Song came to be interpreted by Protestant reformers as a figure expressing not simply the spiritual renewal of the individual, but the triumph of God's chosen people in their war against Pope–Antichrist. The New Song is the song of an elect nation: as Henry Bullinger writes in his influential commentary on St John's Revelation, 'no man could learne that same song, save the electe'.[43] That contemporary audiences should have been struck by what they saw as analogies between the events of the second tetralogy and their own situation is not surprising. For although Shakespeare, like virtually every political dramatist writing in the 1590s, is careful for obvious reasons to avoid topical allusion in his presentation of pre-Reformation history,[44] the problems that confront his characters – the nature of regal authority; whether and in what circumstances rebellion could ever be justified; the legalities of succession; the risk of foreign war – were essentially those that concerned his contemporaries. Indeed, it was precisely the events of 1533–4 that gave them a particular urgency. With the revival of a cult of royal quasi-divinity in the militaristic environment of the 1590s, when bellicose pamphleteers were predicting the imminent destruction of Antichrist[45] and the notion of *patria* had begun to acquire a powerfully emotive significance,[46] the New Man ruthlessly suppressing rebellion has an inescapably topical meaning, particularly when he is represented as a 'true louer of the holy Church' (*H5*, I.i.23). He is an essential element in that opportunistic political mythology which England's break with Rome made necessary.

In exploiting religion for political purposes Hal is doing no more than Scroop does in cynically turning 'Insurrection to Religion' (*2H4*, I.i.201). Each in effect 'Deriues from heuen, his Quarrell, and his Cause' (*2H4*, I.i.206), because in doing so he knows that there is no more effective way of legitimizing his authority than to represent it as an expression of God's will and thus part of the natural order of things. Once the seed of the myth of the reformed prodigal had been sown in the popular mind it needed only the voice of rumour to nurture it and bring it to fruition. By the sixteenth century the myth of the New Man had become reified as each of the major chroniclers hands on the story to his successor.[47] In Holinshed, Shakespeare found the following account:

But this king even at first appointing with himselfe, to shew that in his person princelie honors should change publike manners, he determined to *put on him the shape of a new man*. For whereas aforetime he had made himselfe a companion unto misrulie mates of dissolute order and life, he now banished them all from his presence.[48]

It is this traditional identification of the newly crowned king with the New Man of St Paul that Hal exploits for political purposes. But *Henry IV* is no mere recital of facts and legends. As a self-consciously theatrical work of art that repeatedly draws attention to its own dramatic nature, the play lays bare the strategic role of myth in the drama of political life. Such is the power of symbolic spectacle that an act of judicious treachery can assume an almost hagiological status until, promoted by the church and circulated by a multitude playing on the pipe of rumour, it becomes an emblem of those 'traditional ideals of public service' that constitute our national ideology.

Insofar as it engages with questions of kingship and authority, *Henry IV* is just as much part of the contemporary discourse of power as a historical chronicle, a political pamphlet, an editor's address to his reader or a royal pageant. This is true however carefully the play avoids open commitment to any particular political position. But to pretend that there is no essential difference between literature and other forms of discursive practice[49] is to deny to drama, not only its political function as a discloser of ideology, but also – more absurdly – that aesthetic appeal which alone is capable of capturing the imaginations of theatre audiences and holding their attention for the two hours' traffic of the stage. There can be few plays that illustrate more effectively the truth of Macherey's contention – later substantially modified – that 'literature establishes myth and illusion as visible objects'.[50] It is just such a way of seeing that *Henry IV* offers its audiences.[51] That Shakespeare's Henry V wins the hearts and minds of his subjects, both by his respect for parliament and by his sympathy with the common man, is indisputable and underlines the fact that love of the people was widely regarded as a more important qualification for kingship than impeccable hereditary credentials. But that should not disguise the fact that he is also a ruthless military opportunist who follows his father's advice in busying 'giddie mindes / With forraine quarrells' (*2H4*, IV.v.213–14). By bringing conflicting points of view into unresolved collision and denying its audience a single authoritative voice, *Henry IV* invites us to construct from within the play a critique of the ideology it dramatizes, an ideology of such talismanic power that it is capable of safeguarding the reputation of a militaristic ruler for posterity and persuading us that the authoritarian regime of which he is a symbol and type is the earthly form of a divine pattern of social harmony, 'congreeing in a full and natural close, / Like Musicke'.

CHAPTER 3

Prospero, King James and the myth of the musician-king

Prospero's masques are ... vanities indeed, having no basis in economic and political reality.
(David Lindley, 'Music, Masque and Meaning in *The Tempest*')

The masque is basically an elite private entertainment, very much to do with symbols and emblems and allegories. And anybody who has seen my cinema will know that metaphors and allegories fascinate me enormously.
(Peter Greenaway on *Prospero's Books*)

In the central stanzas of his hymn *On the Morning of Christ's Nativity* Milton describes a visionary masque in which, summoned by the power of music, the allegorical figures of Truth and Justice return once more to the earth 'Orb'd in a Rain-bow'.[1] Milton's imagined masque is a conflation of two traditional themes: the Neoplatonic belief that if our hearts were purified we should once again hear the music of the spheres; and the idea, expressed in Virgil's Fourth Eclogue, of the restoration of the age of Saturn.[2] Echoes of the wedding masque in the fourth act of *The Tempest*, in which Juno and Ceres descend on a rainbow singing of Golden Age peace and fecundity, are probably intentional: Milton would have recognized that Prospero's spectacle was not the escapist fantasy it is often accused of being, but a qualified expression of human potentialities. As he explains in an essay on the music of the spheres, only if human nature were to be reformed would 'all things turn back to the Age of Gold, and we ourselves, free from every grief, would pass our lives in a blessed peace which even the gods might envy'.[3]

Like Milton's hymn, *The Tempest* offers its audiences a vision of social harmony in which discords are resolved by the magical power of 'solemne musicke'. In the sixteenth and early seventeenth centuries the most widely used vehicle for the Neoplatonic belief in the rehabilitative function of the arts is the myth of the musician-king (see Introduction, pp. 2–7). But in adapting this myth and making it the basis for a parable of good government, *The Tempest* is not just another *speculum principis*, or even for that matter a *speculum mundi*. This is no piece of mimetic art holding the mirror up to nature, but the work of a poet freely ranging within the zodiac of his own wit, creating magical visions in which music, song and spectacle combine, in Puttenham's words, to 'inueigle and appassionate the mind'.[4] As it repeatedly exposes these visions for the fictions they are, *The Tempest* suggests that it is finally up to us what kind of social order we create. In doing so it deconstructs, as it were, the experience of the newly fashionable theatre of spectacle, self-consciously disposing of the notion of dramatic texts as authoritative and inflexible sources of meaning and proposing instead a more fluid view of art in which meaning is generated by a dialogue between play and audience.

Like the earlier romantic comedies *The Tempest* harmonizes disjunctions in a symbolic marriage of opposites. But in all these plays closure is provisional. In *A Midsummer Night's Dream* the happy union of the two pairs of lovers is undercut by an alternative ending in which the conflict between authority and passion ends not with reconciliation, but with death. In *As You Like It* the seemingly miraculous resolution of love's problems is presented as hypothesis: only *if* (and the word is repeated thirteen times in the space of fifty-odd lines) Orlando is prepared to believe in the power of Rosalind's 'magic' will his wishes will be realized. As Touchstone remarks, 'much vertue in if' (v.iv.97).[5] Closure has a similarly provisional nature in *The Tempest*: not only are some characters excluded from the play's valedictory scene of repentance, forgiveness and reconciliation, but even the happiness of the lovers is conditional. Like *As You Like It*, *The Tempest* implies that there may be 'much vertue in if'; in asking us to entertain a hypothesis, it demands that we consider the contingent nature of the myths that form the basis of our sense of political reality. By ignoring those myths recent criticism has not so much deconstructed as misconstrued a play that is never less than fully conscious of its own affective devices.

I

Post-structuralist historicists on both sides of the Atlantic emphasize the gulf that separates their own principles and methods from the 'worn-out formalism', the 'potted history of ideas' and the 'myopic historiography' that is said to be the stock-in-trade of traditional Renaissance scholarship.[6] Claiming that traditionalists, in their preoccupation with transcendent meanings and universal human truths, effectively strip the texts they study of any political meaning, post-structuralist historicism aims to relocate literature in its authentic historical context and in this way to show how subjectivity is discursively produced. For a number of critics this means, in practice, reading *The Tempest* as part of the English colonial experience. As Francis Barker and Peter Hulme explain, it is this 'ensemble of fictional and lived practices' that provides the play's 'dominant discursive con-texts'.[7]

There are, of course, many discourses at work in *The Tempest* – humanist, Christian, Neoplatonist, monarchist, paternalist, colonialist – to name only those that might be regarded as serving to articulate the interests of the court before which *The Tempest* was first performed by the King's Men in 1611.[8] Colonialism undoubtedly provides an important key to some of the play's latent meanings. But to privilege this motif and say that it dominates all others is to reduce the play's significance. *The Tempest* is so elusive in its protean ability to accommodate different interpretations that any attempt to pin it down in this way is inevitably to falsify it. Nevertheless, insofar as discourses generate patterns of symbolic imagery and enlist mythological narratives to articulate their particular view of reality, the play may be said to belong to the general discursive field of Neoplatonism, elements of which had a special interest for James I.[9] It is not so much a matter of this discourse, with its characteristic images of musical harmony and discord, providing Shakespeare with a source of metaphors for articulating the problems of colonial rule as the other way round: in travellers' reports of the New World and its inhabitants Shakespeare found a test of what Johnson called 'the contest about the original benevolence or malignity of man'[10] – one that apparently confirmed his belief in the need for responsible autocracy. Such a political philosophy may not accord with modern common-sense notions of social justice;[11] but in the early seventeenth century common sense told a very different story from the one it tells us in the late twentieth century. It said first of all that you cannot have social justice if you violate that complex ensemble of mutual obligations and responsibilities that Renaissance political philosophers called natural law.[12] And as *King Lear* reminds us, that is something that can just as easily be done by a prince as by his meanest subject. To argue, as Kiernan Ryan does, that a 'hierarchical ideology which divides people into masters and servants ... has no natural foundation or validity'[13] begs a rather large philosophical question.

Natural law is a notoriously slippery term in this period. John Donne said he had read it countless times before he understood it once;[14] Montaigne claimed that it was inaccessible to human reason.[15] However, as I shall argue more fully in chapter 5, it would be quite wrong to conclude that a vigorous debate about the meaning of nature meant that there was any significant abandonment, in the first half of the seventeenth century at least, of those Neopythagorean principles of order that inform the great bulk of cosmological, anthropological and political thinking in Renaissance England. Right up to the outbreak of war in 1642 the leaders of the parliamentary opposition continued to argue that monarchy was superior to any other form of government.[16] Since the universe is like a vast musical instrument played by the hand of God, it followed from the law of correspondence that social harmony could only be achieved if the strings of state were similarly played by a single hand. A harmonious state, says Hooker in the *Laws of Ecclesiastical Polity*, is like a well-tuned instrument responding to the skilful touch of the musician-king:

Where the *King* doth guide the state and the lawe the *King*, that commonwealth is like an harpe or melodious instrument, the stringes whereof are tuned and handled by one hand, following as lawes the rules and canons of Musicall science.[17]

However, if it was generally believed that, in Castiglione's words, 'the worlde is made of musike, and the heavens in their moving make a melodie, and our soule is framed after the verie same sort',[18] it was also recognized that, owing to the corruption of human nature at the Fall, the fragile web of social concord could all too easily be destroyed. This is the burden of the frequently quoted speech on degree in *Troilus and Cressida*: 'Take but degree away, vntune that string', warns Ulysses, 'And harke what discord followes' (i.iii.109–10). In a fallen world it is the task of the musician-king to restore harmony to a divided society. One of the central ironies of *Richard II* is the fact that a prince who claims he has 'the daintinesse of ear / To checke time broke in a disordred string' is himself responsible for contributing to a state of national crisis in which 'time is broke and no proportion kept' (v.v.43–6). 'Wolde god that now were on / An other such as Arion', wrote John Gower during the period of civil turmoil that culminated in his deposition in 1399:

> if ther were such on now,
> Which cowthe harpe as he tho dede,
> He myhte availe in many a stede
> To make pes wher now is hate.[19]

In echoing Horace's allegorization of the Orpheus story,[20] Gower is making a thinly concealed apology for his own poem. Spenser makes a similar defence of his own political role when he appeals in *The Faerie Queene* to Orpheus as a type of the poet-musician who restores harmony to a discordant world by means of 'wise words with time concented' (IV.ii.1–2).

A parallel tradition going back to the early Church Fathers substituted King David for Orpheus.[21] According to St Ambrose (*c.* 340–97) it was David who, in instituting psalmody, provided fallen man with the means of raising himself spiritually.[22] In the sixteenth century King David was popularly regarded as a 'celestial Orpheus'.[23] Like his classical prototype, the psalmist is a tamer of the wayward human spirit. Puttenham explains how it was these musician-kings with their 'discreete and wholesome lessons vttered in harmonie and with melodious instruments' who first civilized humanity.[24] This myth, or rather Shakespeare's critical adaptation of it, is central to the *The Tempest*'s political and artistic vision.

II

'Sweet musicke' and its antithesis, cacophonous noise, are an essential (and for an audience inescapable) part of the symbolic fabric of *The Tempest*. Opening with a scene of confusion in which the 'tempestuous noise' of the elements mirrors the disruption of customary social relations on board the foundering ship, *The Tempest* tells a story of authority reasserting dynastic rights, quashing new rebellions and establishing social harmony. Shakespeare's immediate source for his tale of shipwreck and mutiny was William Strachy's report of the loss of the *Sea Adventurer* off the Bermudas in 1609. Drawing on Strachy's account of 'those infortunate (yet fortunate) Ilands', where shipwrecked sailors experience a seemingly miraculous

deliverance from 'tempests, thunders and other fearefull objects',[25]
Shakespeare gives his play the romantic setting of a fertile island
magically filled with sounds and sweet airs. In this idealized world of
harmonious natural forces where rebels are, for the most part,
laughably ineffectual and at least some sinners are brought to
repentance, music is an omnipresent agent of reconciliation and
rehabilitation. Recollecting his crime against Prospero, Alonso cries,

> O, it is monstrous: monstrous:
> Me thought the billowes spoke, and told me of it,
> The windes did sing it to me: and the Thunder,
> (That deep and dreadfull Organ-Pipe) pronounc'd
> The name of *Prosper*: it did base my Trespasse.   (III.iii.95–9)

Ariel's magical music leads not only to repentance, but also to love.
Thinking, possibly, of the story of Orpheus and Jason's crew of
Argonauts, Shakespeare shows Ferdinand led not by '*Syren* teares' to
'ruin'd loue' (*Sonn.* 119), but instead by Ariel's magical songs to
chaste Miranda and the romantic union that will eventually join the
feuding houses of Milan and Naples.[26]

   The identification of music and love with social harmony is a
commonplace of medieval and Renaissance thought. In his *Schoole of
Abuse* (1579) Stephen Gosson writes:

The politike lawes in wel gouerned common wealthes, that treade downe
the proude and upholde the meeke; the loue of the king and his subiectes,
the father and his chylde ... are excellent maisters to shewe you that this is
right musicke, this perfect harmony.[27]

Music and love are complementary aspects of the same cosmological
principle.[28] In one of the most widely read of all late classical texts,
the *Consolation of Philosophy*, Boethius develops this traditional idea,
explaining that it is love 'that gouernythe both the land and the sea,
and likewyse commaundeth the heuen, and kepyth the world in due
order and accorde, that is to saye: causythe ye due seasons of the
yere to come successyuely according to their nature'.[29] Because the
same principles of order and disorder govern every plane of existence, the well-regulated society will manifest that loving concord
which underlies the elemental harmony of the universe. It is the
same love, Boethius explains, which 'conserueth vertuous folke, and
suche as be ioyned together in the bond of frendship ... [and]
knytteth together the sacrament of wedlocke, with chast loue
betwene man and wyfe'.[30]

Boethius is describing an ideal world. Love may be the foundation of universal order; but in a fallen world where *caritas* has been replaced by *cupiditas*, it is a universal source of strife and confusion. 'Howe happye were mankynd', he writes,

yf this loue of God that rulyth heuen, myght rule and gouerne theyr myndes, that is to say: that they myght so agre together in such perfyte frendeshyp, that one myght loue another, and agre as the elements do agre.[31]

It is because man has lost his natural temper that he needs the arts of civilization to harmonize his fallen nature. Symbolic agent of that process is the musician-king. For Ficino, he embodies that love which is the 'perpetual knot or link of the whole universe'.[32]

Whether or not we choose to see Prospero's abjuring of his magic as the playwright's farewell to the stage, it is clear that the exiled Duke of Milan has much in common with the inspired pedagogue of humanist tradition who uses his magical powers to rehabilitate a discordant society. Where the benign but ineffectual Gonzalo is seen by Antonio and Sebastian as a parody of Amphion raising the walls of Thebes (ii.i.89–91), Prospero himself combines elements of both Orpheus and Arion. Like Arion he is the victim of plots against his life; like Orpheus he uses 'heauenly Musicke' (v.i.52) to tame the natural passions, and even has the power to restore the dead to life by his 'so potent Art' (v.i.50). But most important, he is an enchanter (from L. *canere*, to sing) who employs his art in the service of political order.

In 1610, the year before *The Tempest* was first performed, a panegyric to James I, the self-proclaimed poet-prince,[33] linked all three figures in an emphatic claim for the symbolic power of 'sweete concording Musicke':

Behold, how like another Orpheus, Amphion, and Arion, he draweth to the true knowledge of God, very salvage Beasts, Forrests, Trees, and Stones, by the sweet Harmony of his harp: the most fierce and wilde, the most stupid and insenced, the most brutish and voluptuous, are changed and ciuilized by the delectable sound of his Musicke. The which may transport and rauish our eares, at his mellodious touchinges and concordes, and not tickle them with any delicate noyse, tending vnto voluptuous and sensuall pleasure: but rather such, as by well tempered proportions are able to reduce all extravagant rudenesse, and circuites of our soules, though they had wandered from the right way, to the true path of dutie, and settle all thoughts in such a harmony, as is most pleasing vnto them.[34]

Like the idealized James, for whom he serves in part as an epideictic model of both praise and warning, Prospero is a type of the Orphic tamer of wayward human passions.

Reflecting, as it does, on the nature of royal power,[35] *The Tempest* has become an obvious focus of interest for post-structuralist historicists with their declared interest in the question of whether Shakespeare's plays 'reinforce the dominant order' or whether they 'interrogate it to the point of subversion'.[36] But the trouble with a blunt critical instrument of this kind is that it tends to force Shakespeare into the position either of government lackey (New Historicism) or of covert radical (Cultural Materialism) and does not allow for a range of more plausible possibilities in between these two extremes. There is much in Prospero's character that would have appealed to James' vanity. But it is not just the king's poetic pretensions, his interest in magic and his paternalist theory of kingship that are echoed in the play. Early in his reign James had acquired a reputation for neglect of his princely office;[37] it was also public knowledge that he had issued open threats of vengeance against those who challenged the royal prerogative in parliament.[38] If a playwright-manager less adept at resisting clear-cut interpretation than Shakespeare had incorporated such elements in a play about an arrogantly paternalist musician-king who is ousted from his throne, it is unlikely that his company would have kept its royal patent for long. However, the fact that Prospero is vengeful, irritable and (before the action of the play) irresponsible, does not mean that Shakespeare was challenging the principle of monarchy itself. In a period when indiscreet criticism was highly dangerous, epideictic drama traditionally combined praise and blame as an oblique way of moulding royal opinion.[39]

Nor should the fact that Caliban (not himself of indigenous island stock) has some of the best lines in the play necessarily be read as a sign of Shakespeare's egalitarian political views.[40] Because Caliban is the victim of Prospero's punitive anger after the attempted rape of Miranda, and claims that all the spirits of the island hate their new master, it does not inevitably follow that Shakespeare is attacking the principle of autocratic rule, only its abuse. Associated symbolically with the four elements, Ariel and Caliban also figure the twin potentialities of the soul – 'one scale of reason, to poise another of sensuality', as Iago puts it (*Oth.*, I.iii.321–2). Only by confronting the baser elements that are an essential part of his own nature and listening to the counsel offered by 'nobler reason' (v.i.26), can Prospero achieve the self-discipline that the humanist believed was the precondition of any wise action. That is why he must acknowledge 'this Thing of darkenesse' (v.i.275) as his own. Like the castle of the soul in *The Faerie Queene*, besieged on all sides by the rebel forces of passion (II.ix.12–16), Prospero's humanity is never free from the threat posed by his natural desire for vengeance. While it is under that threat Prospero is in danger of becoming a tyrant. For, as Starkey argues, a tyrannical state is like the body of a man 'when reson ys ouer-run and unrulyd affectys gouerne and reyne in hys ordur of lyfe'.[41]

Essential to Renaissance Neoplatonism as an intellectual system is the belief that 'There's nothing situate vnder heauens eye, / But hath his bound in earth, in sea, in skie' (*Err.*, II.i.16–17). This doctrine of limit applies no less to a prince than to his subjects.[42] Indeed, if there is within each of us a Caliban that must be restrained by the rule of reason, it follows *a fortiori* that a monarch must obey those universal laws which it is his task to uphold and guarantee. As Lyly neatly puts in *Campaspe*, 'It were a shame that [a prince] should desire to rule the world, if he could not commaund himselfe.'[43] By portraying the musician-prince as a radically ambivalent figure Shakespeare can appear to compliment James for the harmonizing powers of his 'music' while at the same time obliquely warning him of the dangers of exceeding the limits of royal authority and abusing the power vested in him by parliament.

Within the terms of the Neoplatonic discourse adopted by Elizabethan and Jacobean writers from both ends of the political spectrum, logic dictates that the harp of state must be played by a single hand. However, this is not to say that *The Tempest* is foisting on its audiences one particular version of reality 'at the expense of all the other imaginable versions which it excludes' as Ryan believes.[44] On the contrary, one of the most interesting things about this play is its self-consciousness. By repeatedly adverting to its own dramatic nature, the play insists on the hypothetical nature of this model of social harmony.

III

The quest for the ideal society is a theme that has some nice variations in *The Tempest*. Impressed not so much by the beauty of

Caliban's eloquent account of the island's magical music as by the
fact that this remarkable entertainment is free, Stephano remarks:

> This will proue a braue kingdome to me, where
> I shall haue my Musicke for nothing.   (III.ii.139–40)

Like Gonzalo, and indeed like Prospero himself, Stephano sees the
island as territory for appropriation. All three men are colonizers by
instinct who dream of fashioning a community after their own ideals
or, in Stephano's case, selfish interests. But although the play clearly
reflects the colonial activities of early seventeenth-century England,
the world it portrays cannot be identified finally either with the New
World of the Americas or, as one critic suggests, Ireland.[45] It is a
transparently fictitious world. Indeed, it insists on its own artificiality. It does this by a number of means: by its use of a presenter;
by self-conscious use of retrospective narrative; by repeated interruptions of the dramatic action;[46] by the almost diagrammatic
symmetry of its character groupings and contrasts[47] and by the
dramatic contrast between its two major structural symbols – the
tempest and the rainbow. But most significant is the way the play
draws attention to its own fictional nature by its use of spectacle.

Prospero's wedding masque has been widely criticized for its
irrrelevance to contemporary social problems. In *Drama Within
Drama* Robert Egan writes, 'As a comprehensive image of the real
world, the masque is bound to fail. Since it ignores the realities of
earthly existence, it is incapable, as art, of comprehending or coping
with the disorder of that existence, in particular the innate propensity for evil in human kind.'[48] Egan's misgivings have recently been
echoed by David Lindley, who writes 'Prospero's masques are ...
vanities indeed, having no basis in economic and political reality'.[49]

It is true that the vision of pastoral peace and fecundity evoked by
Juno and Ceres is an idealized one. But to say that the masque fails
because it ignores reality suggests either a failure to appreciate the
significance of those distancing devices that effectively establish its
fictional status, or else an odd prejudice against non-illusionist forms
of art. Peter Greenaway has no such prejudice. A non-illusionist
artist himself, he knows that the dramatic mode of *The Tempest* is
self-evidently not that of social realism, but of 'symbols and emblems
and allegories'.[50] Prospero's appeal to the traditional analogy
between the world and the stage is a reminder to the young couple of
the ephemerality of the sensible world. But the ultimate effect of his

words is not, as Anne Righter suggests, to blur the distinctions between art and life,[51] but rather to insist on their difference. Though his intentions are quite different, the results of Prospero's cancellation of his masque and his reflections on it are similar to the crudely naive interpolations of Bottom and his friends in the text of their play. In both cases disruption of the narrative has the effect of breaking the spell that theatre casts on its audiences and calling attention to the fictional nature of the dramatic world within which these inset-plays are framed.

The point of Prospero's masque is precisely that it is not life, but art. A similar kind of distancing effect can be seen in the sixth book of *The Faerie Queene*, where Spenser also shows a lover's utopian dreams of a life of pastoral bliss shattered by a cancelled masque.[52] The vision that Calidore glimpses through the trees on Mount Acidale (vi.x.6ff) is a stylized emblem of harmony expressed in that favourite Elizabethan symbol of order, the dance. When Calidore intrudes on this magical scene, Colin Clout the shepherd-minstrel angrily breaks his pipe and the dancers vanish. Not until the next canto, when Calidore finds that his own make-believe world of pastoral romance has also vanished (vi.xi.26), does the full significance of Colin Clout's poetic vision become clear: namely, that it is vain to deceive yourself with false hopes of finding perfect happiness in a fallen world. Having failed to understand this truth when Meliboe had tried to impress it on him (vi.ix.20ff), Calidore must be shown the wisdom of the old man's Boethian counsel by other means. Unlike Meliboe the rural philosopher, Colin Clout is a poet-musician; his medium is not 'sensefull words' (vi.ix.26), but spectacle. It is because Calidore mistakes that poetic vision for reality that Colin Clout must destroy his masque in order to assert its fictive status: for the visionary artist, disenchantment is as important as enchantment.

Like Colin Clout, Prospero, too, is a visionary. Instead of setting out to educate his subjects by holding the mirror up to nature, he creates through music and spectacle an image, not of what is, but of 'what may be'.[53] The ethical and ontological significance of his wedding masque is a function of the part it forms in the play's complex pattern of symbolic contrasts and parallels. The masque begins with the slow and spectacular descent, to the accompaniment of 'Soft musick' (sd, iv.i.59), of Juno from the heavens on a rainbow. This archetypal Christian covenantal symbol of hope is a dramatic contrast to the emblematic violence of the play's opening scene with its 'tempestuous noise of Thunder and Lightning' (sd, i.i.1) and carries with it the promise of new life. As Juno alights from the rainbow, Ceres offers the bridal couple her benediction:

> Earths increase, and foyzon plentie,
> Barnes, and Garners, neuer empty.
> Vines, with clustring bunches growing,
> Plants, with goodly burthen bowing:
> Spring come to you at the farthest,
> In the very end of Haruest.
> Scarcity and want shall shun you,
> *Ceres* blessing so is on you.　　　　　　　　　(iv.i.110–17)

Ceres' stylized pastoral vision is self-evidently unrealistic. Its Ovidian echoes of a world in which spring and Harvest coexist in fecund abundance recall another pastoral vision. Gonzalo's dream of an egalitarian utopia where all is 'foyzon, all abundance' (ii.i.168) also draws on the *Metamorphoses* (1.89–112), filtered this time through Montaigne's imagination. But though both visions look back to Ovid's version of the Golden Age myth, the use they make of that mythical material is very different. Where Ceres, goddess of agriculture, evokes an image of idealized farmers filling their barns with the fruits of honest labour, Montaigne's noble savages have not yet been 'bastardized' by the corrupting effects of civilization: 'no manuring of lands, no use of wine, corne or mettle'.[54] Like Montaigne, Gonzalo is a primitivist, believing that if the legal and commercial restrictions of civilization could be dispensed with, men and women could live virtuous lives in harmony with nature: 'all men idle, all: / And Women too, but innocent and pure: / No Soueraignty' (ii.i.148–50). The naivety of this primitivist fancy is made clear by the sardonic interruptions of Antonio and Sebastian: with villains like these the prospects for a benign anarchism are not good. As Thomas Starkey bluntly remarked earlier in the century, it is because 'man by nature ys so frayle and corrupt' that such utopian schemes are 'playn impossybul'.[55]

Gonzalo's utopian vision is based on a conflation of two myths, one of which rewrites the other. Both represent an attempt to account for human suffering. In Ovid's account of the four ages of the world we see humanity degenerate from primitive innocence to a barbarity so terrible that the father of the gods is impelled to destroy the entire race in a tempest that inundates the whole world. But

Gonzalo makes no mention of man's fall from his primal state of innocence. According to the primitivist myth of natural virtue it is not our innate wickedness that is the cause of human suffering, but the unnatural constraints of civilization that have corrupted and contaminated our native dignity. Thus, although Gonzalo's ideal commonwealth is recognizably Ovidian, the philosophy that underpins it is the antithesis of Ovid's.[56]

Ceres' vision of human happiness is also rooted in myth. But where Gonzalo's utopian scheme relies on the principle of natural innocence, her vision is based on order and control. Like Orpheus, Ceres is a symbolic civilizer of fallen humanity.[57] Ovid explains how it was she who first taught men the sciences of agriculture and law:

> Dame *Ceres* first to breake the Earth with plough the maner found,
> She first made corne and stover soft to grow upon the ground,
> She first made lawes: for all these things we are to *Ceres* bound.[58]

In casting Ceres in the central role of his masque Prospero is, in effect, reinforcing one myth of civilization in terms of another. If Gonzalo is a sentimentalist, Prospero is a pragmatist: he knows that unless his audience has a true understanding of the conditional nature of this dramatic vision, it will never be more than a figment of the poet's imagination. Adapting Frank Kermode's distinction between myth and fiction – the one inviting absolute, the other conditional assent – it could be said that Gonzalo's is a simple, and Prospero's a complex, response to myth.[59] When Ferdinand, like Calidore, asks if he can remain forever in this pastoral paradise with its idealized nymphs and picturesque reapers, Prospero reminds him that these creatures are no more than spirits summoned by art to enact a prince's 'present fancies' (IV.i.120–2).

IV

As a prince who employs the arts of poetry, music and spectacle to civilize his subjects and restore harmony to his kingdom, Prospero has much in common with the divinely gifted poet-musician of classical and medieval tradition. James must have been flattered by the obvious comparison, provided, that is, that he was no more astute than some modern critics and did not notice the rather damaging criticism that the play levels at him by implication. But it would be wrong to press the Orpheus comparison too far, because in

some ways Prospero is quite different from the traditional pedagogue who seeks to reform society by a Horatian combination of
pleasure and instruction. Where Gower's poet-musician is essentially a reteller of ancient stories who uses his eloquence to promote
the cause of *humanitas*, Prospero – and here we have to drop the
comparison with royal poetasters and see Shakespeare's magus as a
figure for the genuine artist – employs his magic to turn a 'bare
Island' (Epil. 8) into a world in microcosm, a world complete with
its own pantheon of beneficent spirits. Prospero the ruler may be
subject to many of the infirmities that the flesh is heir to. But
Prospero the artist is a god-like figure. As he raises a storm and sets
his bow in the heavens it would be difficult to think of a more
complete embodiment of the Neoplatonic idea of the artist as creating god. In 1607 Federico Zuccaro claimed that the artist, by
'imitating God as it were, and rivalling nature . . . [has] the ability to
make a New Paradise appear on earth'.[60] It is just such a power that
Prospero possesses.

   Italian theories of the artist as creator were well known in Elizabethan England.[61] Puttenham begins his treatise with the claim that
poets are like 'creating gods';[62] Sidney's *Defence of Poesie* is a compen-
dium of such ideas. Following Scaliger's threefold classification of
poets according to their interests and subject-matter, Sidney discusses first the theological poet, second the philosophical and last
what he calls those 'indeed right Poets' who 'range . . . into the
divine consideration of what may be and should be'.[63] The 'right
poet', says Sidney, is not simply a maker of verses, drawing for his
materials on nature's world of sensible objects, but a creator,
god-like in his powers of invention, who generates an imaginative
heterocosm independent of nature's world. Such a poet, he declares
in a celebrated passage in the *Defence*,

lifted up with the vigor of his own invention, doth grow in effect into an
other nature: in making things either better then nature bringeth foorth, or
quite a new, formes such as never were in nature: as the *Heroes*, *Demigods*,
Cyclops, *Chymeras*, *Furies*, and such like; so as he goeth hand in hand with
nature, not enclosed within the narrow warrant of her gifts, but freely
raunging within the Zodiack of his owne wit.[64]

   Shakespeare's most explicit, and also most playfully ironic,
treatment of the Neoplatonic poetic is Theseus' cynically dismissive
view of the inspired poet in *A Midsummer Night's Dream* (v.i.7–22).[65]
By linking the poet with the lunatic and the lover and rejecting the

very notion of imagination, Theseus is in effect dismissing Shake-speare's own technique of dramatizing serious matters by non-realis-tic means. The result is a witty affirmation of what Theseus denies: after the dramatic subtleties of the play's first four acts, only a pedant or a blockhead would refuse to concede the power of what Hyppolyta calls 'fancies images' (v.i.25).

Unlike the mimetic artist, the Neoplatonic visionary makes no pretence of producing a copy of the phenomenal universe. He can create whatever worlds he likes: he can conjure up scenes of social anarchy, or of harmonious order; he can portray irresponsible tyrants, or benevolent patriarchs; he can invent harsh, punitive gods, or beneficent, loving ones. Although he knows that in the real world fate is inscrutable and injustice apparently endemic, on his stage he is free to imagine a world ruled as if by kindly gods, a world where princes have learnt to be wise and just and where, under responsible government, subjects are united in loving harmony. Indeed, this is all he can do: at a period in history when new philosophies are undermining old religious certainties; when the gods seem to have withdrawn from the world of human affairs; and when social order is coming to be seen, not as a natural, but as an artefactual phenomenon, the intellectual has no choice but to read, as George Steiner puts it, '*as if*'.[66] The visionary who invents an idealized world where threatening seas turn out to be merciful in the end, and who then dismantles this vision, showing it to be no more than an artist's fancy, has more in common with Montaigne's whimsical brand of philosophic scepticism than he has with either the religious fideism of Luther and Calvin or the Christian human-ism of Hooker. He is not so much inferring the existence of a rational pattern in nature[67] as suggesting that there could be such a pattern. But although this idealized world would be merely a fiction, it is no more inherently implausible than the one that human wickedness has actually created. Whether or not it could be realized depends ultimately on whether humanity – ruler and subject alike – is capable of abnegating the destructive passions that have been the root cause of human suffering since the Fall. Such, at least, is the essentialist view of human history expressed in Milton's essay (see note 3) on the music of the spheres; in its imaginative treatment of myth, *The Tempest* would seem to suggest that it is also Shake-speare's.

But given such an essentialist view of things, is it realistic to suppose that human behaviour can be modified in this way? In Renaissance poetics the traditional answer to this question is an appeal to the affective power of the arts. As late as 1704 John Dennis claimed that 'the great Design of Arts is to restore the Decays that happen'd to human Nature by the Fall, by restoring Order';[68] it is precisely this function that Marcelline ascribes to James I when he praises Britain's own musician-king for civilizing even 'the most brutish and voluptuous' of his subjects by 'the delectable sound of his Musicke'. In practice, however, even a sentimental Neoplatonist like Lorenzo understands that there are some individuals who, having no music in themselves, are unmoved by the 'concord of sweet sounds' (*Mer. V.*, v.i.84). Prospero knows that if his vision is to have any chance of becoming a reality he will need the willing co-operation of an audience that is prepared to commit itself to an act of faith, and, moreover, that is not going to mistake art for life. It is a similar act of faith that Rosalind playfully demands of Orlando when she tells him he must believe in her powers of magic; or, in a more serious vein, that Paulina asks of Leontes when, persuading him to believe she can restore his long-lost wife, she tells him: 'It is requir'd / You doe awake your Faith' (*Wint.*, v.iii.94–5). *The Tempest*, too, asks for a knowing suspension of disbelief. This is why in the play's epilogue Prospero, giving new life to a familiar theatrical convention, must supplicate for applause. But he can do so only after he has stepped out of his stage role. Insofar as it concerns itself with the way drama works, *The Tempest* acknowledges that audiences will inevitably interpret plays in the light of their own interests or prejudices. Indeed, where there is no common ground of shared artistic or intellectual assumptions, dramatist and spectator may well find themselves talking at cross-purposes; Ferdinand's ingenuous questions about the meaning of Prospero's wedding masque are a case in point. As with stage audiences, so with theatre audiences. Having enchanted his audience, Prospero must now disenchant them. If that audience rejects his hypothesis, the 'proiect fails'; if it applauds it, the play will have done its work.

v

In his analysis of Spenser's Bower of Bliss Stephen Greenblatt argues that Guyon's refusal to kill Acrasia illustrates how authority depends on its other as a means of legitimating its own exercise of power (see chapter 1, pp. 38–9). Recent Shakespeare criticism makes the same point about *The Tempest*. Malcolm Evans claims that by representing the play as a rich repository of universal human truths, traditional criticism has suppressed the uncomfortable political realities latent in the text. However, if we can forget this mystifying rhetoric and read the play deconstructively as part of a contemporary colonialist discourse, says Evans, then it becomes clear that the master–slave relationship is not something that is given by nature, but is socially produced: in reality it is only by subjecting others – constructing them as existential and political subjects – that Prospero is able to establish his own identity as master. Like Guyon, Prospero *needs* his other as an affirmation of his own authority, argues Evans.[69]

The fact that a number of other critics have made exactly the same point about *The Tempest* does not, in itself, limit the value of what they are saying. Irrespective of what Shakespeare meant his audiences to see in the play, *The Tempest* is now part of our common European racial mythology.[70] But as with Greenblatt's analysis of the Bower of Bliss, the political truth that this analysis reveals is not one that is historically specific to the sixteenth century. It is something that is true of any kind of colonizing activity, literal or metaphoric. Virginia Woolf makes the same point in *A Room of One's Own* when she observes how, in our own society, men have traditionally 'colonized' women, constructing femininity as a way of asserting their own masculine superiority.[71] Indeed, Evans makes the same point himself when he shows how traditional scholarship, represented by Frank Kermode's introduction to the 1954 Arden edition of *The Tempest*, 'colonizes' the play. In 'mastering' *The Tempest* and reducing its uncomfortable political realities to a bland declaration of universal truths, Kermode has 'colonized the text of *The Tempest*' and made it safe for polite critical debate.[72] Ironically, it is precisely the same process of metaphoric 'colonization' that is at work in Evans' own discussion. In order to assert his own critical superiority he must demonize traditional literary scholarship; in fact he even goes so far as to suggest that, like the witches in *Macbeth*, it tells us truths, wins us with honest trifles, to betray us in deepest consequence.[73] As Carol Neely points out, the calculated effect of systematically debunking the traditional scholarship on which poststructuralist historicism is so heavily dependent is mastery – 'mastery over earlier criticism and scholarship, now rendered "old" and hence irrelevant. Mastery above all and most successfully in the profession.'[74]

Insofar as it insists on the ideological nature of common sense, post-structuralist historicism offers a critical approach that is considerably more sophisticated than that of a Neomarxist like Ryan, who attempts anachronistically to enlist Shakespeare in the struggle for 'equality and community',[75] or Patterson, whose own common sense tells her that it is unlikely that so popular a dramatist as Shakespeare would have entertained anti-populist political views.[76] However, in its overriding concern to identify trans-historical paradigms, post-structuralist historicism is not so much locating texts in history, and thereby showing how subjectivity is discursively produced, as taking them *out* of the cultural history of their own time and showing – contrary to its own most fundamental theoretical axioms – that there are certain constants in human behaviour that transcend historical and cultural boundaries. If we are indeed such stuff as ideologies are made on, we cannot afford to ignore the symbols, the emblems and the allegories that go to make up the discourses within which Shakespeare wrote, however unpalatable those discourses may be to us. Only by recovering the terms in which it is cast can we enter into constructive dialogue with an open-ended play like *The Tempest*, endorsing or rejecting the hypotheses it offers us.

PART II

Defining the essential: a humanist iconography

CHAPTER 4

The ladder of love: verbal and musical rhetoric in the Elizabethan lute song

> I was that silly thing that once was wrought
>   To practise this thin love;
> I climbed from sex to soul, from soul to thought
>   But thinking there to move,
> Headlong I rowled from thought to soul, and then,
> From soul I lighted at the sex agen.
> (William Cartwright, No Platonique Love)

'Shall I strive to a heauenly Ioy / with an earthly loue'? asks the singer in one of the elegant bagatelles with which Dowland intersperses his more solemn airs.[1] His problem – whether it is true that the sensuous apprehension of beauty is capable of inspiring a love of virtue – is one that is common to all the great medieval and Renaissance metaphysics of love,[2] and touches on an issue that is fundamental to the Renaissance debate on human nature. His questions continue:

> Shall I think that a bleeding hart
>   or a wounded eie,
> Or a sigh can ascend the cloudes so hie?

But as the singer ponders his conundrum, the facile charm of his melody and the sprightly syncopations of his lute suggest that his speculations may not be entirely serious. We shall see later that they are not.

When Dowland sets the antithesis in lines 3–4 ('heauenly Ioy ... earthly loue') he uses the simple device of a rising and falling scale. As you might expect, the Elizabethan songbooks are full of such devices. Notable examples are Campion's *Follow thy fair sun* and *My sweetest Lesbia* (1601), Ford's *Go passions to the cruel fair* (1607), Jones' *Arise my thoughts* (1601), Pilkington's *Climb, o heart* (1605) and Rosseter's *Reproue not loue* (1601). In all these cases – and there are many others like them in the lute-song repertory – the composer is doing what Thomas Morley advises in his observations on the art of 'dittying' and illustrating his subject in musical terms:

You must haue a care that when your matter signifieth ascending, high heauen, and such like, you make your musicke ascend: and by the contrarie where your dittie speaketh of descending loweness, depth, hell, and others such, you must make your musicke descend.[3]

Unlike the examples I have just cited, however, *Shall I sue?* is more than simple word-painting. To express the singer's mounting hopes the poet employs a rhetorical figure of climax, piling clause upon clause until the subject has persuaded himself that he is in Elysium. When Dowland sets these words to rising and falling musical scales he is doing more than simply illustrating the phrases 'heauenly Ioy', 'ascend the cloudes' and 'earthly loue': it is the idea of love's progress as it is expressed by the rhetorical figure *quaestium* that he is imitating in musical terms. *Quaestium* is a form of amplification. Henry Peacham the Elder defines it as a figure 'by which the Orator doth demaund many times together, and vse many questions in one place ... this figure serueth ... to moue affections'.[4] It is this paralleling of verbal patterns in musical terms that is my subject in this chapter.[5]

I

The Elizabethan lute song was the product of a self-consciously humanist intellectual environment. It is true that there were no formal humanist academies in Elizabethan England, and we have no proof that the nearest approximation to one – the Areopagus – ever discussed in detail the sort of matters debated by Zarlino and Galileo in Italy and Baïf and Ronsard in France.[6] Nevertheless, it is clear from the scattered remarks made by Dowland and Campion in their prefaces that English composers were inspired, like their continental counterparts, by a classical ideal of *eloquentia*. The lute song was seen by the more serious composers of the age as an attempt to recapture the lost art of Greek song.

Campion tells us in the preface to his *Two Bookes of Ayres* that his intention is to 'couple ... Words and Notes louingly together'.[7] Prettily as it is expressed, his frequently cited credo is misleading insofar as it implies an equal balance between the claims of music and poetry.[8] The true nature of the relationship is more accurately defined by the character of Orpheus in Campion's *Lords Maske* of 1612:

> Happie is he whose words can moue,
>   Yet sweet notes help perswasion.
> Mixe your words with Musicke then,
>   That they the more may enter.[9]

In these lines Orpheus makes it clear that although the persuasive power of his songs is due to the combined effects of music and poetry, music's function is a strictly subsidiary one: the words come first and the composer's job is to amplify their meaning. The point is spelled out by the pedagogue Francis Clement in his *Petie Schole* in the authentic style of the schoolmaster:

Thou hast hard, I am sure, of the meruelous sweete harmony of Orpheus his harpe, how it moued mountaines and hard rockes, it shooke the blockish and senselesse trees, it stayed the wilde, cruell & savage beastes, all were rauished with the wonderfull delectation and pleasure of his melodie: but trowest thou it was his wodden harpe that made that golden stirre? no, no child, it was his gallant, eloquent and learned tongue.[10]

What Clement is here impressing on his pupils is a commonplace of humanist thought; and it is this humanist emphasis on the primacy of the word that was in part responsible for the increasingly picturesque quality of sixteenth-century secular music.[11] Songs like Bartlet's *Surcharged with discontent* (1606), Johnson's *Arm, arm* (c. 1616) or Jones' setting of Campion's *There is a garden in her face* (1608) with their charmingly meretricious imitative effects are in the truest sense popular songs. I am concerned, not with word-painting, but with a different kind of musical mimesis. Although it would not be entirely true to describe such accessible songs as Dowland's *Come again: sweet loue doth now inuite* (1597) or Rosseter's *No graue for woe* (1601) as *musica reservata*, they nevertheless depend for some of their subtlest effects on devices to which only a classically educated audience would be fully responsive.

Brian Vickers has warned of the dangers of arguing for specific and particular identities between the two arts of rhetoric and music: although the subject aroused lively interest among theorists, there is no proof that any contemporary composer actually took these discussions as prescriptions for composition.[12] Indeed, given the radically different natures of music and poetry as affective arts, there is only a limited sense in which such a programme would have been practicable. Vickers' *caveat* needs to be taken seriously: when one speaks of the 'language' of music one is speaking metaphorically; and any analogy between this and the language of poetry has a strictly limited application. But while it is true that music cannot reproduce the effects of figurative language it can imitate *schemata verborum*: 'hath not Musicke her figures, the same which Rhetorique'? asks Henry Peacham the Younger in *The Compleat Gentleman* (1622), 'what is a *Revert* but her *Antistrophe*? her reports, but sweet *Anaphoras*? her counterchange of points, *Antimetaboles*? her passionate Aires but *Prosopopoeas*? with infinite other of the same nature'.[13] In an equally well-known passage from *Sylva Sylvarum* Bacon makes the same claim: 'There be in Musick certaine *Figures*, or *Tropes*; almost agreeing with the *Figures* of *Rhetorike*; And with the *Affections* of the *Minde*, and other Senses.'[14] For reasons that will become clear, Elizabethan composers were particularly interested in the musical setting of a group of related rhetorical figures whose purpose is amplification.

II

Quintilian defined rhetoric as 'the science of speaking well'.[15] But it was more than simply a wish to instil in their pupils a facility with words that led the great Tudor educators to formulate curricula of such daunting proportions.[16] Behind the unremittingly arduous training that the Elizabethan grammar-school boy received in grammar, logic and rhetoric lay a belief in the civilizing power of language. According to the ancients it was the power of speech that first enabled men to form civil communities. Thomas Starkey, echoing Cicero, explains that 'by perfayt eloquence and hye phylosophy men were brought, by lytyl and lytyl, from the rude lyfe in feldys and wodys, to thys cyvylyte, wych you now se stablysched and set in al wel rulyd cytes and townys'.[17] Some twenty years later Thomas Wilson makes the same point in *The Arte of Rhetorique* (1553):

whereas men liued brutishly in open fealdes, hauing neither house to shroude them in, nor attire to clothe their backes, nor yet any regard to seeke their best auaile: these appointed of GOD called them together by vtteraunce of speech, and perswaded with them what was good, what was badde, & what was gainful for mankind.[18]

Similar claims continued to be made until the end of the century and beyond.[19]

Rhetoric was more than simply the art of speaking and writing well. It was the product of a philosophy of civilization that believed that the business of the arts was to repair the defects of man's fallen nature, or, as John Dennis puts it, 'to restore the decays that happen'd to human Nature by the Fall, by restoring Order'.[20] But although the purpose of poetry, as the Renaissance conceived it, was to instruct by pleasing, Renaissance poets are not always insistently didactic in practice. Relishing their new-found powers of eloquence, they often fill their poetry with rhetorical schemes that serve not so much a moral as a decorative or a mimetic function. When Milton describes Satan's epic voyage through Chaos in the second book of *Paradise Lost* he evokes the physical sensations of someone floundering through swampy terrain by means of a combination of two similar rhetorical devices, *asyndeton* (the absence of connecting particles), and *polysyndeton* (a superfluity of connecting particles):

> As when a Gryfon through the Wilderness
> With winged course ore Hill or moarie Dale,
> Persues the *Arimaspian*, who by stelth
> Had from his wakeful custody purloind
> The guarded Gold: so eagerly the Fiend
> Ore bog or steep, through strait, rough, dense, or rare,
> With head, hands, wings, or feet persues his way,
> And swims or sinks, or wades, or creeps, or flyes ...[21]

A rather more subtle form of rhetorical mimesis occurs in Spenser's description of the Bower of Bliss in the second book of *The Faerie Queene*. When the hero arrives at Acrasia's magic island he is temporarily diverted by two seductresses. Taking an obvious delight in her task, the more forward of these two sirens laughs at the confusion into which Guyon is thrown by her blatantly erotic invitation:

> Withall she laughed, and she blusht withall,
> That blushing to her laughter gave more grace,
> And laughter to her blushing as did fall. (II.ix.68)

As blushes and laughter alternate, creating doubt in the hero's mind as to whether to read these signals as marks of modesty or provocation, so the repetition of the words themselves imitates the effect they describe. The rhetorical figure Spenser is using in these lines is *antimetabole*. Puttenham defines this scheme as 'a figure which takes a couple of words to play with in a verse, and by making them to chaunge and shift one into others place they do very pretily exchange and shift the sence'.[22]

I have taken these two examples of rhetorical mimesis more or less at random; similar devices could be found on almost any page of an anthology of Renaissance poetry. However, rhetoric may be used to imitate not simply physical actions, but also ideas. When Shakespeare parodies the language of Euphuistic rhetoric in the following speech by Rosalind from the fifth act of *As You Like It*, the scheme he employs serves a mimetic function of a different kind from the ones I have just described:

your brother, and my sister, no sooner met, but they look'd: no sooner look'd, but they lou'd; no sooner lou'd, but they sigh'd; no sooner sigh'd but they ask'd one another the reason: no sooner knew the reason, but they sought the remedie: and in these degrees haue they made a pair of staires to marriage. (v.ii.31–7)

On a first reading Rosalind's mocking words sound longwinded, as indeed she intends them to. But the truth is that her account of the way Celia and Oliver meet, fall in love and agree to marry parodies with some precision the Neoplatonic belief that physical beauty should lead the mind by degrees to a love of virtue. Not only does Rosalind actually describe this process in the phrase 'in these degrees haue they made a pair of staires to marriage', but the rhetorical scheme she uses – *gradatio* – is itself a kind of stairway or ladder. In fact Scaliger actually defines *gradatio* as 'the ladder form, whereby the same words repeated links the step preceding to the one following'.[23] *Gradatio* is a technique of amplification in which the speaker seeks to generate suspense leading to a climax by the accumulation of clauses linked by a repeated phrase. And 'climax', which is the Greek word for ladder, is another name for this figure. Rosalind's words artfully mime the process she is describing to the presumably bemused Orlando.

The belief that eloquence can lead the mind by degrees from earthly to spiritual matters is fundamental to Renaissance poetics. It is the corollary of a conception of human nature that goes back to Plato and the school of Pythagoras (see chapter 5) and that was still a commonplace in the eighteenth century. It finds its most impressive articulation in the Renaissance in a well-known passage from Pico della Mirandola's *Oration on the Dignity of Man* (1486). Pico imagines the voice of God telling mankind:

We have made thee neither of heaven nor of earth, neither mortal nor immortal, so that with freedom of choice and with honor, as though the maker and molder of thyself, thou mayest fashion thyself in whatever shape thou shalt prefer. Thou shalt have the power to degenerate into the lower forms of life, which are brutish. Thou shalt have the power, out of thy soul's judgement, to be reborn into the higher forms, which are divine.[24]

If man occupied a unique position in the universal scheme of things, sharing with the brutes a propensity to obey natural impulses, yet blessed with a god-like reason that had not been entirely obliterated by the Fall, then the arts could assist him in his efforts to ascend the *scala naturae*. As Sidney puts it in *The Defence of Poetry*, the final end of poetry is to 'lead and draw us to as high a perfection, as our degenerate soules made worse by their clay-lodgings, can be capable of'.[25]

The idea of progressive ascent is an integral feature of the structure of the pre-modern universe. A classic sixteenth-century account of this principle is the well-known defence of order in Sir Thomas Elyot's introduction to *The Governour* (1531).[26] Sir Thomas Browne makes the same point more succinctly in his *Religio Medici* (1635): 'There is in this Universe a Stair, or manifest Scale of creatures, rising not disorderly, or in confusion, but with a comely method and proportion.'[27] It is because the universe was conceived as a series of interlocking hierarchies that the images of scale, chain and ladder are found so universally in medieval and Renaissance arts (illus. 4). Originating in ancient Greek philosophy,[28] this prototypal image of multeity reduced to unity is rarely absent from medieval and Renaissance discussions of world order, and was not finally abandoned as a model for social and personal harmony until the middle of the eighteenth century. When Shakespeare's Ulysses says in his famous speech on order that degree is 'the ladder of all high designs' (*Troil.*, I.iii.102–3) he is articulating a commonplace with which no member of his audience, however slightly educated, could conceivably have been unfamiliar.

In the Middle Ages the Chain of Being was conflated with two other images: the Golden Chain of Zeus (*Iliad*, VIII.19–27) and Jacob's Ladder (Gen. 28:12) (illus. 5). Neither originally had any connection with the idea of hierarchical order. In Homer the golden chain with which the father of the gods challenges the assembled company on Mount Olympus to a celestial tug-of-war is no more than a device for asserting Zeus's supremacy. However, a long

4. Diagrammatic representation of the cosmos showing the various levels of
creation linked together by the Great Chain of Being. Didacus Valades, *Rhetorica
christiana* (Perugia, 1579)

5. 'And he dreamed, and behold a ladder set up on the earth, and the top of it reached to heaven; and behold the angels of God ascending and descending on it' (Gen. 28:12). *Jacob's Ladder*, Giovanni da Vecchi and Raffaelino da Reggio

tradition of misinterpretation saw in this image a symbolic affirmation of the hierarchical structure of the universe. The influential
Macrobius, writing at the end of the fourth century, asserts that

From the Supreme God even to the bottommost dregs of the universe there
is one tie, binding at every link and never broken. This is the golden chain
of Homer which, he tells us, God ordered to hang down from the sky to the
earth.[29]

Variations on this idea in the Renaissance are legion.[30]

In a similar fashion the visionary ladder on which the sleeping
Jacob sees angels ascending and descending was widely interpreted
as a symbol of cosmic harmony. 'Being in itself', writes Peter Sterry,

in its universal Nature, from its purest heighth, by beautiful, harmonious,
just degrees and steps, *descendeth* into every Being, even to the lowest shades.
All ranks and degrees of Being, so become like the mystical steps in that
scale of Divine Harmony and Proportions, *Jacobs Ladder*. Every form of
Being to the lowest step, seen and understood according to its order and
proportions in its descent upon this *Ladder*, seemeth as an *Angel*, or as a
Troop of Angels in one, full of all Angelick Musick and Beauty.[31]

When Sterry refers to the created universe as a 'scale of Divine
harmony and Proportions' he is reflecting a tradition that goes back
to Pythagoras of describing natural order in musical terms. By late
antiquity the Pythagorean doctrine of the music of the spheres had
become elaborated into the system of universal harmony that
Boethius describes in the *De musica*. Fundamental to Boethius' view
of the cosmos is the analogy between *musica mundana* and *musica
humana*, the former being the audible expression of those mathematical relationships that are the ultimate constituents of reality, and the
latter those same principles as they are manifested in the microcosm
of man's own being.[32] Refined and developed over centuries,
Boethius' picture of a universe united at all levels by arithmetic and
harmonic proportions became the standard model for medieval and
Renaissance treatises on cosmic order. In a well-known woodcut
that forms the frontispiece of his *Practica musice* (1496) Franchino
Gaffurio represents the universe as a graduated scale beginning with
earth, lowest of the four elements, and rising to the heavens. Represented at precise tonal intervals are the nine planets (including
earth) and the corresponding muses (illus. 6).

Whether it was seen as a chain or a ladder, the *scale naturae* was not
simply a static symbol of world order: for pagan and Christian alike

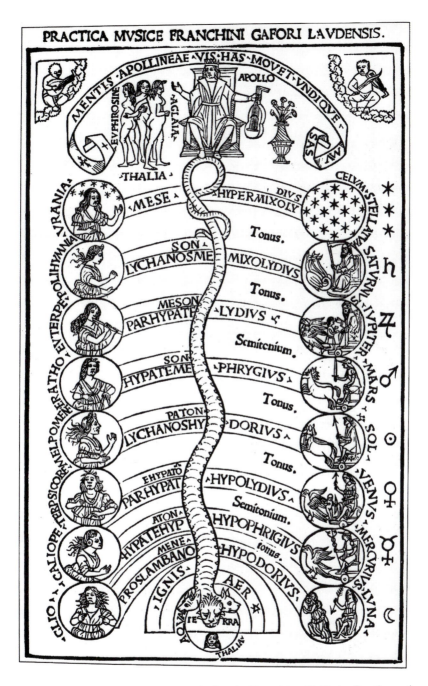

6. The universe as a graduated musical scale. Franchino Gaffurio, *Practica musice* (Milan, 1496)

7.   The Lady Philosophy, her head touching the clouds, with sceptre and books, and ladder symbolizing the mind's ascent to higher spheres of knowledge. Bas-relief on the west portal of Notre-Dame de Paris (thirteenth century)

it was a dynamic image expressive of the soul's potential for either amelioration or degeneration. According to St John Chrysostom (born *c.* AD 347) Jacob's Ladder signified 'the gradual ascent by means of virtue, by which it is possible for us to ascend from earth to heaven'.[33] Chrysostom was not alone among the early Church Fathers in using the ladder as a figure for the spiritual life;[34] indeed the 'soul ladder' has a long history going back to Greek and Egyptian antiquity.[35] An important late classical source for medieval representations of the ladder of perfection was Boethius' *Consolation of Philosophy*. In his introductory portrait of the Lady Philosophy Boethius describes his visitor as a woman of immense height carrying

8.   Eleventh-century Ms of Joannes Climacus, *The Ladder of Divine Ascent* (late sixth century), showing the author expounding his work, Garrett Ms 16 fol. 194ʳ

books and a sceptre. But the most significant aspect of her appearance is her garments. Embroidered on her robe is a symbolic ladder, with clearly marked rungs, representing the mind's ascent to higher principles.[36] Identical figures, corresponding in every significant detail to Boethius' description of Philosophy, appear in medieval ecclesiastical statuary[37] (illus. 7).

But it was another sixth-century treatise, *The Ladder of Divine Ascent* by the anchorite Joannes Climacus, that appealed most vividly to the medieval imagination. Joannes' *Ladder* is a classic of monastic literature; with the exception of the Bible and the service books it was more widely read in the Middle Ages than any other Eastern Christian text.[38] With its graphic conception of the spiritual life as a ladder stretching from earth to heaven (illus. 8), Joannes' treatise inspired not only such devotional classics as Walter Hilton's *Scale of Perfection* (late fourteenth century), but also a wealth of visual representations in panel icons, frescoes and illuminated manuscripts of the soul's struggle to achieve perfection.[39] These often take the form of a realistically portrayed ladder on which Everyman is accompanied by allegorical figures representing the virtues and vices by which he is assisted or hindered (illus. 9).

Conflating pagan and Christian elements, the ladder of perfection is a powerful symbol of the spiritual life; as an iconographic tradition it survives, at least in the title pages of music books, beyond the Enlightenment.[40] A well-known sixteenth-century representation of the soul's ascent is Dürer's engraving of *Melencolia*. If we accept Frances Yates' reading of Dürer's allegory, the winged figure of meditation represents not the suffering of frustrated artistic genius, as Panofsky argues,[41] but the first stage of that divine inspiration which the Neoplatonist believes can lead the mind to higher things. Melancholy's angelic character is suggested, Yates argues, 'not only by her angel wings, but also by the ladder behind her, leading, not to the top of the building but generally upwards into the sky, Jacob's ladder on which the angels ascend and descend'[42] (illus. 10). When the singer in Robert Jones' *Come sorrow come* (1601) appeals to 'sorrows sweet scayle / By the which we ascend to the heauenlie place'[43] he could almost have been composing a gloss on Dürer's engraving.

If man was, in Sir Thomas Browne's words, an '*Amphibium*, whose nature is to live in divided and distinguished worlds',[44] there was general agreement among Neoplatonists that the means by which he

9. Medieval ladder of virtue combining the social with the ethical scale. The climbers, representing the various social classes, are attacked by vices and assisted by virtues. Copy of Herrad of Landsberg, *Hortus Deliciarum* (late twelfth century; original destroyed in 1870)

10.   The Neoplatonic ladder of perfection. Albrecht Dürer, *Melencolia I*
(1514)

was able to purge himself of the baser elements of his nature and ascend the ladder of perfection was love. 'Love', writes Milton in *Paradise Lost*,

> refines
> The thoughts, and heart enlarges, hath his seat
> In Reason, and is judicious, is the scale
> By which to heav'nly love thou maist ascend.　　(VIII.589–92)

The doctrine that Milton's Raphael is expounding in these lines was a central tenet of Neoplatonic thought; it has its origins in the *Symposium*. The neophyte who wishes to be initiated into the mysteries of love, Diotima tells Socrates,

must for the sake of that highest beauty be ever climbing aloft, as on the rungs of a ladder [ὥσπερ ἐπαναβαθμοῖς χρώμενον] from personal beauty he proceeds to beautiful observances, from observance to beautiful learning, and from learning at last to that particular study which is concerned with the beautiful itself and that alone; so that in the end he comes to know the very essence of beauty.[45]

Just as the Golden Chain of Zeus was identified in the Middle Ages with Jacob's Ladder, and both with the *scala mundi*, so the Platonic ladder of love was conflated with the biblical image of a stairway of the angels. One of the most memorable passages in Dante's *Paradiso* is the scene in which the poet sees the figure of Beatrice standing on a ladder which rises into the empyrean (*'vid'io uno scaleo eretto in suso / tanto, che nol seguiva la mia luce'* (XXI. 29–30)) and beckoning his soul towards heaven. Platonic and biblical traditions are here fused in an image of great expressive power. This iconographic image is also widely represented in Renaissance art.[46]

For Dante, as for the Platonists of the Florentine Academy a century and a half later, love is the principle that impels the sequestered soul to return to its spiritual home. In what was undoubtedly the most influential, as well as the most eloquent, popularization of these ideas, Castiglione's Pietro Bembo explains how, as the courtier climbs the 'stayre of love', he progressively abandons the world of the senses until, reaching the final degree of perfection, he is able 'to beholde the beautie that is seene with the eyes of the minde, which then begin to be sharpe and throughly seeing, when the eyes of the bodie lose the floure of their sightlinesse'.[47] But before it can ascend the *scala coeli* the discordant soul must attune itself to the harmony of the universe. By reviving in man a memory of the perfect harmony of the spheres, music is capable of inspiring a love of that divine beauty which is true harmony. Precisely what form this process of musical induction actually took was a matter of extensive speculation. In the sixteenth century it was the Pléiade poet and philosopher Pontus de Tyard who gave the most ambitious theoretical account of the soul's migration. Drawing extensively on Ficino's commentaries on Plato, Tyard describes in complex detail the various stages through which the soul must pass in its re-ascent of the celestial ladder. But the process cannot begin until the discords of man's fallen nature have been resolved by the animating power of the Platonic *furor poeticus*. Tyard explains how this poetic enthusiasm achieves its effects: it works first 'by awakening the drowsy part of the soul by the tones of Music, and soothing the perturbed part by the suavity of harmony'; then it 'chases away the dissonant discords' by the 'well-accorded diversity of musical accords'; finally, it restores order by 'the gracious and grave facility of verses regulated by the careful observance of number of measure'.[48] In this way poetry and music work together to set in motion the process of initiation that will eventually lead to the higher spheres of knowledge.

III

When the singer in Dowland's *Shall I sue?* muses on the possibility of ascending to heavenly joys by means of an earthly love and amplifies his words with corresponding musical figures, it would seem that here is a clear example of a composer putting into musical practice precisely those speculative theories that had preoccupied philosophers like Ficino and Tyard. Renaissance Neoplatonism came late to England. But when it did begin to permeate Elizabethan thought some 250 years after the great Italian literary efflorescence of the fourteenth century, it was often treated in a sceptical and critical manner. Like so many Elizabethan songs, *Shall I sue?* mocks the ideas it appears to enact, exposing the singer's credulity and self-deception to ridicule. In fact, the whole song is an example of the rhetorical figure *antipophora*, that is to say, a scheme in which the speaker or singer supplies the answer to his own question: 'Silly wretch', he tells himself in the second stanza, 'forsake these dreames, / Of a vaine desire.' Neoplatonic theories of love may have their appeal; but experience tells us that felicity is 'not wonne with words, /

Example 1 John Dowland, *Shall I sue? The Second Booke of Songs (1600)* (lute accompaniment omitted)

Or a sigh can as-cend the cloudes to at-taine so hie.

Nor the wish of a thought' (stanza 3). It is impossible for music to express such reversals of meaning in a strophic song where the melody is repeated for each stanza. It could be argued, however, that by setting the final line of the first stanza – 'To attaine so hie' – to a falling figure (Ex. 1), Dowland was hinting at the disillusionment to follow, thus creating a kind of prospective irony.

Dowland was not the only Elizabethan composer who consciously attempted to reproduce in musical terms the rhetorical schemes of his lyrics. There is a similar paralleling of rhetorical and musical figures for ironic effect in Rosseter's *No graue for woe* (1601). Unlike Campion the Neoclassicist, whose lyrics tend, if I may generalize, in the direction of syntactical simplicity, Rosseter chooses for this song a poem of some rhetorical complexity:

> No graue for woe, yet earth my watrie teares deuoures,
> Sighs want ayre, and burnt desires kind pitties showres,
> Stars hold their fatal course my ioies preuenting,
> The earth, the sea, the aire, the fire, the heau'ns vow my
> tormenting.
>
> Yet still I liue and waste my wearie daies in grones,
> And with wofull tunes adorne dispayring mones,
> Night still prepares a more displeasing morrow,
> My day is night, my life my death, and all but sence of sorrow.[49]

Because his subject is one of almost banal simplicity – a slighted lover's anguish – the poet can afford to indulge his Elizabethan taste for the florid. In the first stanza traditional Petrarchan paradoxes are expressed in terms of a single controlling metaphor, that of the four elements. To the Renaissance mind the analogy between elements and humours was a real one. Graphic illustration of this basic law of human nature can be seen in the beautifully ingenious diagrams with which Robert Fludd illuminated his treatises on universal harmony. Although Fludd's attempt to provide a pseudo-scientific account of the process of musico-spiritual anamnesis looked bizarre even to his own contemporaries,[50] the underlying

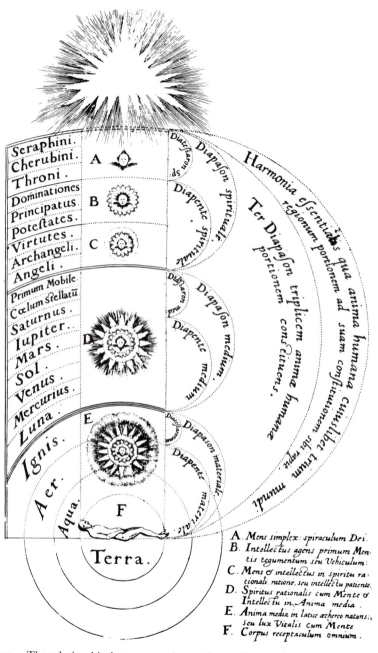

The relationship between *musica mundana* and *musica humana*. Robert Fludd,
Utriusque cosmi ... historia (Oppenheim, 1617–19)

basis of his whole philosophy – the analogy between macrocosm and microcosm – was entirely traditional. Illus. no. 11 is from his *Utriusque cosmi ... historia* (1617–19); it sets out in diagrammatic form the idea, fundamental to Neoplatonic thought, that man's own ascending degrees of spirituality (listed by Fludd in the bottom right-hand corner of his diagram) correspond to the hierarchies of nature. Rosseter's song parodies this familiar idea. Man may be, in Donne's words, 'a little world made cunningly / Of elements', but here there is no harmony between microcosm and macrocosm: the earth devours his tears, but offers no solace for his woe; nature extorts signs of anguish, but denies him air to breath; a sun-like beauty inflames his desires, but refuses to quench the fire of his passion. These paradoxes are then rehearsed and summarized in lines 3–4. This recapitulatory figure is known as *ordinatio*, a scheme that Thomas Wilson defines as a 'reckoning ... when many things are numbred together ... By this figure wee may enlarge that, by rehearsing of the partes, which was spoken generally, and in fewe wordes.'[51]

Into this short four-line stanza the poet has compressed a number of rhetorical figures: *paradoxon* (My day is night'), *zeugma* ('Sighes want ayre, and burnt desires kind pitties showres'), antithesis ('No graue for woe, yet earth my watrie teares deuoures'), *ordinatio* (see above), *alliteratio* ('sence of sorrow') and *auxesis* ('The earth, the sea, the fire, the heau'ns ...'). However, is is only the last that the composer has made any attempt to imitate in musical terms. John Hoskins defines *auxesis* as a scheme 'which by steps of comparison scores every degree till it come to the top'.[52] So nicely is this verbal ladder matched with a corresponding musical scale, moving by step and punctuated by rests to signify the singer's sighs,[53] that it is difficult to avoid the conclusion that the composer's intention was to amplify the poem's ironic view of the Neoplatonic *scala*, particularly since he gives to the treble and bass parts of the lute accompaniment for these bars a rising sequence identical to that of the cantus and forming a strict canon with it at the distance of one minim beat (Ex. 2).

No graue for woe is typical of Elizabethan attitudes towards Neoplatonic ideas. Sidney may claim in the *Defence of Poesie* that poetry can lead the mind to heavenly matters, but the view of rhetoric he gives us in his poetry is not a sanguine one: ostensibly an agent of moral rehabilitation, it all too easily becomes an instrument of

Example 2   Philip Rosseter, *No graue for woe, A Book of Ayres (1601)*

self-deception. When the eponymous lover in *Astrophil and Stella* attempts to scale the Neoplatonic ladder of love he is forced, like the singer in *Shall I sue?*, to recognize that his idealistic hopes are simply 'dreames / Of a vaine desire'. Sidney is quite flagrant in his mockery of Astrophil's winningly ingenuous idealism. However, in Jones' *O he is gone* (1609) the slippery nature of love's scale is not explicitly remarked on, but rather implied by a musical irony. The subject of the song is once again the sorrows of rejected love:

> O he is gone, and I am here
> Aye me why are wee thus diuided?
> My sight in his eyes, did appeare
> My soule by his soules thought was guided
> Then come againe my all my life, my being,
> Soules zeale, harts ioy, eares geste, eyes only seeing.
>
> Come sable care sease on my heart,
> Take up the roomes that ioyes once filled,
> Natures sweet blisse is slaine by Art.
> Absence blacke frost lives spring hath killed
> then come againe, my love, my deere, my treasure,
> My blisse, my fate, my end, my hopes full measure.[54]

In both stanzas the climax of the singer's grief is expressed by the rhetorical figure *articulus*, a form of staccato speech in which single words or short phrases are separated by commas. But instead of setting these lines to a simple ascending scale. Jones employs a series of falling thirds, each a tone or semitone higher than the previous interval. In this way he amplifies the rising tide of emotion expressed in the poem's rhetoric, while at the same time hinting at the disillusionment that must inevitably follow such emotional self-

Example 3 Robert Jones, *O he is gone, A Musicall Dreamee: or The Fourth Booke of Ayres (1609)*. Partsong version (altus omitted) plus lute accompaniment

indulgence. From the version for voice and lute it might appear that Jones confines his musical 'translation' to the cantus. However, the partsong version printed opposite it reveals a more elaborate response: here the tenor anticipates the cantus a major sixth below, to form a strict canon at one minim's distance (ex. 3).

The songs I have been discussing are mock-serious love songs; their purpose is entertainment. Although they employ quite complex rhetorical schemes, they are not intended for moral improvement, or seduction or, for that matter, persuasion of any kind. Indeed, in a song where the singer's grief is occasioned precisely by the absence of his beloved, there is no one to persuade. It is sufficient for him if his grief is recognized. As the poet says in Dowland's *If my complaints could passions moue* (1597), 'Die shall my hopes, but not my faith / That you that of my fall may hearers be'.[55] Although these songs depend for their effect on the presence of an audience, the listener is cast in the role, not of recipient of edifying truths, but of eavesdropper overhearing what, by tacit agreement, we pretend to believe is an artlessly naive confession. They are the product of a world in which it was expected that a poet would be 'a dissembler in the subtilties of his arte'.[56] The complaint is a traditional form that makes no great demands of its audience. However, it is often wittily used by Renaissance poets as camouflage to conceal another lyric kind – the seduction poem. A particularly brilliant example is Donne's *The Dampe*, which, under cover of a typically lachrymose piece of Petrarchan self-pity, performs a number of adroit syllogistic manoeuvres, finally springing on the unsuspecting reader a proposal of an outrageously erotic nature. Like Donne's poem, Dowland's *Come again: sweet loue doth now inuite* (1597) is a seduction song masquerading as an innocent complaint. It begins with what appears to be a polite and decorous invitation to a reluctant mistress:

> Come again sweet loue doth now inuite,
> Thy graces that refraine,
> To do me due delight,
> To see, to heare, to touch, to kisse, to die,
> With thee againe in sweetest sympathy.[57]

But the invitation in the last two lines of the stanza, expressed by the rhetorical figure of *auxesis*, is not as innocent as it appears. A sixteenth-century audience would be likely to notice, not just that it culminates in the standard euphemism for sexual climax, but also that there is something familiar about the form of the singer's invitation. It is in fact a stylized scheme of seduction that appears in a variety of literary forms. Modern scholars of the period call it the 'ladder of lechery'.[58] The *rhétoriqueur* Lemaire de Belges explains how it works:

Our noble poets state that there are five stages in a love affair, or rather five particular points or degrees, namely, the glance, the conversation, the touch, the embrace – and last, most highly desired of all, and towards which all the others are directed, is that which is decently called the 'granting of favours'.[59]

The ladder of lechery is a parody of the medieval devotional five-point *gradus amoris*,[60] itself a Christian adaptation of the Neoplatonic ladder of love. Although music was supposed to remind man of, and induce in him a longing for, his celestial origins, it was notoriously susceptible of abuse – hence the deep suspicion with

12. The ladder of lechery. In Bosch's satirical allegory the ladder of love leads not to virtue, but to concupiscence, here represented by musicians seated on a wagon of hay (symbol of vanity). Hieronymus Bosch, *The Hay Wain*

Example 4   John Dowland, *Come again: sweet love doth now inuite, The First Booke of Songes (1597)*

to see,   to heare,   to touch,   to kisse,   to die

which it was regarded by many Reformation prelates. In theory the *gradus amoris* should lead to spiritual beatitude; in practice it was likely to lead to bliss of a more terrestrial nature. The point is neatly illustrated in Bosch's *The Hay Wain* (illus. 12), where the ladder placed against the wagon of hay – symbol of vanity – leads, not to heaven, but to a bower of bliss where concupiscence is fomented by the 'lasciuious pleasing of a lute' (*Richard III*, 1.i.13). *The Hay Wain* is the profane counterpart of Dürer's *Melencolia*.

Under the surface of the polite-sounding lyrics that Dowland has chosen to set there lurks, then, some rather artful innuendo. Just as the poet employs a rhetorical figure of climax to persuade his mistress to climb the ladder of love, so Dowland illustrates these words by using a scale, or ladder, of rising fourths that reach their climax as the singer anticipates his own (ex. 4). The five steps of the *gradus amoris* are confirmed by the treble and bass parts of the lute accompaniment: as with Rosseter's accompaniment to *No graue for woe*, these take the form of a rising scale punctuated by rests. Like so many Renaissance seduction lyrics, *Come again* uses, or rather abuses, rhetoric in order to move the mind of the listener. In doing so both poet and composer employ schemes that mime the process they seek to initiate. The result is a nicely decorous indecency.

It would be wrong to suggest that Elizabethan lutenist song-writers were never entirely serious. Rhetorical figures may be, in Puttenham's words, 'abuses or rather trespasses in speach, because ... they be occupied of purpose to deceive the eare and also the minde';[61] but few listeners can doubt the seriousness of Dowland's intentions in writing *Flow my tears* (1600), for example, or Danyel's in *Griefe keep within* (1606). Yet for all its emotional profundity, *Flow my tears* has no more to 'say' than songs like Rosseter's *No graue for woe* or Jones' *O he is gone*. Its interest is largely musical and owes very little to the words, which were a later addition to a pre-existing pavan. Indeed, with lyrics as inconsequential as these it would be unwise, in the absence of concrete evidence of Dowland's intellectual affiliations, to read precise philosophical meanings into the song.

By contrast, Danyel's *Grief keep within* has a very precise meaning. It is a funeral elegy that argues for the disciplined avoidance of tasteless shows of sorrow:

> Greefe keep within and scorne to shew but teares,
> Since Ioy can weepe as well as thou:
> Disdaine to sigh for so can slender cares,
> Which but from Idle causes grow.
> Doe not looke forth vnlesse thou didst know how
> To looke with thine owne face, and as thou art,
> And onely let my hart,
> That knowes more reason why,
> Pyne, Fret, Consume, Swell, Burst and Dye.
>
> Drop not myne eyes nor Trickle downe so fast,
> For so you could doe oft before,
> In our sad farewells and sweet meetings past,
> And shall his death now haue no more?
> Can niggard sorrow yeld no other store:
> To shew the plentie of aflictions smart,
> Then onely thou poore hart,
> That knowst more reason why,
> Pyne, Fret, Consume, Swell, Burst and Dye.
>
> Haue all our passions certaine proper vents,
> And sorow none that is her owne?
> But she must borow others complements,
> To make her inward feelings knowne?
> Are Ioyes delights and deathes compassion showne,
> With one lyke face and one lamenting part?
> Then onely thou poore hart that know'st more reason why,
> Pine, Fret, Consume, Swell, Burst, and Dye.[62]

Unlike *Flow my tears*, which is in effect, a celebration of melancholy, *Griefe keep within* counsels self-restraint. It was well known that music was capable either of allaying or inflaming passion. These two songs are a good example of music's dual powers. Where Dowland apostrophizes his tears, encouraging them to flow the more freely,

Example 5   John Danyel, *Griefe keep within, Songs for the Lute Viol and Voice (1606)*
(Lute accompaniment omitted)

Example 6   *Griefe keep within*, stanza 2

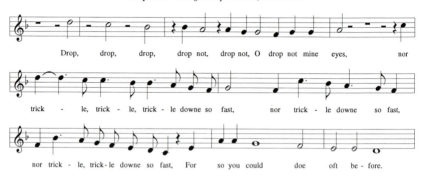

Danyel's lyrics do the opposite: 'Drop not myne eyes', writes the
poet, 'nor Trickle down so fast.' His reason is that, since the outward
marks of sorrow signify nothing and may as easily arise from trivial
as from serious causes, death's shrine should not be desecrated by
something as superficial as tears. The heart must mourn in private.

Although each stanza of the song has a different melodic and
harmonic structure, Danyel uses repetition to some effect in his
setting of the refrain. The rhetorical figure of *auxesis* in the emotive
final line is set, as one would expect, to an analogous musical figure,
moving by step, that reaches its climax on the word 'Dye' (ex. 5).
The emotional tension generated by this line is then dissipated in the
opening bars of the second stanza, where Danyel imitates the falling
of the singer's tears in a series of descending scale figures (ex. 6).
Danyel repeats his setting of the refrain in stanzas 2 and 3. In each
case, however, the final line is set twice, first to the rising scale used
in stanza 1, and second to a falling figure that brings the singer back
to the key note on 'Dye' (ex. 7, 8).

The effect of these repeated refrains is to enrich the poetry and to
suggest ambiguity where none exists in the words alone. Whereas in
the first stanza it is the grieving singer who anticipates her own
death, the music of the second and third stanzas implies that it is not
the subject, but her grief that is now expiring. The stoicism that is

Example 7   *Griefe keep within*, stanza 2

Example 8   *Griefe keep within*, stanza 3

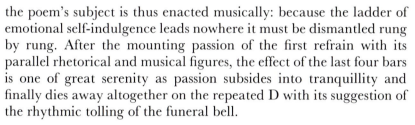

the poem's subject is thus enacted musically: because the ladder of emotional self-indulgence leads nowhere it must be dismantled rung by rung. After the mounting passion of the first refrain with its parallel rhetorical and musical figures, the effect of the last four bars is one of great serenity as passion subsides into tranquillity and finally dies away altogether on the repeated D with its suggestion of the rhythmic tolling of the funeral bell.

IV

In late sixteenth-century England there was something of a flowering of interest in the occult traditions of Renaissance magic, and it is sometimes suggested that hermetic Neoplatonism may account for the melancholy that was so fashionable at the time (see chapter 8). That hermeticism enjoyed a vogue in Elizabethan England is undeniable. But while occultism may have attracted the deeper spirits of the age, it is alien to the general tenor of Elizabethan thought. This is not to suggest that the stoicism of *Griefe keep within* is to be preferred to the inspired melancholy of magical tradition, merely that, of the two, it is Danyel's ideal that is more representative of the age. The view of rhetoric and music that informs his song is one that has its origins in Cicero and the Roman manuals of rhetoric. If Orpheus was seen by Renaissance writers as the symbolic embodiment of civilization, it was not because of his ability to inspire passion, but because it was by his 'prudent art of perswasion [that people] were conuerted from that most brutish condition of life, to the loue of humanitie & pollitic government'.[63] It is this belief in the civilizing power of the arts that is the subject of Campion's *Lord's Maske*. As Mania, goddess of madness, is drawn from her cave by the sound of Orpheus' music, she is compelled 'T'abandon darkenesse which my humour fits.'[64]

In realizing Morley's ideal of a 'harmonicall concent betwixt the matter and the musicke',[65] the Elizabethan lute song forms a unique chapter in the history of song; it also represents a significant stage in the history of metaphysical anthropology. Fundamental to Renaissance humanism was a belief in the rehabilitative power of the arts, and of poetry and music in particular: if the 'musicke of mens liues' was in some mysterious way organically related to a harmony that was implicit in the structure of the universe, then the arts could assist humanity in the attempt to recover its lost equilibrium. Of course, those theories could only survive while their metaphysical premises remained intact. But it was to be many decades before the old structures finally lost their imaginative power. Despite recent claims by materialist critics to find evidence of widespread scepticism in this period concerning essentialist theories of human nature, those beliefs survive well into the eighteenth century. It is true that most Elizabethan humanists are sceptical of the more extravagant claims of speculative Neoplatonism. But it is their sense of man's innate and essential limitations, rather than any wish to decentre their human subject, that makes them suspicious of poets or composers who attempt, in Boccaccio's words, 'to raise flights of symbolic steps to heaven'.[66]

CHAPTER 5

Microcosmos: symbolic geometry in the Renaissance lute rose

> To call ourselves a Microcosm, or little world, I thought it onely a pleasant trope of Rhetorick, till my neare judgement and second thoughts told me there was a reall truth therein.
>
> (Sir Thomas Browne, *Religio Medici*)

How could an intellectual living in the post-Copernican world of early modern England seriously believe that there was any 'reall truth' in the proposition that man is an epitome of the universe? The question is one that interests political historians as well as students of the history of anthropology. If you believe, as so many writers in this period claim to do, that correspondence between macrocosm and microcosm is the expression of an immutable law of nature, then anything like a truly democratic form of government becomes, quite literally, unthinkable: it would be a denial of one of nature's most fundamental principles. As Sir John Hayward puts it in a classic Elizabethan expression of the doctrine of correspondence: 'As one God ruleth the World, one master the family ... so it seemeth no less natural that one state should be ruled by one commander.'[1]

It was, of course, highly convenient for successive Tudor and Stuart governments and their supporters to be able to claim that the existing social structure was part of the natural order of things; and no doubt many people accepted this 'official' version of reality without question. But how many intellectuals gave credence to the doctrine of correspondence? In recent years it has been suggested that the answer is, very few. It has been argued that the very notion of an essential human nature that transcends cultural boundaries and is more or less constant throughout history is a comparatively recent invention.[2] If you go back to the fifteenth century you find that the representative human being, as portrayed in the literature of the period, 'has no unifying essence'.[3] Instead, subjectivity is shown to be discursively produced: it was recognized, the argument goes, that our sense of individuality is an illusion generated by ideological forces that shape not only our attitudes and beliefs, but even our apparently most spontaneous feelings. It is claimed that the historical moment when this materialist view of the self is abandoned can be pinpointed with some precision: 'the unified subject of liberal humanism is a product of the second half of the seventeenth century', writes Catherine Belsey.[4] It is only since the Enlightenment that we have been in thrall to a bourgeois-liberal ideology of the self conceived as an independent self-determining entity. Before that, intellectuals had a much clearer understanding of the way the individual is constructed by ideology.[5] If this fact has not been generally understood by Renaissance scholars, it is because traditional historical scholarship has painted a false picture of Renaissance intellectual life, argues Jonathan Dollimore. In *Radical Tragedy* he claims that it is historically incorrect to read the period 'through the grid of an essentialist humanism'.[6]

It is always gratifying to identify in those writers from the past whom we admire a preoccupation with ideas and problems that concern ourselves. John Donne is a signal case in point. Sardonic, anxious, sceptical, he has appealed to several generations of modern critics who have seen in him a kindred spirit who seems to anticipate our own twentieth-century sense of intellectual crisis. That early modern England was also a period of crisis is not in dispute. However, in making common cause with the past there is a danger that we may replace one form of historical distortion with another. This is particularly true of revisionist versions of Elizabethan anthropology. E. M. W. Tillyard has been rightly criticized for his schematic picture of Elizabethan intellectual life. But it is arguably less misleading to present a one-sided view of the period (as Tillyard did) based on first-hand knowledge of a wide range of primary texts than it is to attribute wholly anachronistic ideas to a small and heterogeneous group of Renaissance writers, and then to erect on that basis a revisionist view of the entire Western intellectual tradition. To claim, as a number of recent critics have done, that there is in this period a significant body of anti-essentialist thought that challenged the notion of an irreducible human essence is profoundly misleading, the more so since the claim is made with little reference either directly to the contemporary debate on human nature, or to the substantial body of modern scholarship on the subject of Renaissance metaphysical anthropology. It is true that there is a growing scepticism in this period concerning traditional world views; but the scientists and thinkers who were doing most to change traditional conceptions of the universe were in many cases people who also believed passionately in the reality of what Boethius called *musica mundana*; they believed, that is to say, in a universe whose inherent harmonies were a function of mathematical principles.

In this chapter I shall consider the implications of that belief as they concern Elizabethan ideas about human nature. My point of reference will probably be unfamiliar to students of English literature. It is an abstract geometrical pattern, one that is repeated, with many variations, in practically every Renaissance lute rose. The lute rose is more than just a piece of pleasing decoration. Its geometry symbolizes precisely that mystery which fascinated Sir Thomas Browne, namely, the mystery of a musico-mathematical universe in which the microcosm can truly be said to be 'an Epitome or Compend of the whole creation'.[7] The subject is arcane. Despite enormous modern interest in early music, even lutenists have been unaware, until recently, of the symbolic meanings their instrument originally possessed.[8] But I suggest that it is better to acknowledge that the past is another country where they do things differently than to try to remake its inhabitants in our own image.

I

In his *Obseruations in the Art of English Poesie* Thomas Campion gives an example of the kind of metre that is suitable for poems that are intended 'to be soong to an instrument':

> Rose-cheekt *Lawra*, come
> Sing thou smoothly with thy beawties
> Silent musick, either other
>   Sweetely gracing.
>
> Louely formes do flowe
> From concent deuinely framed;
> Heau'n is musick, and thy beawties
>   Birth is heauenly.
>
> These dull notes we sing
> Discords neede for helps to grace them;
> Only beawty purely louing
>   Knowes no discord,

> But still mooues delight,
> Like cleare springs renu'd by flowing,
> Euer perfet, euer in them-
>   selues eternall.[9]

Campion says that trochaic metres of this kind are fit for expressing 'any amorous conceit'.[10] We should not be misled by his typically casual disclaimer: Campion's song is actually a remarkable piece of elegant compression in which Pythagorean, Platonic and Boethian ideas are combined with an apparently effortless ease. When we read the words on the page we are likely to miss much of the song's intended effect. This is not because the ideas it alludes to are particularly inaccessible, but because with a song that is meant 'to be soong to an instrument' the iconography of the performance is part of its meaning. When the singer apologizes for his own 'dull notes' and reminds us that this *musica instrumentalis* is merely a poor echo of celestial music (*musica mundana*), the instrument he is playing serves as a visual symbol of the fact that 'Heau'n is musick'.

The idea that the universe is like a vast lyre goes back to classical antiquity.[11] John Donne sums up a commonplace of this period – one that provided Elizabethan poets and dramatists with an endless repertory of metaphors for describing psychological, social and political realities – when he writes: 'God made this whole world in such an uniformity, such a correspondency, such a concinnity of parts, as that it was an Instrument, perfectly in tune.'[12] As the modern equivalent of the classical lyre, the lute was widely interpreted as a symbol of the cosmos. William Drummond elaborates this familiar conceit in the style of an emblem-book writer:

> GOD binding with hid *Tendons* this great ALL,
> Did make a LVTE which had all parts it giuen;
> This LVTES round *Bellie* was the azur'd Heauen,
> The *Rose* those lights which Hee did there install;
> The *Basses* were the Earth and Ocean,
> The *Treble* shrill the Aire: the other *Strings*
> The vnlike Bodies were of mixed things.[13]

But the lute is more than just an emblem of a harmonious universe. At its centre is a device that has its own symbolic language, a language as precise as that of any medieval cathedral rose window. Campion's singer says it is 'From concent deuinely framed' that all earthly forms of beauty emanate. The Pythagoreans taught that, in

Castiglione's words, 'the worlde is made of musike, and the heavens in their moving make a melodie'. From this principle there followed another of equal importance, namely, that 'our soule is framed after the verie same sort'.[14] The lute rose is a symbolic reminder of this mysterious musical correspondence between macrocosm and microcosm. The geometric forms through which that meaning is articulated have a long and complex history.

II

In a seminal article on the construction of Renaissance and baroque lutes Friedemann Hellwig noted that the large number of different rose patterns that characterize the instruments of this period can be reduced to a few basic motifs. The most frequent of these is the six-pointed star formed by the interlacing of two equilateral triangles. Hellwig suggests that this design may have been intended to symbolize 'the permeation of the visible and invisible world'.[15] A glance at its origins suggests that, in broad terms, he is undoubtedly right.

Unlike most of its wire-strung relatives, whose roses were usually of gothic design, the lute retained the geometric motifs of its Arabic origins. Basing his design on a few simple forms such as the circle, the triangle and the square, the Islamic artist developed a highly sophisticated system of symbolism whose purpose was to reveal the hidden laws of the universe.[16] The characteristic idiom of this symbolic language was a complex geometrical pattern interwoven with floral arabesques. The interlacing strapwork that is a feature of most Renaissance lute and archlute roses has its origins in the ubiquitous Islamic rosette, a design that originated in the tenth century and is found in countries as widely separated geographically as Turkey, Egypt and Spain (illus. 13). By repeating an infinitely extendible geometrical motif the artist gives us, in effect, an incomplete picture of a pattern that exists in its entirety only in infinity.[17] In this way he is able to suggest the idea, fundamental to Islam, that man is a transient being whose earthly existence must be seen as part of a unified eternal order. Informing the geometric motifs of Islamic art is a long tradition of representing the cosmos by means of number expressed diagrammatically.

The belief that numbers are the basis of all physical reality originates in the school of Pythagoras (sixth century BC). According

13. Detail from a wall decoration from the Alhambra, Granada

to ancient legend it was Pythagoras' discovery that musical intervals are a function of mathematical ratios that led him to the portentous conclusion that number represents not just a way of explaining the physical world, but the ultimate building-blocks of reality. As Aristotle explains in the *Metaphysics*:

since [the Pythagoreans] saw that the properties and ratios of the musical scales are based on numbers, and since it seemed clear that all other things have their whole nature modelled upon numbers, and that numbers are the ultimate things in the whole physical universe, they assumed the elements of numbers to be the elements of everything, and the whole universe to be a proportion or number.[18]

It was the belief that they had discovered a fundamental law of nature that led the Pythagoreans to attribute mystic significance to certain numbers. Expressed diagrammatically, such numbers constituted a secret language that was accessible only to the initiate. Galileo writes:

Philosophy is written in that vast book which stands forever open before our eyes, I mean the universe; but it cannot be read until we have learnt the language and become familiar with the characters in which it is

written. It is written in mathematical language, and the letters are triangles, circles and other geometric figures, without which means it is
humanly impossible to comprehend a single word.[19]

For the Pythagoreans mathematics was a key that could unlock
the hidden mysteries of a universe created on harmonic principles: it
explained the revolutions of the heavens; the harmonious rhythms of
the natural world; even the life of the individual soul. It was Plato
who first proposed an exact correspondence between the music of
the spheres and the harmonies of the soul. In the *Timaeus* he explains
how the gift of music was bestowed on man for the purpose of
harmonizing the spirit:

harmony, which has motions akin to the revolutions of the Soul within us,
was given by the Muses to him who makes intelligent use of the Muses, not
as an aid to irrational pleasure ... but as an auxiliary to the inner
revolution of the Soul, when it has lost its harmony, to assist in restoring it
to order and concord with itself.[20]

In comparing the revolutions of the soul with 'the revolutions of
Reason in the Heaven' (47c), Plato laid the basis for the doctrine of
analogy between macrocosm and microcosm, a principle that dominated medieval and Renaissance metaphysical anthropology and
that was to survive well into the seventeenth century. By charting
the correspondences between the manifold levels of existence, the
numerologist provided a quasi-scientific account of human nature
and its place in the universal scheme of things.

One of the principal channels through which these ideas were
transmitted to the Middle Ages was Arabic philosophy. In the work
of Avicenna (980–1037), greatest of the Arabic philosophers, the
traditional analogy between microcosm and macrocosm was
extended and developed into a highly complex psycho-physical
theory. Soon after his death Avicenna's works made their way to
Spain, and from there to Christian Europe. He was a well-known
authority in fifteenth- and sixteenth-century England through John
Trevisa's and Stephen Batman's translations of the encyclopaedic
De proprietatibus rerum of Bartholomaeus Anglicus (*fl. c.* 1220–40).
Avicenna has been described as one of the supreme names in the
history of ideas, 'an epoch-making thinker who determined the
course of much Western thought'.[21] As a Neoplatonist he was
particularly interested in the means by which music was able to
rehabilitate the soul and, in Plato's words, 'restore it to order and

14. Fourteenth-century Egyptian Ms illustration of an *'ud*. Nationalbibliothek,
Vienna, Ms AF9 fol. 42

concord with itself'. Although Plato claimed that music could have a therapeutic effect on the soul, he did not explain how this process actually worked. Arab Neoplatonism attempted to provide that explanation. The result was an elaborate system of correspondences in which the four bodily humours were attuned to their equivalent elements through the agency of music. The most important instrument in Arab philosophy was the *'ud* (illus. 14), the direct ancestor of the Renaissance lute. The *'ud* was a symbolic focus for the system of correspondences that is fundamental to Pythagoreanism. Its four strings were conventionally identified both with the elements and with the corresponding humours and were dyed accordingly: yellow for bile, red for blood, white for mucous and black for black bile.[22] The encyclopaedic *Rasa'il* of the tenth-century *Ikhwan as Safa*, a community of scientists and mathematicians that aimed to combine philosophy and religion, describes the metaphysical properties of the *'ud*'s four strings in terms that anticipate Wither's seventeenth-century cosmic lute:

> The treble string is like the element of fire, its tone being hot and violent.
> The second string is like the element of air; its tone corresponds to the humidity of air and to its softness.
> The third string is like the element of water; its tone suggests water-like moisture and coolness.
> The bass string is like the heaviness and thickness of the element earth.[23]

As well as being identified with the elements and humours, the four strings of the *'ud* were associated with the signs of the zodiac, winds, seasons, periods of life and times of the month and of the day. These were related in turn to human temperament and to the faculties of both body and soul.[24]

The *'ud* occupies a place of special honour in medieval Arabic philosophy; indeed it was known as the 'philosopher's instrument'. According to the ninth-century philosopher and music theorist al-Kindi, every detail of its construction has an arithmetical or geometrical basis in philosophy or astrology.[25] It is at once a symbol of the cosmos – its arched belly was compared to the dome of the heavens[26] – and a practical means of realizing the rehabilitative function of music that is central to Arabic Neoplatonism. As it became assimilated into European musical life in the later Middle Ages through the brilliant Islamic society that flourished in Spain from the tenth century,[27] the *'ud* brought with it a complex body of Pythagorean musical lore. That lore was to survive into the Renaissance.

III

In the prestige it accorded to literature and the arts, the Islamic civilization of medieval Spain far surpassed anything that Western Christendom was able to offer and had a profound influence on the course of European culture.[28] In the twelfth century there was a revival of interest in Pythagoreanism, notably at the School of Chartres.[29] The principles of Pythagorean number symbolism were already familiar in the West from the work of well-known writers like Macrobius and St Augustine. But with the impetus of new ideas from the Islamic world there was renewed interest in numerology. Number symbolism is a fundamental aspect of the medieval artistic imagination;[30] insofar as it was capable of showing that all fixed aggregates defined by the same number were related to one another, numerology provided the Christian writer not just with a way of structuring his work, but with a means of imparting knowledge of man, of nature and consequently of God. As Sir William Ingpen puts it, since the created universe is 'an harmonious body, containing number, order, beauty, and proportion', the best way to know its author is 'to begin with numbring'.[31] In the Middle Ages the most dramatic monuments of Pythagorean symbolism were not works of literature but buildings. The medieval gothic cathedral was designed as a visible embodiment of divine order; in the words of Robert Jordan, it was 'an analogue of creation itself, a concrete microcosm of the abstract, musico-mathematical perfection of the universe'.[32] One of the most remarkable features of the Gothic cathedral is the rose window. According to Painton Cowen, the sudden appearance of rose windows in France at the beginning of the thirteenth century is a mystery.[33] Miraculous as this exotic and beautiful flowering may seem, it is less mysterious when it is seen as a programmatic expression of the philosophic ideals of the School of Chartres.[34] Adelhard of Bath (*fl.* early twelfth century), who had travelled as far as Syria and committed himself to making Arab philosophy known to the Christian world, believed that through a study of the seven liberal arts, man is capable of intuiting the *musica mundana* and participating in its harmonies.[35] A roundel in a twelfth-century pontifical from the School of Rheims represents these ideas in schematic form. Illus. 15 shows the spheres of *musica mundana* and *musica humana* spanned, as in a Vitruvian diagram, by the figure of man himself, the *nodus et vinculum mundi*.[36] A similar vision inspired the great rose windows of the thirteenth century. In the silent music of their geometry each of these windows embodies the fundamental principles of the Pythagorean universe. In his analysis of the rose in the north transept of Chartres cathedral (illus. 16) Cowen explains how everything in the window is derived from three basic figures; the equilateral triangle (representing the Trinity or the soul); the square (unfolding the relation between spirit and matter, Father and Son) and the circle (symbolizing the perfection of the cosmos itself).[37] In effect it is a mandala whose hidden geometry symbolizes the interpenetration of microcosm and macrocosm. It is this principle that Alain de Lille (*c.* 1128–1202), most influential of the Chartrian Neoplatonists, describes in a key passage from the *Plaint of Nature*. Man's own nature, says Alain, is formed

according to the exemplar and likeness of the structure of the universe so that in him, as in a mirror of the universe itself, Nature's lineaments might be there to see. For just as concord in discord, unity in plurality, harmony in disharmony, agreement in disagreement of the four elements unite the arts of the structure of the royal palace of the universe, so too, similarity in dissimilarity, equality in inequality, like in unlike, identity in diversity of four combinations bind together the house of the human body.[38]

The Neoplatonists of the twelfth-century Renaissance believed that through an understanding of this universal mystery man could come to know his true essence and thus realize Timaeus' ideal of rational self-control based on a knowledge of the laws of nature.

With the Neoplatonic revival of the fifteenth and sixteenth centuries there was a reaffirmation of the belief that the harmony of the universe was a function of mathematical laws. Revival of interest in the principle of universal harmony is reflected in the flood of Renaissance treatises with titles such as *De harmonia mundi totius* (Francesco di Giorgio, 1525), *Harmonices mundi* (Kepler, 1619) and *Harmonie universelle* (Mersenne, 1636). It is reflected also in the preoccupation of Renaissance painters, sculptors and architects with Vitruvius' theories of architectural proportion.[39] In claiming that temples should be modelled on the proportions of the human body, Vitruvius (first century BC) was endorsing the traditional Pythagorean belief that man is the measure of all things. As the

15.   Drawing of twelfth-century Ms illustration from the School of Reims showing the Boethian categories of *musica mundana*, *musica humana* and *musica instrumentalis* linked together by a human figure (Aer) representing the principle of poetico-musical inspiration, Pontifical Ms, School of Reims, Chapitre de Notre Dame.

Italian mathematician and friend of Leonardo da Vinci, Luca Pacioli (1445–1509), wrote in a treatise entitled *De proportione*, 'from the human body derive all measures and their denominations and in it is to be found all and every ratio and proportion by which God reveals the innermost secrets of nature'.[40] The well-known figure of

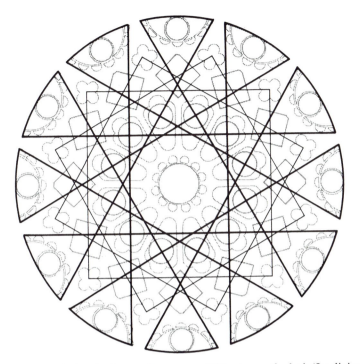

16.   Rose window in the north transept of Chartres cathedral. 'Its divine
geometry is among its finest glories. Everything in the window is generated
from the properties of the square within the circle'
(Painton Cowen)

the Vitruvian man inscribed in a circle within a square (illus. 17) is a
symbolic representation of this idea. By basing their designs on
Vitruvian principles, architects like Alberti (1404–72) and Palladio
(1508–80) were not so much celebrating man himself as attempting
to reproduce in microcosm the harmonies of a mathematical
universe.

In Renaissance England the Pythagorean revival manifests itself
in a variety of ways – in a renewed interest in astrology and magic;
in works of popular astronomy; in architectural treatises; in theatre
design; and in number symbolism of all kinds.[41] The greatest Elizabethan example of the numerologist's art is *The Faerie Queene*. Spenser's description of the House of Alma is a symbolic restatement of
Vitruvian architectural principles:

17.   Leonardo da Vinci, Vitruvian man

> The frame thereof was partly circulare,
>   And part triangulare, O worke diuine;
>   Those two the first and last proportions are,
>   The one imperfect, mortall, foeminine;
>   Th'other immortall, perfect masculine,
>   And twixt them both a quadrate was the base,
>   Proportioned equally by seuen and nine;
>   Nine was the circle set in heauens place,
> All which compacted made a goodly diapase.   (II.ix.22)

The House of Alma is a whimsical allegory of the human body: the turret ('Like highest heauen encompassed around') represents the head; the hall the stomach; the kitchens the internal organs; and so on. But as with any Vitruvian building, its structural principles are identical with those of the cosmos.[42] The geometric figures on which it is based – circle, triangle and square – are the basis of all Pythagorean representations of the universe and serve to articulate the interpenetration of microcosm and macrocosm. The same figures form the basis of the Renaissance lute rose.

IV

Like the poet, the painter and the architect, the Renaissance luthier made conscious use of Vitruvian principles in the design of his instruments.[43] Just as a temple based on the proportions of the human body was thought to express the harmony of a mathematical universe, so the 'body' of the lute, consisting of 'belly', 'back' and 'ribs', was based on formalized geometrical principles. Those same Pythagorean principles are articulated in microcosm at the lute's centre.

As Hellwig points out, the classic Renaissance lute rose is based on the hexagram. This device is inherited from the Arabic *'ud*, where the six-pointed star formed by two interlocking triangles conventionally signifies the union of the human and the divine, the corporeal and the spiritual, the visible and the invisible. In Pythagorean lore the limits of the physical universe were defined by the decade, and as a result each of the first ten integers was endowed with its own symbolic quality. As the sum of its aliquot parts ($1 + 2 + 3$), six is regarded as the first perfect number. Ingpen describes it as 'in every way full, perfect, divine'.[44] Its identification with harmony is probably due to the fact that six is the number of intervals in the Greek

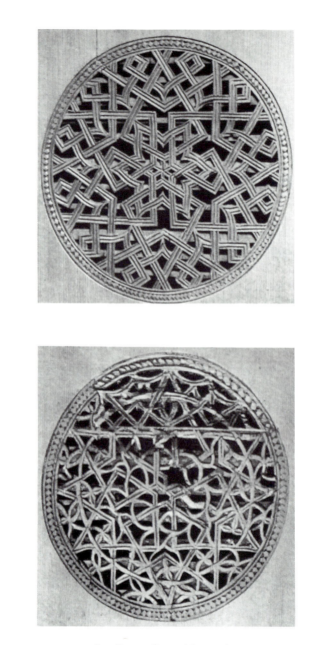

18. Roses of two chittaroni

scale. The hexagram is thus a fitting form of decoration to incorporate in a musical instrument that was itself treated as a symbol of the cosmos (one of the meanings of the word *kosmos* is 'decoration').

On this basic figure the Renaissance luthier superimposed a second hexagram. In doing so he created a more complex pattern in which a number of quadrilateral figures appears. The roses of two early seventeenth-century chittaroni in the Victoria and Albert Museum may serve as typical examples (illus. 18). Despite the obvious differences in the treatment of their arabesques, the same geometrical pattern is present: from whichever of the eight cardinal points of the compass the roses are viewed, the eye perceives either a hexagram or a rectangular figure that divides the circle into four main compartments.

The number four has particular importance in Pythagorean lore. If six, the first perfect number, is associated with harmony, four is the very basis of the cosmos. 'All the foundation of every deepe studie and invention must be settled upon the number fower, because it is the roote and beginning of all numbers', writes Pierre de La Primaudaye in *The French Academie*.[45] The fourth integer was a key to the cosmos because it bound together macrocosm and microcosm in a system of linked tetrads that subsumed every level of creation. At one extreme were the four celestial elements that went to make up the World-Soul; at the other were the four virtues that characterized the sensible part of man's own soul – that part which Shakespeare's Regan calls 'the precious square of sence' (*Lr.*, 1.i.76).[46] The same pattern was repeated at every level of creation. Each of these tetrads was related to the others in an integrated whole. The harmony of the cosmos depended on the unique stability of the tetrad. In its simplest form this stable union of four conflicting elements was represented diagrammatically in cosmographical treatises as four interlocking circles (illus. 19). Derivations of this motif are frequently found in lute roses either as a simple quatrefoil (illus. 20), or, in a more stylized form, as a series of interlocking quadrangles (illus. 21). Although it is unusual to find a rose whose geometry is unrelieved by arabesques, this underlying pattern of interlocking quadrangles is in fact extremely widespread, and, as illus. 22 shows, it often forms the basis of roses that have lost all trace of geometrical strapwork.

The inherent stability of the cosmos was explained by the fact that the four elements were bound together in a configuration of two

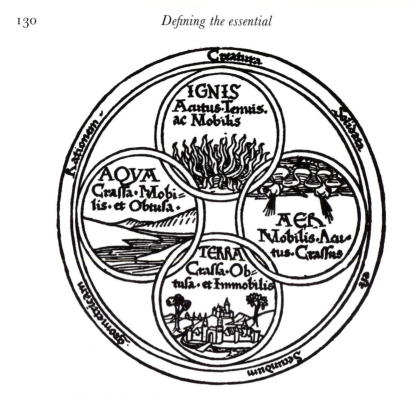

19.   Tetrad from Isidore of Seville, *Liber de responsione mundi et astrorum ordinatione*
(Augsburg, 1472)

pairs of opposites linked together by their two mean terms. This arrangement was the principle on which God had created the universe. The clearest account of the way the four elements are united by their mean terms is by Macrobius (*fl.* 400). In his *Commentary on the Dream of Scipio* he explains how the Creator gave to each of the four elements two qualities, one of which it shared with the element closest to it in character. Thus:

Earth is dry and cold, and water cold and moist; but although these two elements are opposed, the dry to the wet, they have a common bond in their coldness. Air is moist and warm and, although opposed to water, the cold to the warm, nevertheless has the common bond of moisture. Moreover, fire, being hot and dry, spurns the moisture of the air, but yet adheres to it because of the warmth in both. And so it happens that each one of the elements appears to embrace the two elements bordering on each side of it by single qualities: water binds earth to itself by coldness, and air by moisture; air is allied to water by its moisture, and to fire by warmth; fire mingles with air because of its heat, and with earth because of its dryness;

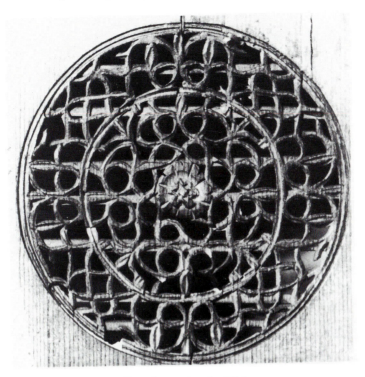

20.   Rose from a lute by Hieber

earth is compatible with fire because of its dryness, and with water because of its coldness. These different bonds would have no tenacity, however, if there were only two elements; if there were three the union would be but a weak one; but as there are four elements the bonds are unbreakable, since the two extremes are held together by two means.[47]

In a poem entitled *Vicissitudo Rerum* John Norden gives an Elizabethan version of the same idea. In answer to the question why discord is essential to the harmony of the cosmos, Norden explains that if the mutually antagonistic elements were not kept in check by one another the result would be an imbalance in nature:

> Yet thus, this *disagreement* must bee set,
> As in the *discord* bee no power to wrong:
> For why? supremest have no fatall let,
> But will preuaile, as they become too strong.
> Therefore such *meane* must them be set among,
>   As though things bee compact of *contraryes*,
>   They must by *ballance*, have like quantities.[48]

21. Rose from an early sixteenth-century lute

The tetrad is the foundation of cosmic harmony. It was commonly represented by Renaissance cosmographers with great precision in diagrammatic form. In illus. 23 the elements are arranged at equal intervals round the circumference of a circle. Between them are their four properties which, acting as mean terms, serve to bind the warring elements together in a stable union. The complex nature of the relationships within the tetrad described by Macrobius is illustrated by a network of intersecting lines. The same pattern of concordant discord is repeated at the microcosmic level. Illus. 24 shows how the four elements have their counterparts in the four seasons and the four bodily humours. This time the elemental mean terms have been doubled. This arrangement of elements and mean terms has the effect of dividing the circle into twelve sections, one for each month of the year. The circle itself is an ancient symbol of perfection. John Norden writes:

22. Rose based on a damaged instrument by Graill

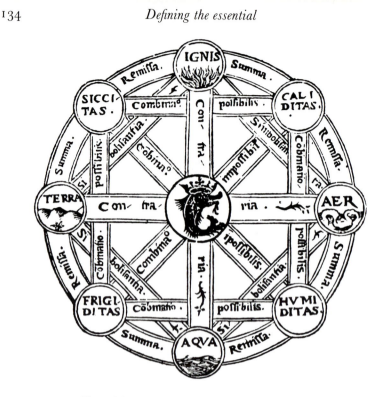

23. Tetrad from Oronce Fine, *Protomathesis* (Paris, 1532)

The *Heauens* in their peereles pryde may bost,
That they in their orbiculer figure
Are farre the freest, and by change vntost,
Keeping by turne, their *Reuolutions* sure:
Though still reuoluing yet alike endure.
  As *Orbes* and *Circles* figure perfectest,
  Held by all *Artistes* to excell the rest.[49]

The whole diagram thus symbolizes the world, the year and man himself. The idea – implicit in illus. 24 – that man's life is part of an endless cycle of time is expressed pictorially in illus. 25 where the twelve months of the year are each identified with a typical human activity. The total integration of microcosm and macrocosm is suggested by the arabesque in illus. 24 that interweaves and binds together the concentric circles that symbolize these related planes of existence.

  The lute rose can be read in a similar way. It is true that in some

24. Tetrad from Isidore of Seville, *Liber de responsione mundi* (Augsburg, 1472)

late Renaissance lutes and archlutes the geometric strapwork that the instrument inherited from its Islamic origins has disappeared, and the rose consists entirely of floral arabesques. This type of non-geometric rose may in some cases have no symbolic meaning. However, the great majority of Renaissance lute roses are 'written' in that traditional mathematical language described by Galileo. Like a medieval rose window or a Renaissance Vitruvian diagram, the lute rose is a mandala – a symbolic expression of a universe in which *musica instrumentalis* is, in Sir Thomas Browne's words, 'an Hieroglyphical and shadowed lesson of the whole World'.[50] Illus. 26 shows a typical late Renaissance rose interpreted in such a way. Though the details of my reading are conjectural, the figures on which the rose is based – the circle, the square and the triangle – are so ubiquitous in Renaissance cosmology, anthropology and

25.   Roundel from Bartholomaeus Anglicus, *De proprietatibus rerum* (Lyons, 1485)

architectural theory that there can be little question of their general significance.

The typical Renaissance rose is a roundel formed by a sequence of hexagrams made up of interlocking triangles representing, as Hellwig suggests, the interpenetration of spirit and matter. More precisely, the triangles may represent the soul for, as Stephen Batman puts it, whereas the 'soule *Vegetabilis* is lyke to a Triangle in Geometrie ... the soule *Sensibilis* maketh two triangles of virtue'.[51] The repeated triangles also form a series of quadrangles representing the proliferating tetrads of the natural world: elements, seasons, bodily humours and so forth. These corresponding planes of being are interlaced and bound together by an arabesque. The circle that encloses the tetrad of elements, seasons and humours probably represents that fifth element which the Greeks called 'orbis', and which John Gower describes as the 'firmament ... / In which the sterres stonden alle'.[52] But because, as Castiglione says, 'our soule is

26. Renaissance lute rose symbolizing relationship between *musica mundana* and *musica humana*

framed after the verie same sort', it may also represent the soul *rationalis*, which, as Batman notes, is traditionally likened to a circle 'because of his perfection and conteining'.[53] Where the strapwork approaches the perimeter of the rose it divides the circle into twelve equal sections, one for each sign of the zodiac, thus symbolizing in the same figure both the annual unit of time and the eternal revolution of the heavens. The harmonious integration of microcosm and macrocosm is recapitulated in the hexagram. As man was believed to be 'a little world made cunningly' whose own constitution mirrored that of the universe, so the hexagram occurs twice: once as a series of repeated figures filling the entire rose, and again in microcosm at its centre. Together the tetrad and the hexad embrace the entire cosmos; for their sum is the decad, the most important of all numbers and basis of the sacred Pythagorean tetraktys.[54]

V

In his memorial of Sir Philip Sidney, Fulke Greville tells the familiar story of how, on his deathbed, England's national hero called for music 'to fashion and enfranchise his heavenly soul into that everlasting harmony of angels whereof these concords were a kind of terrestriall echo'.[55] Sidney's last wish is a piece of pure, or rather a piece of Christianized, Pythagoreanism. Whether he believed literally in the power of music to restore the soul to harmony, or whether this was merely the rhetorical gesture of a dying aristocrat, is impossible to say. The world of 1586 was a radically different place from the world of even fifty years earlier. As the medieval cosmos was gradually superseded by the Copernican universe, the doctrine of correspondence began to lose its power as an anthropological model, and eventually became simply a figure of speech without any basis in reality. The mathematical language of circles, squares and triangles that had once been the lingua franca of Renaissance philosophers, architects and instrument-makers became, in the work of an eccentric like Robert Fludd,[56] a dead language.

However, it would be quite wrong to imply that the new astronomy was the immediate cause of the demise of Pythagoreanism as an intellectual system, or that there was anything like a clean break with the old ideas. On the contrary, it was Pythagorean principles that inspired the great Renaissance astronomers. It was their search for a universal model that was more harmonious, more rational and above all simpler than the old Ptolemaic model that led Copernicus, Kepler and Galileo to formulate their new theories.[57] Indeed, without his passionate conviction that the harmony of the solar system was expressible in musical notation, Kepler would never have discovered the celebrated Third Law of the *Harmonices Mundi* (1619), the law that was eventually to lead to Newton's theory of gravity.[58] Based, as it was, in mathematics, Pythagoreanism seemed to promise an account of the universe that was more scientific than the traditional medieval model with all its beautifully labyrinthine complexities.

It was the same search for a more scientific method of enquiry that led political philosophers to look for a key to the meaning of human society in nature rather than in God's will. For example, when the sixteenth-century Italian historian Gasparo Contarini explains the lengendary stability of the Venetian republic, he appeals to Pythagorean principles of natural harmony:

Every institution and gouernment of man, the neerer it aspireth to the praise of perfection and goodnesse, the nearer shold it imitate nature, the best mother of all thynges...

With this reason therefore was the Senate ordayned and established in this commonwealth of ours, & likewise the councell of tenne ... and are (as it were) the meane or middle, which reconcileth and bindeth together the two extreames, that is, the popular estate represented in the great councell, & the prince bearing a shew of royaltie. So saith *Plato* are the extreame elementes, the earth and the fire, ioyned and bound together with the middle elementes, as in a well tuned dyapason the extreame voyces are concorded together by the middle tunes of the Dyatessaron and Diapente [as in a well-tuned musical scale the octaves are harmonized by the intervals of the fourth and the fifth].[59]

A similar concern to discover the universal laws of nature can be seen in Renaissance metaphysical anthropology. Among the most influential of the Neopythagorean philosophers of the fifteenth century is Pico della Mirandola with his systematically mathematical view of the universe.[60] It has recently been suggested that Pico is typical of a growing tendency in this period to de-centre man, to show, that is to say, that human nature is not a trans-historical datum, but is discursively produced.[61] This could hardly be further from the truth. Far from de-centring man, Pico is concerned to locate man precisely at the centre of the universe ('medium mundi').[62] Like Alain before him, Pico sees man as a kind of alembic in which are distilled all the materials of nature; he is, to use a particularly appropriate modern metaphor, the interface between God and nature ('interstitium et quasi cynnus natura').[63] Because man is a microcosm of the whole universe, he can acquire a knowledge of nature's laws through an understanding of his own essence: hence the importance for Pico of the ancient maxim 'know thyself'.[64] Man's celebrated freedom of choice is a function, not of his lack of a nature that is uniquely and essentially human,[65] but of his precisely defined location on the map of cosmos. Just as Alain imagined the voice of God explaining how there will always be contradictory principles at war within man, the one with the power of corrupting him and changing him into a beast, the other capable of transforming him into a god,[66] so Pico's deity makes it clear that, if man allows himself to be ruled by the sensual side of his nature he will become brutish, but that if he cultivates the rational side, he may become like an angel.[67] Like the Neoplatonists of the twelfth-century Renaissance, Pico sees the final stage in this process of spiritual rehabilitation as an intuitive sympathy with the *musica mundana*:

> If through moral philosophy the forces of our passions have by a fitting agreement become so intent on harmony that they sing together in undisturbed concord ... then we shall ... drink the heavenly harmony with our inmost hearing.[68]

Pico composed his *Oration* in 1486 (though he was prevented by the church from delivering it). The same formulaic view of man's essentially divided nature is rehearsed in the sixteenth, the seventeenth and the eighteenth centuries.[69] The gulf that separates the fifteenth-century psychologist from his eighteenth-century counterpart is vast. Yet, despite the revolutionary changes in scientific method that divide the pre-modern from the de-mythologized modern world, traditional patterns of thought die hard. When Alexander Pope proposes to reduce 'the science of Human Nature' to 'a few clear points' he is writing as a true representative of the Enlightenment. But his characterization of man as an oxymoronic figure ('darkly wise and rudely great') teetering insecurely on the isthmus between angels and brutes,[70] would have made immediate sense to Alain some six centuries earlier, or indeed to St Augustine seven centuries before him.[71] In the light of such a long and continuous tradition of essentialist anthropology it would seem unwise to speak of an anti-essentialist Renaissance *épistème* or to claim, as Foucault does, that 'man is only a recent invention, a figure not yet two centuries old'.[72]

It is true that in fifteenth-century Italy there was a reaction against the rhetorical and lyrical celebration of human rationality and freedom that characterizes the early humanist movement, and a recognition, especially in Pomponazzi and his followers, of the illusory nature of man's supposed powers of self-determination. But this reaction takes place within an essentialist view of humanity.[73] After the Reformation the meliorist view of human nature came under increasing attack. The new challenge came from two main quarters: from radical Protestants on the one hand, and from primitivists on the other. Neither of these positions can be described as anti-essentialist. The former replaced Pythagorean essentialism with an uncompromising assertion of the innate and absolute corruption of the natural man, the latter with a belief in his inherent goodness.[74] Donne's *Hymn to God my God, in my sickness* is a good example of just such a substitution of one form of essentialism for another. Beginning with what looks like a classic Pythagorean statement of the perfectibility of the soul through attunement to the *musica mundana*, the poem performs the kind of *volte-face* that is so typical of Donne and concludes with an acknowledgment of the fact that it is only by accepting his own innate and essential depravity that the writer can entertain any hope of salvation. Only by a total obliteration of the old Adam can Donne learn to sing the New Song and thus hope to join the 'Quire of Saints'. To argue, as Catherine Belsey does, that Donne's *Hymn* de-centres its human subject[75] is to misunderstand either the whole drift of the poem, or the soteriology that it articulates with such ingenious precision, or perhaps both. However, if humanists – and it has to be emphasized that in the sixteenth century this means both conservatives and radicals – continued to assert that man is 'an Epitome or Compend of the whole creation' they should not be dismissed simply as representatives of the tail end of a pre-scientific mysticism.[76] Although modern scholarship commonly uses the term 'principle of analogy', to describe the doctrine of correspondence between microcosm and macrocosm, what this theory actually refers to is not the metaphoric, and therefore strictly speaking improper, comparison of the teleology of one category with that of another, but the operation of an identical law throughout the universe: a state is not, strictly speaking, *like* a human body; rather, states and bodies are different structures that happen to obey the same universal laws. Just as Kepler's empirical observations convinced him that behind the confusing phenomena of nature was a harmonious world of unchanging mathematical realities, so the anthropologist believed that a study of the *telos* that defines the true essence of human nature could lead to an understanding of those same laws of universal nature.

Thanks to the research of A. K. Hieatt, Christopher Butler, Alastair Fowler and other scholars it is now common knowledge to all students of this period that Elizabethan poets were in the habit of organizing their works in accordance with Pythagorean structural principles. But because the best-known Elizabethan numerologist (Spenser) happened to be an antiquarian, it has been popularly assumed that Pythagoreanism was a quaint and unrepresentative eccentricity even in the sixteenth century. Only recently has it begun to be clear just how false that view is. As T. McAlindon shows in *Shakespeare's Tragic Cosmos*, the age's most profound imaginative attempts to understand man's psychological, political and ethical life are informed by an essentialism that is deeply rooted in Pythagorean tradition.[77] If the empirical observations of a scientist like Kepler seemed to confirm the reality of the music of the spheres, perhaps it is not so surprising that a simple tavern song could lead Sir Thomas Browne to the same conclusion:

Whosoever is harmonically composed delights in harmony; which makes me much distrust the symmetry of those heads which declaim against all Church-Musick. For my self, not only from my obedience, but my particular Genius, I do embrace it: for even that vulgar and Tavern-Musick, which makes one man merry, another mad, strikes in me a deep fit of devotion, and a profound contemplation of the First Composer. There is something in it of Divinity more than the ear discovers: it is an Hieroglyphical and shadowed lesson of the whole World ... In brief, it is a sensible fit of that harmony which intellectually sounds in the ears of God.[78]

CHAPTER 6

The orpharion: 'a British shell'

There let me oft, retir'd by Day,
In Dreams of Passion melt away,
  Allow'd with Thee to dwell:
There waste the mournful Lamp of Night,
Till, Virgin, Thou again delight
  To hear a *British* shell!

(William Collins, *Ode to Pity*)

To emphasize the classical credentials of their songs many of the
Elizabethan lutenist song-writers make a point of specifying, as an
alternative to the lute, an accompanying instrument of unmistak-
able, though spurious, ancient origins. That instrument was the
orpharion (illus. 27).[1] Like the *lira da braccio*, the orpharion is a
product of the humanist attempt to revive the musical practice of
classical antiquity. In contrast with the lute, which has a long and
well-documented history going back ultimately to the primitive
gourd instruments whose shape it still bears, the orpharion has only
a mythical genealogy. It was invented, possibly by the viol-maker
John Rose, towards the end of the sixteenth century.[2] In naming his
new instrument after the two most celebrated legendary exponents
of the art of accompanied song, Rose (or whoever was responsible
for the appellation)[3] clearly wanted to evoke a humanist ideal of
eloquence. Precisely how that ideal should be realized was the
subject of vigorous debate.[4] But however much the humanist
academicians of the sixteenth century might have disagreed on the
question the merits and demerits of contemporary music, they
were unanimous in their belief that the secret of the magical power
of ancient song lay in the affective setting of poetic texts for solo
voice with instrumental accompaniment.[5] It is a belief that is
perhaps best summed up by Giraldi in his *Dialoghi della vita civile*:

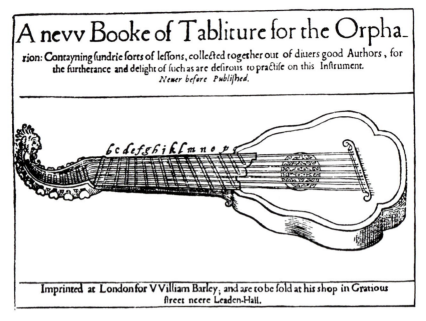

A nevv Booke of Tabliture for the Orpha_
rion: Contayning fundrie forts of leſſons, collected together out of diuers good Authors, for the furtherance and delight of ſuch as are defirous to practiſe on this Inſtrument.
Neuer before Publiſhed.

Imprinted at London for VVilliam Barley; and are to be ſold at his shop in Gratious ſtreet neere Leaden-Hall.

27.   Orpharion. Title page, William Barley, *A New Book of Tabliture for the Orpharion* (London, 1596)

if that ancient kinde of musicke … were now knowne and used, which kinde was then set forth with the learned and grave verses of excellent Poets, we should now also see magnificall and high desires stirred up in the minds of the hearers. Which verses contained the praises of excellent and heroicall personages, and were used to be sung at the table of great men and Princes, to the sound of the Lyra; whereby they inflamed the mindes of the hearers to vertue and generous actions. For the force of Musicke with Poesie, is such, as is of power to set the followers and lovers thereof into the direct way that leadeth them to their felicity.[6]

Of course, Giraldi no more knew what ancient music actually sounded like than did Ronsard and Baïf, or Dowland and Campion. What inspired all these poets and composers was a mythical and sentimental, rather than a strictly historical, ideal. It is an ideal that is embodied in the cult figures of Orpheus and, to a lesser extent, Arion.

I

Luis de Milan broke new ground when he published a collection of instrumental music in 1536. *El Maestro* was the first, and arguably the

28. Orpheus taming the beasts. Woodcut from Luis de Milan, *El maestro*
(Valencia, 1536)

most distinguished, of the ten or so volumes of printed music for the vihuela that appeared in Spain in the sixteenth century. For the frontispiece of his collection Milan chose a woodcut showing a young musician dressed in antique costume with flowing hair and a wreath of laurel (illus. 28). As he plays, a group of wild animals listens, spellbound by his music. The setting for this primitive *concert champêtre* is bleak – a stony plain with only two trees to shade the player from the sun. In the distance there is a river where a ferryman plies his trade; if you look closely you can just make out a pair of horns on the ferryman's head. Beyond the river is a burning town.

Even without the inscription, the musician's identity is obvious. So well known to the Middle Ages and the Renaissance was the Orpheus legend that a few crudely represented details were all that was necessary to recall the main events of his story: a burning city – conventional shorthand for hell in medieval iconography – as a reminder of his pilgrimage to the underworld in search of his dead bride; a Christianized devil symbolizing Charon's refusal to allow him to recross the Styx after he has lost Eurydice for the second time; two trees representing the grove that miraculously gathers round to shade him as he sings of his grief; a small menagerie; and finally some rocks, whose stony nature has also been intermitted by the magic of his songs. Ironically it is those same rocks, deafened by the shrieks of the enraged Maenads as they stone the man who has abjured all women, that are to be the instruments of his death, though there is no hint of this in Milan's woodcut.

By prefacing his collection with a portrait of Orpheus, Luis de Milan hoped to arrogate to himself something of the talismanic prestige associated with the legendary poet-musician of antiquity. In case the point should be missed, he spells it out in the words that frame his picture: 'El grande Orpheo, primero inuentor: si el fue primero, no fue sin segundo' – renowned Orpheus, chief among poets: if he was the first, he was not without a second. Milan was not alone in encouraging his readers to see in him the rebirth of classical antiquity; in fact there was a long tradition in the Middle Ages of poets and composers referring to themselves as the new Orpheus.[7] Two years after the publication of *El Maestro* Luis de Narvaez printed a portrait of Arion being carried ashore by the dolphin as the frontispiece to his *Los seys libros del delphin*. In England John Dowland audaciously invited comparison between his own songs and those of Orpheus. In the dedication to his *First Booke of Songes*

(1597) he explains that although instrumental music 'easily stirres vp the mindes of the hearers to admiration and delight', it must be considered inferior to that kind of music which

to the sweetnesse of Instrument applyes the liuely voyce of man, expressing some worthy sentence or excellent Poeme. Hence (as all antiquity can witness) first grew the heauenly Art of Musicke: for Linus Orpheus and the rest, according to the number and time of their Poems, first framed the numbers and times of Musicke.[8]

Thomas Campion similarly attempts to establish ancient precedent for his first collection of songs when he reminds his readers that 'The Lyricke Poets among the Greekes, and Latines were the first inuentors of Ayres.'[9] When we meet the character of Orpheus himself in Campion's *The Lords Maske* we find him attired, like Milan's vihuelist, 'after the old Greeke manner, his haire curled and long; a lawrell wreath on his head'.[10]

Dowland's and Campion's evocation of the legendary figure of Orpheus is one expression of a contemporary cult of the antique that looked for its inspiration, not to the historical past, but to an idealized pre-historical Golden Age.[11] It was a cult that involved strong nationalistic sentiments. When George Puttenham calls for a revival of the art of poetry he asks 'why should not Poesie be a vulgar Art with vs aswel as with the Greeks and Latines, our language admitting no fewer rules and nice diuersities than theirs?'[12] It is no coincidence that the progress poem has its origins in this period.[13] The progress poem is a variation on the theme of the old British History.[14] The medieval chronicler who invented fictional genealogies tracing his nation's ancestry back to Troy sought to show that the ancient Britons were not barbarians, but had been marked out by providence for a special purpose. When Elizabethan writers took up the theme and traced their own queen's ancestry back to the legendary Brutus, great-grandson of Aeneas, they conflated the Troy story with the prophecies in Virgil's fourth *Eclogue*: Astraea, virgin goddess of justice, had returned to the earth – more precisely to England – and Troynovaunt was about to witness a restoration of the legendary Golden Age of antiquity.[15] The progress poem makes similar claims for Britain's cultural destiny. By tracing the arts to their origins in classical antiquity, and by describing their continuous historical and geographical progress westwards, it set out to demonstrate that it was the British who were the true heirs to the civilizations of the ancient world. As a result of the efficiency of the royal propaganda machine, the British History was so familiar in the final years of the century that when Elizabethan writers of songs and masques evoked the figure of Orpheus, the nationalist message was unavoidable: Britain had been providentially chosen as the site of a revival of ancient arts. It is this fashionable obsession with the antique, epitomized by long-haired Orpheus, that Marlowe wittily satirizes in his mock-heroic portrait of the romantic Leander with his 'dangling tresses that were never shorne'.[16]

Underlying the Elizabethan cult of the antique is a traditional view of the universal human condition – a view, shared by Christian and humanist alike, that saw man as an innately flawed and erring creature. As in so much else, Edmund Spenser is the unofficial spokesman of his age. In the famous proem to the fifth book of *The Faerie Queene* he describes the progressive degeneration of the world from its primal state:

> So oft as I with state of present time,
> The image of the antique world compare,
> When as mans age was in his freshest prime,
> And the first blossome of faire vertue bare,
> Such oddes I finde twixt those, and these which are,
> As that, through long continuance of his course,
> Me seemes the world is runne quite out of square,
> From the first point of his appointed sourse,
> And being once amisse growes daily wourse and wourse.
>
> (v.proem.1)

But the corollary of a classic view of human nature is the need for powerful authority. Orpheus may have romantic associations for lovers of music and poetry but, as the conversation between Lorenzo and Jessica in moonlit Belmont reminds us, he is also a political figure. The fate that was likely to meet those Elizabethans who, sceptical of their queen's claims to be *Astraea rediviva*, had the temerity to engage in 'treasons, stratagems, and spoils' is embodied in another musical fable. The contest between Apollo and Marsyas, one representing stringed instruments, the other wind instruments, has traditionally been seen as an allegory of the battle between reason and passion. As Edgar Wind explains, the flaying of Marsyas by the victorious Apollo was interpreted by Renaissance mythographers as an ordeal of purification in which baser elements are stripped away to reveal the nobler side of human nature.[17] But the story of the defeated challenger whose skin is ceremonially removed so that, in Ovid's words, 'the sinews lie bare, his veins throb and quiver with no skin to cover them: you could count the entrails as they palpitate, and the vitals showing clearly in his breast'[18] – this story has a more sinister meaning. To readers who had actually witnessed the spectacle of rebels and heretics being hung, drawn and quartered in public it was a drama that was all too familiar. In his recent adaptation of Sophocles' *Ichneutae* Tony Harrison spells out the political lesson underlying the horrific details of Marsyas' punishment: 'Whenever in the world there is prison and pain / the powerful are playing the Marsyas refrain.'[19] Though the discussion that follows does not claim to be anything more than a chapter in the history of Elizabethan humanist iconography, we should do well to recall a truth that *The Merchant of Venice* insists on, namely, that however tempting it may be to try to sequester the world of love, music and poetry from that of politics and finance, the two are actually inseparable.

II

That the orpharion owes its genesis to the contemporary interest in the revival of classical culture is well known to organologists. It is surprising therefore that the unusual shape of the instrument – a design that is as significant as its name – should have received so little attention. In a series of articles on the iconography of Renaissance musical instruments Emmanuel Winternitz has suggested that in some cases the physical details of an instrument may serve not a functional but a symbolic purpose. Winternitz' discussion of the cittern is particularly interesting in this context, because it is from the cittern that the orpharion is generally considered to have been developed. We know from Galilei's remarks on the cittern in his *Dialogo della musica antica e della moderna* that the instrument was popularly regarded as a revival of the classical kithara.[20] Winternitz argues that its classical origins may be detected in the stylized scrolls or 'buckles' that are a standard feature of the Renaissance cittern.[21] These, he claims, are vestigial echoes of the arms of the ancient kithara: atrophied to nothing more than decorative curlicues, they are nevertheless a reminder of the cittern's noble ancestry.

Whether or not Winternitz is justified in his claim to have discovered an unbroken line of descent from the classical kithara to the Renaissance cittern is not important; what seems remarkable is that

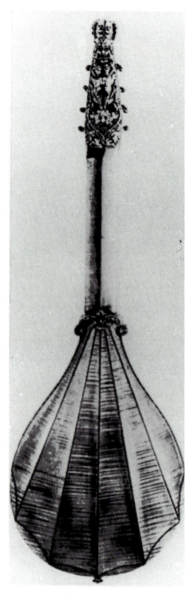

29.   Cittern attributed to Antonio Stradivari

30. Hermes with a tortoise-shell lyre. Drawing of detail from a fifth-century
Greek vase painting

in his analysis of the cittern Winternitz does not mention the feature
of the instrument that would be most likely to have struck the
contemporary observer with an eye for symbolic detail, namely its
resemblance to a shell. If the cittern in illus. 29 is taken as an
example, it will be seen that the basic shell-like shape of the body has
been emphasised by the use of multiple tapering ribs with scalloped
purfling, while the scrolls at the top of the body suggest the 'ears' of a
stylized scallop shell.

The reason for this emphasis on the shell-like features of the
cittern is not far to seek. According to classical legend the lyre that
Hermes gave to Orpheus was made from a shell (illus. 30). The story

of its invention is told in the Homeric *Hymn to Hermes*. Offspring of Zeus and the nymph Maia, Hermes rivals even our own Solomon Grundy in precociousness. On the morning of his birth, says the poet, he leapt from the immortal knees of his mother and, finding a tortoise, saluted the unfortunate creature with the words:

> Better to be at home than out of door,
>   So come with me; and though it has been said
> That you alive defend from magic power,
>   I know you will sing sweetly when you're dead.[22]

Removing the animal from its carapace, Hermes then covered the empty shell with oxhide and attached two horns and a bridge to carry seven strings of sheep gut. Thus it was that Hermes 'first made the tortoise sing'.[23] Use of the tortoise shell for a resonator survives to the present day in folk instruments such as the North African guembrie.

Christian versions of the myth attribute the discovery of the *testudo*, or tortoise-lyre, to Jubal. In the second volume of his great poem on the creation Du Bartas explains how the father of all instrument-makers[24] happens to find

> An open Tortoise lying on the ground,
> Within the which there nothing else remained
> Save three drie sinewes on the shell stiffe-strained,
> This empty house *Jubal* doth gladlie beare,
> Strikes on those strings, and lends attentive eare.
> And by this mould, frames the melodious Lute
> That makes woods harken, and the winds be mute;
> The hils to daunce, the heav'ns to retro-grade,
> Lyons be tame, and tempests quickly vade.[25]

Though the cosmogony of *La semaine* is of course Christian, Du Bartas' tribute to the persuasive powers of music is a conflation of classical and biblical ideas: Jubal's lute is indistinguishable in its effects from Orpheus' lyre.

Gradually, Jubal's instrument began to lose its association with the tortoise and was referred to simply as a shell. Thus Dryden, in the *Song for St Cecilia's Day*, writes:

> What Passion cannot MUSICK raise and quell!
>   When *Jubal* struck the corded Shell,
>   His list'ning Brethren stood around
>   And wond'ring, on their Faces fell

To worship that Celestial Sound.
Less than a God they thought there cou'd not dwell
  Within the hollow of that Shell
  That spoke so sweetly and so well.
What Passion cannot MUSICKE raise and quell![26]

Eventually, by a process of metonymy, the shell becomes a symbol of the music it produces and, by an extension of the figure, of verse.[27] Indeed for a brief period in the eighteenth century it becomes the standard fashionable term for poetry.[28] For example, when William Collins, like Puttenham before him, takes upon himself the task of reviving the fortunes of English poetry, he tells his muse that he hopes she will once again 'delight / To hear a *British* shell'.[29]

If, as Galilei and other writers tell us, the cittern was regarded as a revival of the classical kithara, then we must suppose that its shell-like shape was intended to symbolize the affective power of music. It would seem reasonable, also, to assume that the design of the orpharion was likewise intended as an allusion to the legendary instrument that Hermes/Mercury gave to Orpheus. The close similarities between the cittern and the orpharion are best illustrated in the instrument by John Rose at Helmingham (illus. 31). The body of the Rose orpharion is little larger than that of a Renaissance cittern and shares some of its structural features.[30] From the front its gracefully scalloped outline suggests a stylized shell. On the back of the instrument is a large piece of decorative carving. This device serves no obvious functional purpose and has given rise to some speculation as to its significance. The author of an article on this instrument suggests that it may be 'perhaps a rebus or some other form of conceit'.[31] He is indeed right, for the object represented in fine detail in the carving is a scallop shell (illus. 32).

The Rose orpharion may be seen as a transitional instrument, showing clearly its origins in the six-course cittern, yet anticipating many of the features of the later orpharions that have survived either in the form of contemporary drawings or, in the case of the orpharion by Francis Palmer in Copenhagen, in the form of an actual instrument. By 1596 the familiar shape of the 'stately Orpharion'[32] with its scalloped outline and either one or two incurvations or 'bouts' near the bridge, had become standardized. If, as I have argued, its unusual shape was intended to suggest a stylized shell, then the conclusion seems obvious that the purpose of this design was to serve as a reminder of the instrument's fictional provenance.

31. Orpharion by John Rose. Helmingham Hall, Suffolk

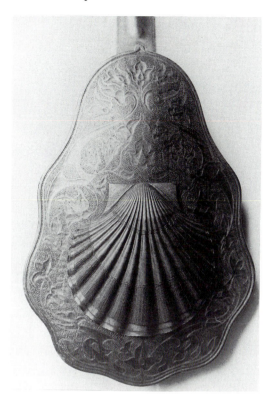

32. Scallop-shell carving on the back of the Rose orpharion

What is not so obvious is why it is a scallop, rather than any other kind of shell, that is represented on the Rose orpharion. To answer this question we need to consider the iconography of the scallop in classical and Renaissance art.[33]

III

The scallop shell is probably best known as the emblem of St James the Greater. Through its association with his burial place and pilgrimage shrine at Compostela it became familiar in the Middle Ages as the identifying badge of the pilgrim.[34] However, the use of the scallop both as a decorative and a symbolic device antedates the Christian era by several centuries. As an architectural motif it has been popular since classical times.[35] Its use in both pagan and

33. Pompeian fresco showing Venus transported to shore on a scallop shell,
House of Venus

Christian architecture and funerary monuments suggests that it may
have been employed for other than purely decorative reasons.

The religious associations of the scallop are of ancient origin. Its
first appearance in European art is in representations of the birth of
Aphrodite. According to Greek legend, Aphrodite was born from
the spume produced when Cronus threw the severed genitals of his
father, Uranus, into the sea. The earliest account of this gruesome
event is in Hesiod's *Theogony* (*c.* eighth century). The following is an
Elizabethan version of the story: 'The Poets', writes the astrologer
John Maplet, 'have it in opinion that Venus was bred first and came
of the froth or bloud that flowed forth from the Privities of Coelus
whom Saturne gelt, and cut of, and threwe them into the sea.'[36]
Hesiod makes no mention of a shell, and it is not until the fourth
century that we find an example of the scallop that is such a familiar
feature of Renaissance representations of Aphrodite's nativity. A
burial urn dated *c.*400 BC excavated at Olynthus shows the goddess
rising from between the half-open valves of a scallop.[37] It later
became usual to portray Aphrodite being carried to shore on an
upturned scallop shell (illus. 33), and it is thus that she is depicted in

what is probably the most famous version of the story – Botticelli's
Birth of Venus.

As symbols usually acquire their meaning by a process of association, so the scallop becomes the emblem of Aphrodite serving, as
Titian's *Venus Anadyomene* shows, to identify the goddess, even
though its original functional purpose may have been disregarded
by the artist. In fact medieval mythographers frequently describe
Aphrodite – or Venus, to give her her Roman name – not as
transported on a shell, but carrying it in her hand.[38] But this
complete functional inversion of the symbol does not affect its
iconographic purpose, which is to identify the goddess and to reveal
her essential nature. A creature popularly believed to be 'engendred
of the Ayer, & dewe',[39] the scallop is symbolic of Venus' own
astrological character. For, as John Maplet says, 'among the
Elements [Venus] holdeth a pozician in the ayre and also in the
water'.[40] Though Venus' elemental nature might not at first seem to
be of relevance to this discussion, it is in fact the key to that aspect of
her character that most concerns us, namely, her association with
music.

Of the many illicit relationships contracted by the goddess of love,
the most significant for the mythographer was her liaison with Mars.
Astrologically, Venus and Mars are polar opposites: she is of a
loving, sanguine disposition; he, being hot and dry, like the planet to
which he gives his name, is characterized by his choleric temperament. When united with Venus, however, the fiery excesses of his
nature are tempered by her moist influence. As Maplet explains,
Venus is

a pacifier of Mars in his great fury, and malice, and fiery fervency, quieting
him with friendly and amiable Aspect, in such wise, as a beautifull and
lovinge Woman doth appease and still the rage, and anger of her Husband
being incensed.[41]

Respectable Elizabethan that he is, Maplet glosses over the fact
that this was an adulterous relationship. Nor does he mention the
crucially important fact that it was from this union of opposite
principles that harmony was born. 'It is well known', writes Plutarch in an essay on Isis and Osiris, 'that, in the fables of the Greeks,
Harmony was born from the union of Venus and Mars: of whom the
latter is fierce and contentious, the former generous and pleasing.'[42]
Elsewhere Plutarch explains the philosophic principle that was

embodied in this myth: 'when the contraries, high and deep, are tempered by a certain proportion, a marvellous consonance arises between them'.[43] In the Renaissance the myth of Mars and Venus came to be seen as an allegory of the Creation itself. The idea that the harmony of the cosmos consisted in the amicable reconciliation of fundamentally opposed qualities in a uniquely stable union is of ancient origin.[44] Traditional also is the belief that it is love that is the architect of this *discordia concors*.[45] In the well-known apostrophe to Venus in the introduction to the *De rerum natura* Lucretius celebrates the goddess of love as the very source of life itself; in the following Elizabethan paraphrase of Lucretius, Venus is hailed as the author of universal harmony:

> Great *Venus*, Queene of beautie and of grace,
>   The ioy of Gods and men, that vnder skie
>   Doest fayrest shine, and most adorne thy place,
>   That with thy smyling looke doest pacifie
>   The raging seas, and makst the stormes to flie;
>   Thee goddesse, thee the winds, the clouds doe feare,
>   And when thou spredst thy mantle forth on hie,
>   The waters play and pleasant lands appeare,
> And heavens laugh, and al the world shews ioyous cheare.
>
> (*Faerie Queene*, IV.x.44)

Venus is inseparable from the idea of harmony, for it is she, the goddess of love, who resolves the discords of the world. Those who are born under her planetary influence are, in John Maplet's words, 'such as do greatly delight in Musicke'.[46]

But the goddess of love has another aspect. When the ancients spoke of the power of Venus they made it clear that there were in truth two Venuses: *Venus coelestis*, the source of universal harmony, and *Venus vulgaris*, goddess of sensuality.[47] It is the latter whose destructive powers are recorded in the emblematic temple frescoes in Chaucer's *Knight's Tale*:

> The broken slepes, and the sikes colde,
> The sacred teeris, and the waymentynge,
> The firy strokes of the desirynge
> That loves servantz in this lyf enduren.[48]

Depicted rising from the waves with a cittern in her hand,[49] Chaucer's Venus is a more powerful deity even than Mars, the god of war; indeed, such is her irresistible influence that she is able to

34. Carving depicting the birth of Venus, on a cittern by Girolamo Virchi

rule the world just as she pleases (III.1950). The medieval association of *Venus vulgaris* with the cittern may perhaps explain the significance of the naked figure emerging from a shell carved on the base of the fingerboard of the instrument by Virchi in the Kunsthistorisches Museum in Vienna (illus. 34). Though it is true that it is not a scallop shell from which she is rising, the allusion to the well-known story of Venus' nativity seems unambiguous.

Because music is notorious for its ability to arouse the venereal passions, it is an essential feature of the medieval garden of love.[50] The symbolic garden survives as a typical feature of Renaissance allegorical love poetry.[51] However, one of the most explicit examples in Renaissance art of the symbolic association of music with the pleasures of Venus is not a garden but an interior scene. The painting, illus. 35, is by the seventeenth-century genre artist Jacob Ochtervelt. The aphrodisiac effects of both music and food – represented here on the one hand by the shell-like cittern, and on the other by a dish of oysters – were common knowledge. By linking these two most powerful weapons in love's armoury by the motif of

35. Jacob Ochtervelt, *The Oyster Meal*. Colección Thyssen-Bornemisza, Madrid

36.   Allegorical figure of Music beneath a scallop-shell canopy. Joos van
Wassenhove

the shell, the painter has created a 'speaking picture' whose apparent artlessness conceals a very precise meaning.

IV

Through its association with the ambivalent figure of Venus, the scallop shell acquires a dual symbolic significance. 'The fairest instrument that can be, beinge of natures makinge',[52] it may stand either for the pleasures of the senses, or, paradoxically, for the idea of harmony in its broadest sense of cosmic concord. It is as a symbol of the latter that the scallop appears in Renaissance allegorical representations of music. Illus. 36 shows the figure of Music seated beneath a scallop-shell canopy. The shell canopy is an ancient architectural motif. So widespread is its use in Renaissance and baroque architecture that it would be foolish to claim that it always had a symbolic significance. However, it was originally used to suggest specific religious or cosmological meanings. A familiar device in both pagan and Christian architecture is the vision of heaven depicted in decorated domes and ceilings. Karl Lehman has argued that this tradition of representing the heavens in symbolic form has its origins in antiquity and, flourishing in Byzantine ecclesiastical art, survives in medieval, Renaissance and baroque religious architecture. The symbolism may take a naturalistic form and employ realistic figures of the divinities that rule the world, or it may be purely abstract. In its more complex forms, the decorated vault evokes not just a generalized, ornamental allusion to the sky, but a comprehensive symbolic representation of the cosmos.[53] The most complex form of vaulting ever devised is the late gothic fan-vault. As Walter Leedy suggests, the beauty and the regularity of these immensely complex three-dimensional geometric patterns creates the impression of 'circles or wheels revolving in space',[54] a clear allusion to what Sir John Davies calls 'the turning vault of heaven',

> Whose starrie wheeles he hath so made to passe,
> As that their movings doe a musicke frame.[55]

Where an architect is working with an apsidal half-vault it is perhaps inevitable that the naturally shell-like shape of the canopy should be emphasized by painted or carved fluting and stylized scrolls. One of the examples Lehman discusses – a painted apse

37. Ptolemy of Alexandria with armillary sphere. Woodcut from Cayo Julio
Higino, *Poeticon Astronomicon* (Venice, 1482)

decoration from the *Domus Aurea* in Rome – takes the form of a
scallop shell bordered with waves. At its centre is the figure of the
nascent Venus. In this case the shell motif with its mythological
associations has been assimilated to that of the decorated canopy of
heaven. The shell-shaped prayer niche is a characteristic form in
Islamic architecture; it probably owes its form to the fact that the
shell is thought of as the ear to the heart. Just as it was believed that
pearls formed when the shell rises to the surface of the water on a

38. Bass viol by Gaspar Tieffenbrucker (modernized) with decorated back
    showing Pythagoras seated beneath a scallop-shell canopy

spring night and opens up to receive a dewdrop, so in prayer the ear receives the dewdrop of the divine word.[56] The most remarkable Islamic scallop shell-niche is the *mihrab* in the Great Mosque at Cordoba, which served as a model for countless prayer niches in Spain and North Africa. The shell canopy is also a familiar feature of early Christian basilicas and is used as a symbol of the heavens throughout the Middle Ages;[57] it survives in both religious and secular forms in the Renaissance. Illus. 37 is the frontispiece to *Poeticon Astronomicon* (1482), the first printed book on astronomy. It shows the figure of Ptolemy of Alexandria, architect of the medieval cosmos, with armillary sphere and compass, seated beneath a scallop-shell canopy. Complementing this traditional symbol of the heavens is a stylized representation of the zodiac.

The traditional use of the scallop shell to represent the heavens helps to explain its appearance in early Christian sarcophaguses as a symbol of the soul's ascent to its celestial origins.[58] It also explains its use in Renaissance allegorical representations of music's ability to inspire heavenly thoughts (see above, illus. 36). The same iconography can be seen in the painting on the back of the modernized bass viol in illus. 38. Here the figure of Pythagoras is depicted in the classic pose of the pedagogue and seated beneath a scallop-shell canopy, signifying that cosmic harmony whose principles he was the first to discover. The carving on the back of the Rose orpharion serves a similar symbolic purpose.

Unlike the vulgar cittern, the orpharion was a prestige instrument. During the relatively short period of its popularity, it was taken up by the majority of Elizabethan lutenist song-writers. In designing this new instrument in such a way as to suggest a stylized shell the luthier drew on a rich store of symbolism: in part he wanted to suggest the classical lyre of Orpheus, type of the compellingly persuasive musician-king; but he was also exploiting the ancient association of the shell with Venus. The cittern, we know, was popularly identified with the pleasures of *Venus vulgaris* and is widely depicted in Renaissance art as an aid and accompaniment to seduction. Its supposedly aristocratic cousin, the 'stately orpharion', was intended to symbolize the more patrician pleasures of *Venus coelestis*, the 'music of the world'.[59] It is just such a distinction between plebeian and aristocratic musical pleasures that Harrison's Apollo makes when he appropriates 'the sphere of music and of poetry' and excludes the libidinous satyrs from the world of 'high' art:

> This is now *my* lyre and I define
> its music as half-human, half-divine.
> And satyrs, I repeat, must not aspire
> in any way to mastering my lyre.[60]

PART III

The game of love

CHAPTER 7

'Ars amatoria': Philip Rosseter and the Tudor court lyric

> That may be saide to be a verie arte, that appeareth not to be arte, neither ought a man to put more diligence in any thing than in covering it: for in case it be open, it looseth credite cleane and maketh a man litle set by.
>
> (Baldassare Castiglione, *The Book of the Courtier*)

Imagine a typical Elizabethan lute song. *If she forsake me* – no. 17 in Philip Rosseter's *Book of Ayres* – will do. A lover confides in his audience, revealing the dilemma that is tormenting him. The problem, as usual, is how to deal with an indifferent mistress. Should he lay his cards on the table and tell her how he feels about her, or should he continue to play the part of uncomplaining admirer? His problem is insoluble: if he tells her and she laughs at him he will die of grief; if he doesn't tell her and she remains ignorant of his feelings he will die of frustration anyway. So he concludes his song by appealing to death to come and put an end to his sorrows:

> Thus still is my despaire procur'd
> And her malice more assur'd
> Then come death and end my paine.[1]

Not even our own twentieth-century appetite for the catch-22 can make much of such apparently uncompromising banality. Small wonder that literary critics have on the whole politely echoed Edmund Waller's claim that 'Soft words, with nothing in them make a song'[2] and passed on to more rewarding literary material. Here is what one critic says about the lute song lyric:

Such poems rarely attempt to arrest or obstruct the verse's flow to create a dislocation between sense and movement; the words are chosen to please the ear, to soothe the senses. There is, they seem to assert, no need to know anything more than the shimmering surface – to foreground any ambiguity, tension, or urgent personal voice would dislocate the pattern ... Poems like Campion's 'Rose-cheekt Lawra' ... attempt to create the experience of participating in a timeless world. Even given the necessarily sequential pattern of lines and stanzas, such poems try to fix us in a stasis, without any relation to the passing of time in the mutable world outside the experience of reading or hearing the poem.[3]

Like his seventeenth-century namesake, Gary Waller accuses Elizabethan song-writers of subordinating meaning to sound; their lyrics are designed not to provoke, but to allay critical response.

There is clearly some truth in these charges. Much Elizabethan lyric verse, particularly in the miscellaneous collections, is undeniably trite as it mechanically rehearses the age's most stereotyped poetic formulas. However, as a general statement about the lute song Waller's remarks will not do. Unlike the miscellanies, the lute song collections are conceived as integrated units. Although they have no interconnecting narrative, they are like sonnet sequences in that individual songs form part of a dialectic of love, so that to consider a single song out of context would be to misconceive its essential purpose. Moreover, because they are expressly designed for musical performance, their meaning cannot be reduced to a definitive statement: it is the function of an interaction between a performer (playing both to and with his listeners), and an audience finely attuned to those nuances of meaning that are only possible in a culture that still retains powerful oral traditions. They are in a real sense what Barthes or Derrida would call 'playful' texts,[4] though their play often has an uncomfortably ironic edge to it.

I

Philip Rosseter's *Booke of Ayres* is typical of its genre. Musically Rosseter's songs are unadventurous, with chordal accompaniments, a limited range of modulation and none of the dramatic chromaticisms and false relations that characterize Weelkes' Italianate madrigals or Dowland's later declamatory airs.[5] A number of them have pleasantly memorable melodies; a rather larger number are unmemorable; and there is one miniature masterpiece (*What then is love but mourning?*). Their subjects are, as Campion puts it in his 'Address to the Reader', 'for the most part amorous'.[6] They are, in short, classic Elizabethan light airs.

Lacking any kind of consistent narrative, the songs that go to make up Rosseter's *Booke of Ayres* are best seen as a set of twenty-one

variations on the theme of love. The practice of arranging com-
positions in numerically significant groups was normal in the
Renaissance; in fact it might be said to be the rule rather than the
exception. Such ordering might be dictated by an obvious external
temporal scheme, as in Spenser's *Shepheardes Calender* with its twelve
sections, each representing a single month, or it might be based on a
more complex internal system of structural symbolism.[7] Where a
writer based his work on an obvious temporal plan he was often
quite explicit about the way his composition imitated this numerical
order. An example quoted by Alastair Fowler is Pico della Mirandola's account of the creation in the *Heptaplus*. In his preface Pico
explains how he divided the whole work into seven sections:

Add to this that, since the 7 expositions are distributed through 7 books,
and the 7 individual books are divided each into 7 chapters, all the parts
correspond to the 7 days of creation. We have done this according to a most
appropriate and harmonious design, so that just as the seventh day,
according to Moses, is the Sabbath and a day of peace and rest so each of
our expositions always leads in its seventh chapter to Christ, who is the end
of the Law and our Sabbath, our peace and rest, our happiness.[8]

Implicit in Pico's account of his organization of the *Heptaplus* is the
analogy between microcosm and macrocosm. Just as there are seven
ages of the world so man himself has seven 'ages' or stages of physical
development; and corresponding to the seven notes of the musical
scale are the seven changes of the human voice.[9] The ramifications
of this system of corresponding heptads in nature were seemingly
endless.[10] By imitating in the organization of his own work the order
of nature itself, Pico creates what he describes as a 'harmonious
design'. In doing so he is testifying to the belief that, in Sir William
Ingpen's words, since 'God had disposed all things according to
number, waight and measure ... the next [nearest] way to knowe
him perfectly, is, To begin with numbring'.[11] It is possibly because it
was the number seven that articulated with greatest clarity the
relationship between *musica mundana*, or cosmic harmony, and *musica
humana*, the harmonious ordering of the different parts of the human
soul, that Elizabethan song-writers so often published their collections in multiples of seven. In fact, of the thirty-three books of lute
songs published between 1596 and 1622 nearly three-quarters
conform to this pattern, with twenty-one being the favourite
number.

Rosseter's own collection of twenty-one songs encompasses the whole range of human erotic and devotional experience. The mood of the songs swings from the self-torturing anguish of *No graue for woe*, through the naively cheerful idealism of *When Laura smiles*, to the solemn piety of *What hearts content?*; there are petitions to an absent mistress, complaints by a jilted lover at the fickleness of women and songs of ardent seduction; and in conclusion there is a cynical acknowledgment of the vanity of all human wishes. Symbolically placed at the numerical centre of the series is a celebration of the *via media*, a conventional expression of the belief that happiness is to be found in a balance between extremes of joy and sorrow: 'but the meane, the golden meane, / Doth onely all our fortunes crowne' (*Though far from ioy*). In short, the whole collection presents us with a image of *homo amans*, driven by his emotions, but still reflecting imperfectly the unchanging love that 'chaines the earth and heauen' and 'Turnes the Spheares' (*Reproue not loue*).

By pointing to the fact that Rosseter's songs contain serious elements I do not mean to imply that the whole collection has a solemn didactic purpose. *A Book of Ayres* is not a moral treatise, but a musical *speculum* reflecting every facet of man's amatory experience. Fundamental to that experience is the social nature of love. Unlike the Victorian, who typically represents love as means of escape from the restrictions of social life, the Renaissance writer emphasizes its social aspect; his favourite image for love's civilizing power is the dance, an essentially social activity. It is love, like dancing, that is able to link 'all men in sweet societie'.[12] At least that was the theory. In practice the social rituals of love might serve a variety of purposes. In a world where political success or failure was often linked, either in fiction or in reality, with sex, survival depended on being a skilful player in the game of love. And play is what Rosseter's songs are all about. His singer, like the poetic persona in many of Wyatt's lyrics, is a lover, wooing, teasing and confusing his audience. Indeed, his world has much in common with Wyatt's. Both are writing for a court society in which the whole repertory of supplications, pleas, complaints and acts of revenge that traditionally belong to the love lyric are often metaphors for the hazardous game of social or political advancement.[13]

The double-edged nature of Wyatt's playful relationship with his audience is perhaps best illustrated in that favourite anthology piece, *Blame not my lute*. Wyatt's balet is a complaint at the fickleness of love that relies on the presence of an audience to make its point.

The song appears at first to adopt the familiar convention by which the audience is cast in the role of singer's mistress, receiving silently and passively a lover's praises, entreaties or reproofs. The singer begins by telling his mistress not to blame the lute for the kind of 'tune' he is going to sing, explaining that it is her fickleness that is the cause of so 'strange' a song. Repeating his charges of infidelity, he threatens to publish his wrongs unless she repents: 'The faute so grett, the case so strainge, / Of right it must abrode be blown.'[14] But the threat is not carried out, or at least not explicitly. Having created the familiar illusion by which singer and audience/mistress are presumed to be alone, Wyatt subtly dismantles the convention, reminding us that this is not a clandestine meeting between two lovers, but a musical performance among friends. Indeed, it is precisely because they are not *in camera* that the singer is careful to avoid revealing his mistress' name, instead referring obliquely to 'some that use to fayn'. But of course this show of secrecy is merely a game. By the last stanza it becomes clear that although the singer is not going to name his mistress, he is nevertheless going to make it plain to everyone who she is:

> Farwell, unknowne, for tho thow brake
>   My strynges in spight with grett desdayn,
> Yet have I fownde owtt for thy sake
>   Stringes for to strynge my lute agayne;
> And yf perchance this folysh Rymyme
> Do make the blushe at any tyme,
>   *Blame nott my lutte.*   (stanza 7)

As the song concludes with the singer wickedly goading his lover into a visible display of embarrassment, the audience is left glancing at each other to identify the cruel 'unknown' by her blushes. Thus what appeared at first to be an unpleasantly vindictive personal complaint turns out instead to be a light-hearted act of simulated revenge. *Blame not my lute* is essentially a joke. Although it purports to tell the painful story of a 'falsyd faith', its emotions are simple and stereotyped and reveal nothing of the poet's inner feelings. The contemporary setting of it – one of the few for Wyatt's lyrics that have survived – is correspondingly plain: a simple modal melody adapted from an older Italian source, and an equally simple chordal accompaniment for the lute.[15]

But for all its playful wit, this song is not as insouciant as its seemingly artless form might suggest. The success of its joke depends on a recognition of how dangerous such a scenario would be if it were life and not art. Those who entered into clandestine liaisons at court did in a very real sense 'put theimself in daunger' (*They fle from me*, 5), as Wyatt knew to his own cost (from his cell in the Tower he would probably have been able actually to witness the execution of Anne Boleyn for alleged adultery).

In a uniquely illuminating contemporary analysis of the relationship between power and song Thomas Whythorne provides a valuable gloss on the lute song and its social uses. Known chiefly for his two collections of part songs (1571; 1590), Whythorne made his living as a freelance music teacher. His profession gave him ample opportunity for cultivating the sort of quasi-sexual relationships with women that so obviously appealed to the gamesman in him. When his employer happens to be a widow of independent means the relationship between teacher and mistress acquires a special piquancy. In language reminiscent of Wyatt's hunting metaphors Whythorne describes an elaborate game in which the roles of predator and victim are never quite clear even to the players themselves. Receiving what he takes to be signs of a more than purely professional interest on her part, he decides to test his mistress's response:

if shee did dissembull, I to requyt her thouht that to dissembull with A dissembler waz no dissimulasion, and to play with her az the hunter doth, who hunteth A har, asmuch to see her subtyl skips and leaps az for to get her karkas.[16]

Once the game is under way it is conducted almost exclusively through poetry and song. The fact that Whythorne's lyrics are entirely formulaic does not prejudice his suit: indeed, their stereotyped ambiguities afford him precisely the kind of protective façade he will need if it turns out that he has misread her signals. Of one of them he writes: 'I mad this song sumwhat dark & dowtfull of sens bekawz I knew not serteinly how shee wold tak it, nor to whoz handz it miht kumen after that she had read it.'[17] Nor is he unduly worried when she responds with indifference to his stylized declarations of passion, realizing that 'shee did it *az A pollisy* to keep me still in dowt of her, and by that mean to lyv still in A vain hop'.[18] Whythorne may be an indifferent musician and an even worse poet. But he is an exceptionally shrewd analyst of social games-playing. Reflecting on this playful musico-literary liaison he writes: 'she but seemed to loov mee, bekawz shee wold hav mee her slav to triumph over ... and I seeming to bee such A on az she wold hav mee, mor for the kommodyte that I looked to get at her handz, then for any great & overwhot loov'.[19]

The elegant dissimulations of the sixteenth-century lyric may serve no other purpose than entertainment, though as a song like Wyatt's *Take hede betyme leste ye be spyede* suggests, with its repeated hints of the dangers of discovery, the need for secrecy would have been even greater in the politically perilous world of the court than in a small middle-class household. Listening to a singer praising an unnamed lover, warning her of the need for discretion or swearing to be revenged for her betrayal of him, an audience would find it difficult to know whether the affair to which they were apparently being made privy was real or invented; whether the singer was feigning emotion or pretending to feign it for reasons of self-protection.

II

Rosseter entered his *Booke of Ayres* in the Stationers' Register in May 1601. It was no doubt the success of this, his only published collection of songs, together with his judicious cultivation of the influential MP Sir Thomas Monson, that helped to win him the coveted post of court lutenist, a position he held until his death in 1623. Despite the gap of more than half a century that separates his songs from Wyatt's, it is in many ways the same world of studied passion and simulated spontaneity that they evoke. However, it is only in performance that Rosseter's songs reveal their ironic character. *And would you see my Mistris face* is a case in point (illus. 39). On the printed page these lyrics are likely to seem dull. Nigel Fortune describes them as 'comically lame'.[20] But in performance they acquire a different meaning: an apparently conventional blazon cataloguing the charms of a stereotypically aloof young goddess becomes a variation on the familiar guessing-game used by Wyatt as the audience is invited to speculate on the identity of the mistress whose charms are about to be painted with such sweet ambivalence:

> And would you see my Mistris face,
>   it is a flowrie garden place,
> Where knots of beauties have such grace,
>   that all is worke and nowhere space.

It is a fweete delicious morne,
    where day is breeding neuer borne,
It is a Meadow yet vnfhorne,
    whome thoufand flowers do adorne.

It is the heauens bright reflexe,
    weake eies to dazle and to vexe,
It is th'Idæa of her fexe,
    enuie of whome doth world perplexe.

It is a face of death that fmiles,
    pleafing, though it killes the whiles,
Where death and loue in pretie wiles,
    each other mutuallie beguiles.

It is faire beauties frefheft youth,
    it is the fain'd Elizium truth,
The fpring that winter'd harts renu'th,
    and this is that my foule purfu'th.
    H

39.   *And would you see my Mistris face, A Booke of Ayres* (London, 1601)

The song's irony lies in the fact that the traditional comparison of the mistress' face to a garden is a double-edged compliment. So familiar in European literature is the stylized garden of love that Rosseter's contemporary audience could scarcely fail to be aware of its complex and fundamentally ambivalent symbolism.[21] Representing as it does both the pleasures and the dangers of erotic love, the *giardino amoroso* is portrayed by such writers as Guillaume de

Lorris, Chaucer, Tasso and Spenser as an earthly paradise filled with all that is naturally appealing to the senses (see chapter 1). The second stanza of *And would you see* epitomizes the delights of the garden of love (while at the same time obliquely complimenting the lady on her virginity):

> It is a sweete delicious morne,
> where day is breeding never borne,
> It is a Meadow yet unshorne,
> whome thousand flowers do adorne.

But by stanza four a shadow has fallen across the apparently idyllic garden of love. For amongst the 'knots of flowers' is an ironically smiling 'face of death', lurking, like the emblematic *memento mori* in Holbein's illustration of Proverbs 14:12 ('There is a way which semeth right to a man: but the yssues thereof are the wayes of death'), as a reminder of the vanity of human pleasures (illus. 40).

Medieval and Renaissance moralists never tire of reminding us that a life devoted to the pleasures of the senses is death to the spirit. But in the context of the Elizabethan court, where an indiscreet relationship could mean disgrace or worse, the traditional iconographic representation of Venus and Death acquires a new meaning. On one level the singer may simply be punning prettily on the idea – ubiquitous in the poetry of this period – of sex as a *petite mort*. But on a more serious level he is expressing that sense of the precariousness of life which becomes such a marked feature of literature and music at the turn of the century. What began as a glibly extravagant compliment to an unnamed mistress thus modulates into a covert warning against sex.

To be too serious, though, would be to risk being labelled a malcontent. In the final stanza of the song it is the singer himself who becomes the butt of the poet's irony, for it is passion, not reason, that is the victor in this particular round of love's war. Acknowledging with a nicely elliptical paradox that his mistress's beauty 'is the fain'd Eliziums truth' – meaning, in other words, that he has persuaded himself that fiction is reality – he resolves to go on pursuing his illusory dream of happiness. What saves the song from the charge of misogyny is its wit. Setting up certain expectations in its audience by the apparently artless simplicity of its verbal and melodic prettiness, it then mocks those expectations by satirizing the naivety and ultimately the self-deception of the singer.

40. 'There is a way which semeth right to man: but the yssues thereof are the wayes of death' (Prov. 14:12). Woodcut from Hans Holbein the Younger, *The Dance of Death*, (Lyons, 1538)

For all his declarations of passion the singer of *And would you see* no more reveals his true feelings than do Wyatt and Whythorne. The song invites us to share not his private thoughts, but a joke. In other songs, though, we do appear to catch a glimpse of the man behind the mask. Until the latter years of the sixteenth century there was little sense of the lyric poem as a vehicle for the expression of inner feelings. Even apparent exceptions such as Wyatt's *They fle from me* tend to treat the particular and exceptional not as a point of departure for self-analysis, but as a paradoxical illustration of a general truth (the creatures who used to trust him have now reverted to type). However, as the century moves towards its close poets begin to show an increasing concern with the inner life. 'Looke in thy heart and write' is the best advice that Astrophil's muse can give to a young poet wrestling with the problem of how to express his emotions in verse.[22] Composers, too, become increasingly interested in the emotional possibilities of expressive writing. Music's ability to affect the emotions had, of course, been traditionally recognized both by its defenders and by its detractors. But where Whythorne, writing in the 1570s, simply rehearses the well-known stories of music's ability to influence the mind,[23] by the end of the century we find Hooker testifying, not to music's affective, but to its expressive, potential. In the *Laws of Ecclesiastical Polity* he writes of the 'admirable facilitie which musique hath to expresse ... more inwardlie then any other sensible meane the verie standinge, risinge and fallinge, the verie stepes and inflections everie way, the turnes and varieties of all passions whereunto the minde is subject'.[24]

With the gradual collapse of the familiar medieval cosmos the traditional humanist's notion of the well-regulated personality, in which the passions are held in check by reason, begins to give way to a new interest in the integrity of the emotions. 'Surely', writes Montaigne in the celebrated 'Apology for Raymond Sebond', 'we have strangely overpaid this worthie discourse [of reason] whereof we so much glorie, and this readinesse to judge, or capacitie to know.'[25] Perhaps, speculates Montaigne, the secret of human happiness lies, not in the subjection of the wayward parts of the personality to the rule of order, but in a life innocent of the corrupting influence of civilization and its laws.[26] 'The greatest thing of the world', he writes in the essay 'Solitarinesse', 'is for a man to know how to be his owne. It is high time to shake off societie, since we can bring nothing to it.'[27] For Montaigne it is not society, but the

individual who is the test and guarantor of truth: that is why he
claims that the main subject of his philosophy is himself.[28]

Influential as Montaigne's ideas were among Europe's intellectual *avant-garde*, the tradition of philosophic scepticism they form
part of played a less significant role in modifying popular sensibility
than did Reformation theology. A corollary of the belief in justi-
fication by faith was a tendency to introspection. For if salvation
depends not on good works, but on an admission of the inefficacy of
all human effort, then the penitent must for ever be on his guard
against the temptation of arrogating merit to himself: 'not only the
present mode of life but all the past must be dragged into the white
light of conscience, dissected, and examined with a determination to
overlook no slightest failing or secret desire'.[29] It is true that when
Calvin exhorts the penitent to 'descend to loke into himselfe'[30] he
means that he should acknowledge that he is no exception to the
universal human condition. Nevertheless, reflection on the innate
depravity of the human heart inevitably leads to preoccupation with
the feelings that, in Lear's words, breed about it. The analogy
between the puritan who interrogates his conscience in solitude and
the poet who turns away from his manuals of rhetoric to look in his
heart and write is obvious.

One consequence of this growing interest in the inner life and its
emotions is a sceptical mistrust of rhetoric and its meretricious
effects. When rhetoricians like Peacham and Puttenham adapted
classical manuals of oratory they transformed them into poetic
conjuring books. But when lyric poetry is conceived as self-
discovery, the conjurer's art is redundant: with no audience to
address the only person you deceive is yourself. How seriously we
should take the growing chorus of voices deprecating the prestidigi-
tations of rhetoric[31] is difficult to say: sometimes the protest is clearly
authentic; at other times it is equally plainly tongue-in-cheek as, for
example, when Marlowe's Hero, after listening to eighty-odd lines of
amorous platitude from Leander, coyly demands to know 'Who
taught thee Rhethoricke to deceive a maid.'[32] Already by the 1570s
we find Whythorne arguing that 'to flatter, glos, or ly ... requyreth
gloriowz and painted speech wheraz the trewth needeth but A plain
and simpull utterans without glozing or faining at all'.[33] Over the
next century the same sentiments were repeated by poet after poet:
Sidney's Astrophil scorns those poets who imitate Pindar, 'Ennobling new found tropes with problems old';[34] Samuel Daniel claims

that 'Nature ... is above all Arte';[35] Shakespeare professes contempt for 'Arts faulse borrow'd face' (Sonnet 127); Fulke Greville warns that 'Rhetoricke ... is growne a siren in the formes of pleading, / Captiving reason, with a painted skinne / Of many words; with empty sounds misleading / Us to false ends';[36] Thomas Campion asserts that 'Nature art disdaineth';[37] George Herbert deprecates the practice of 'Curling with metaphors a plain intention, / Decking the sense, as if it were to sell';[38] while Thomas Traherne, echoing Herbert, claims that *his* readers will find 'No curling Metaphors that guild the Sence, / Nor Pictures here, nor painted Eloquence; / No florid Streams of Superficial Gems'.[39] By the end of the seventeenth century the anti-rhetorical revolution was complete: 'A Man is to be cheated into Passion', writes Dryden in the Preface to *Religio Laici* (1682), 'but to be reason'd into Truth.'[40]

A song that seems to reflect a contemporary impatience with the restricting forms of conventional poetic language is no. 8 in Rosseter's collection – *And would you faine the reason know* (illus. 41). Usually cast in the role of a lover to be seduced or a cruel mistress to be vilified, the audience is here required to play the part of friend and counsellor to a distracted lover. The song begins in mid-conversation. The singer's friend has been questioning him about his irrational behaviour, and in reply he offers a defence of his own conduct, arguing that true love refuses to submit to the role of reason. Indeed, his own feelings are unique: to deny so self-evident a truth would be to claim that 'proof is false and truth a liar'. Like Sidney's Astrophil, he takes pains to distance himself from the common race of lovers ('my feuer is no others fire'), and asserts the integrity of his emotions. If he appears inarticulate it is because of the pressure of his feelings; and it is those unique and personal feelings, he claims, that dictate the kind of songs he writes: 'They set the noat then tune the Lute.' Sensing that his attempts to justify his strange behaviour are falling on unsympathetic ears, he becomes increasingly irritated with the friend and his censorious questions. By the end of the song his patience has run out and he bluntly tells the friend to stop finding fault with him and let him nurse his wounds in private.

Taken at face value *And would you faine* appears to be one more expression of a contemporary frustration with inhibiting conventions in both art and life. However, what looks on the surface like an ingenuous assertion of individualism and a plea for naturalism in

Nd would you faine the reafon know, why my fad eies fo of- ten flow? my heart ebs ioy when they doe fo, and loues the moone by whom they go.

And will you aske why pale I looke?
    tis not with poring on my booke,
My Miftris cheeke my bloud hath tooke,
    for her mine owne hath me forfooke.

Doe not demaund why I am mute,
    loues filence doth all fpeech confute,
They fet the noat then tune the Lute,
    harts frame their thoughts then toongs their fuit.

Doe not admire why I admire,
    my feueris no others fire,
Each feuerall heart hath his defire,
    els proofe is falfe and truth a lier.

If why I loue you fhould fee caufe,
    loue fhould haue forme like other lawes,
But fancie pleads not by the clawes,
    tis as the fea ftill vext with flawes.

No fault vpon my loue efpie,
    for you perceiue not with my eie,
My pallate to your taft may lie,
    yet pleafe it felfe delicioufly.

Then let my fufferance be mine owne,
    fufficeth it thefe reafons fhowne,
Reafon and loue are euer knowne,
    to fight till both be ouerthrowne.

I 2

41.   *And would you faine the reason know, A Booke of Ayres* (London, 1601)

writing is in fact riddled with paradoxes. Central to the singer's defence of his own eccentric behaviour is the claim that passion has made him mute, and that, anyway, there is more truth in the silence of emotion than can ever be conveyed in words. The irony, of course, is that far from being speechless, the singer is so voluble in his egotistical concern with his own affairs that the friend cannot get a word in edgeways. But at least the words he sings do carry the guarantee of authenticity: it is not musical precept or literary convention that sets *his* notes and tunes *his* lute, but the truth of emotion. Or so he claims. In reality, of course, his conceits are as stereotyped as those of the next court hack writer. By the beginning of the seventeenth century the lover whose emotions ebb and flow like the tides, or whose face is pale because the blood has left it to grace a fairer cheek, had become a laughing-stock of anti-Petrarchan satire. Like Sidney, the poet is wittily employing parody to mock cliché and using the singer as the butt of his satire.

But the song's final irony is the fact that the form in which the singer articulates his plea for individualistic naturalism – the debate with a cynical or disapproving friend – is itself a cliché of Petrarchan poetry. 'Alas have I not paine enough my friend ... But with your Rubarb [i.e. sour] words yow must contend, / to grieve me worse', cries Astrophil indignantly;[41] 'For Godsake hold your tongue and let me love', shouts the equally irritated Donne.[42] Both give a convincing impression of spontaneous exasperation, but both expect their readers to recognize the clever games they are playing with convention. *And would you fain* enjoys an equally ironic relationship with convention, consciously flaunting its intertextuality.

III

In the address 'To the Reader' that he contributed to their joint publishing venture Campion described his own and Rosseter's songs as 'eare-pleasing rimes without Arte'. Analysis of the songs themselves suggests that Campion's apologia should be read, not as an ingenuous statement of fact, but as a typically sly piece of Elizabethan *sprezzatura*. Songs that offer themselves as sincere expressions of artless sincerity make self-conscious use of the conventions they affect to despise; modest deprecations of artifice are couched in the most flamboyant language; tender expressions of love's despair turn out to be no more than exercises in ingenious frivolity. Nor is *A Booke of Ayres* exceptional in its simulated candour. Does Sidney believe, with Whythorne, that 'the trewth needeth but a plain and simpull utterans', or is he satirizing Astrophil's pretensions to naturalism? Does Shakespeare really despise the arts he is master of? Does Daniel truly believe that 'Nature is above all Arte'? There is no simple answer to these questions. Despite its exhaustive anatomies of the lover's motives and actions the typical Elizabethan sonnet sequence leaves us, not with a portrait, but with an enigma.

The poetry of the latter half of the sixteenth century has been commonly represented as illustrating a development from traditional poetic forms relying heavily on inherited convention towards a more candid mode of expression whose impatience with classical rhetoric reflected a growing concern with human individuality.[43] However, although Sidney's Astrophil represents study as the enemy of poetic inspiration, it was mastery of rhetoric that provided Elizabethan poets with new means of expressing emotion. In fact in Puttenham's view, the more powerful the emotion, the more 'affected, curious and ... witty' the language must be.[44] By the end of the century lyric poetry, despite repeated appeals for simplicity, seems paradoxically to have become not only more introspective, but more florid; not only more reflective, but more flamboyant. As Francis Meres noted in 1598:

the English tongue is mightily enriched and gorgeouslie invested in rare ornaments and resplendent abiliments by sir *Philip Sidney, Spencer, Daniel, Drayton, Warner, Shakespeare, Marlowe* and *Chapman*.[45]

The poet who was thought finally to have broken the restricting mould of convention was Donne: 'There were the Petrarchists, carefully ornamental and studiously trite; and there was Donne, colloquial, fervent, and brilliant' is Donald Guss' parody of a commonly held critical view.[46] But, as we know, the rejection of convention is itself often simply a pose. For all his emotional energy and iconoclastic bravura, we no more see the real Donne in his poetry than we do the real Sidney in his.

It is undeniable that Puritanism fostered a distrust of rhetoric: suspicion of the falsely seductive charms of affective language is an essential aspect of a growing Puritan plea for simplicity in liturgy, in dress, in speech, in writing and in music. That Shakespeare's Perdita should be so anxious to dissociate herself from the practice of 'painting' (*Wint*, IV.iv.101) is hardly surprising in view of the increasing tendency to equate simplicity with godliness and artifice with the devil. 'Who can paynte her face', proclaimed a homily of 1563, 'against excess of Apparell',

and curle her heere, and chaunge it into an unnaturall colour, but therein-doth worke reprofe to her maker, who made her? As though she could make her selfe more comely than GOD hath appoynted the measure of her beautie.

What do these women, but go about to refourme that whiche God hath made? not knowyng that *all thinges naturall is the worke of God, and thynges disguysed, unnaturall be the workes of the devyll.*[47]

With the publication of Calvin's *Institutes of the Christian Religion* in 1535 (English translation 1561) Puritan demand for sobriety and frugality in all areas of life received the support of a systematic predestinarian theology. Its influence was enormous. When parliament ratified the Thirty-nine Articles in 1571 it was an essentially Calvinist theology that it marked with the establishment's official stamp.

However, currents of cultural change rarely flow through orderly channels. In the same year that the *Institutes* was published in English translation, another continental book was published in London which was diametrically opposed to the spirit of Calvin's treatise. Indeed, it is tempting to suppose that the remarkable popularity of Castiglione's *Book of the Courtier* owed something to the fact that it supplied an antidote to the growing influence of Calvinism in all spheres of life. Where Calvin sees a frank acceptance of human depravity as man's only defence against his innate propensity for self-deception, Castiglione commends the arts of dissimulation. For him the courtier is like a poet whose art is most effective when it is most skilfully disguised: 'that may bee saide to be a verie arte, that appeareth not to be arte, neither ought a man to put more diligence in any thing than in covering it: for in case it be open, it looseth credite cleane and maketh a man litle set by'.[48] This playful affectation of a careless and negligent grace in the performance of difficult feats, or *sprezzatura*, is the essence of the courtier's art. Underlying the whole book is the principle of *utile et dulce*. As a purveyor of civilized values the courtier is a living embodiment of the humanist's belief that the gracious and pleasing presentation of virtue 'enflameth the minde with desire to bee woorthie'.[49] This is why Castiglione devotes the whole of his first book to discussion not just of his courtier's accomplishments, but of the art of self-presentation. Whether he is reciting a poem or giving a musical performance, the courtier's object is not to express his mind, but to give pleasure to his audience by drawing them into a fictional world of stylized emotions and ideal sentiments. The fact that the passions he displays are not his own serves to create a pleasing disparity between show and reality, and, in Castiglione's words, 'augmenteth the grace of the thing'.[50]

Castiglione is describing an ideal world: Guidobaldo di Montefel-
tro's court is a utopian 'Mansion place of mirth and joy' where 'in
everie mans countenance a man might perceive painted a loving
jocundnesse'.[51] The Elizabethan court was also a world idealized by
its dependants. 'Is not this a Glasse', wrote one of them, 'for all other
countrie to beholde, wher there is not only an agreement in fayth,
religion, and counsayle, but in friend-shyppe, brother-hoode and
lyving?'[52] But the reality was different. In 1591 Spenser described
the truth behind the exotic popular image of court life:

> Full little knowest thou that hast not tride,
> What hell it is, in suing long to bide:
> To loose good dayes, that might be better spent;
> To wast long nights in pensive discontent;
> To speed to day, to be put back to morrow;
> To feed on hope, to pine with feare and sorrow;
> To have thy Princes grace, yet want her Peeres;
> To have thy asking, yet waite manie yeeres;
> To fret thy soule with crosses and with cares;
> To eate thy heart through comfortlesse dispaires;
> To fawne, to crowche, to waite, to ride, to ronne,
> To spend, to give, to want, to be undonne.
> Unhappie wight, borne to desastrous end,
> That doth his life in so long tendance spend.
>
> (*Mother Hubberd*, 895–908)

In the sort of world described by Spenser a talent for dissimulation
was not simply a pleasing social asset: it was necessary for survival.
And it is techniques for survival that the *Book of the Courtier* taught.[53]
To succeed at Elizabeth's court it was necessary to dissimulate – to
play the part of the accomplished, devoted lover in public, but at all
costs to avoid revealing your private emotions. Successful enough at
playing the demanding role of lover to his ageing Virgin Queen, Sir
Walter Ralegh, with his disastrous political career, is an eloquent
reminder of the dangers of indiscretion. In such a world a lover
might well be tempted to adopt the advice of Astrophil's muse and
look in his heart and write. But to act on that advice would be
supreme folly.

If Elizabethan poets repeatedly affirm, in language of increasing
complexity, the values of simplicity and candour we have to assume
that this, too, is in part a pose. Instead of a process in which poets
are, as T. S. Eliot puts it, 'engaged in the task of trying to find the
verbal equivalents for states of mind and feeling',[54] it might be more

true to describe the development of Elizabethan poetry as the opposite: not so much a matter, as Puttenham suggested, of 'drawing [the mind] from plainnesse and simplicitie to a certain doublenesse',[55] as of discovering more sophisticated ways of *concealing* emotion under a guise of sincerity. Only when it was finally liberated from the court and its influence was lyric poetry able to begin finding ways of expressing a true individualism. But that was not to be for more than a century and a half. In Rosseter's world song was above all a social art. The politically ambitious courtier who wanted to cultivate the image of the perfect Renaissance gentleman, accomplished in all the arts of civilization, needed materials to display his talent: poems to recite, masques to perform, songs to sing. *A Booke of Ayres* is perfectly suited to that purpose. If the rhetorically sophisticated lyrics that Rosseter chooses to set seem simple, artless and naive this is because they are meant to. Their melodic prettiness is self-conscious, their simplicity a pose. They are pretending to be naive. And if you cannot take the singer's sentiments at face value, you cannot accept his values unquestioningly either. These songs invite a critical and sceptical response.

If their impression of formal artlessness is a deliberate illusion, so too is the sense they suggest of individual self-expression. When Rosseter's singer offers us his thought on love and women, these are always related to himself so that we seem to be sharing his innermost feelings. Yet the impression of a unique, individuated self whose 'feuer is no others fire' is deceptive, for nothing of the inner self is actually revealed. His songs are affective rather than expressive; they are not so much a series of personal revelations as fragments of a dialogue between singer and audience. And it is in the space between the two that their meaning lies. Unlike the sonneteer whose characters must come to life on the page or not at all, the song-writer can leave it to the performer to give life to his script. But to do this the singer must be an actor professional enough to be capable of creating an illusion of accomplished amateurism, and of drawing his audience into the fictional world of his song so that they too become active participants in the production of meaning. Unlike the actor on the stage, who strives to give life and authenticity to a character that is not his own, the singer must act the part of himself, persuading his audience that the passions he so carelessly and effortlessly declares come from the heart. Because the relationship between singer and audience is essentially unpredictable, their dialogue can have no final closure. Contained within Rosseter's collection of songs is a celebration of the humanist *via media*. But this does not form a conclusion to the collection. The final song in the book offers, significantly, not an exhortation to piety, or even a plea for libertinism, but instead an affirmation of the ancient Stoic maxim that all 'the world is but a play':

> All our pride is but a jest,
> None are worst and none are best,
> Griefe, and joy, and hope, and feare,
> Play their Pageants every where,
> Vaine opinion all doth sway,
> And the world is but a play.

CHAPTER 8

Dowland, Ficino and Elizabethan melancholy

> O eloquent, just, and mighty Death! whom none could advise, thou has perswaded; what none hath dared, thou hast done; and whom all the world hath flattered, thou only has cast out of the world and despised; thou hast drawne together all the farre-stretched greatnesse, all the pride, crueltie, and ambition of man, and covered it all over with these two narrow words: *Hic jacet*.
>
> (Sir Walter Ralegh, *The Historie of the World*)

When Ralegh wrote these words he had good cause for feeling despondent. Eleven years in the Tower under sentence of death had given him ample time for meditating on the wild capriciousness of fate. But if Ralegh's circumstances were exceptional, his sentiments were not. It was, paradoxically, precisely when England was at last able to enjoy a sense of national security the country had not known for two centuries that poets, artists and composers began to display a morbid concern with mutability and death. As chroniclers like Richard Nicols hailed Elizabeth's reign as a return to the Golden Age,[1] Edmund Spenser, her self-appointed panegyrist, wrote wearily of the decay of a world that had

> runne quite out of square,
> From the first point of his appointed sourse,
> And being once amisse growes daily wourse and wourse.
>
> (*FQ,* v.proem.1)

Spenser was writing at the end of a medieval tradition. Fifteen years later John Donne expressed a new sense of cosmic unease when he claimed that alternative philosophies were challenging all the old intellectual certainties. ''Tis all in pieces', he wrote in the celebrated lines from *The First Anniversarie*, 'all cohaerance gone.'[2] Not only in poetry, but in painting and in music too, the spirit of melancholy

became one of the age's most characteristic features, producing, in
addition to the trivia that any artistic movement generates, the most
profoundly serious expressions of the *contemptus mundi* theme. 'You
may', wrote Robert Burton in the *Anatomy of Melancholy* (1621), 'as
soone separate waight from lead, heat from fire, moistnesse from
water, brightnesse from the Sunne, as misery, discontent, care,
calamity, danger, from a man.'[3] In an age justly celebrated for its
remarkable artistic achievements, John Dowland is one of the
supreme exponents of this sombre mood.

I

Many reasons for the Elizabethan preoccupation with the darker
side of life have been suggested.[4] Social change, political instability,
the demolition of intellectual and religious certainties and, perhaps
most of all, the belief that nature herself was decaying – all these
contributed to a *fin-de-siècle* sense of the transience of a civilization
that seemed destined to pass away 'Like courts removing, or like
ended playes'.[5] But for every serious meditation on the decay of
nature or the corruption of the court there are a dozen stereotyped
complaints, such as the following stanza from the inappropriately
named *gorgious Gallery of gallant Inventions* (1578):

> If euer wight had cause to mone
>   or wayle with bitter teares,
> His wretched life and wofull plight
>   that still in launguish weares.
> Then haue I cause that late haue lodgde
>   such loue within my hart,
> With greefe, with payne, with pyning panges
>   my body boyles in smart.[6]

Dowland's most impassioned songs are usually thought of as belong-
ing to this tradition of stylized complaint. Confronted with a wealth
of philosophically interesting material, he chooses to set verses like
the platitudinous *Goe nightly cares* (*A Pilgrimes Solace*, 1612), a lyric
that would not look out of place among the chorus of dying gasps
that goes to make up *A gorgious Gallery*; or the equally stereotyped *In
darknesse let mee dwell* (*A Musicall Banquet*, 1610) with its poetically
jejune evocation of the conventional topography of melancholy.[7]
Unlike the funeral song, which served quite specific religious, personal and social purposes,[8] this type of complaint has no occasional

or didactic function: in a period dominated by humanist poetics it is probably the closest thing you will find to art for art's sake.

This conventional view of Dowland's songs has been challenged by Anthony Rooley. He argues that Dowland's melancholy songs are coded expressions of a profound interest in Hermetic Neoplatonism.[9] Hermetic studies enjoyed something of a vogue in Renaissance England. The cult of philosophic melancholy associated with this movement originates in the teachings of Marsilio Ficino. Ficino believed that by cultivating a state of inspired melancholy man is capable of achieving a mystical union with the *spiritus mundi,* or divine spirit, that animates the universe.[10] The key to this spiritual ascent to higher things is music (see above, chapters 4 and 5). The idea that music may be morally beneficial insofar as it imitates the perfect harmony of the spheres is an ancient and very familiar one; indeed, it is a truism that is repeated throughout the Middle Ages.[11] But Ficino went far beyond a simple reassertion of time-honoured commonplaces. Although the basis of his theory of musical inspiration was traditional, the programme he evolved for realizing this ideal was both complex and original. For Ficino, the type of the persuasive musician is Orpheus. But unlike Horace's prudent social legislator, Ficino's Orpheus is no tamer of wayward human passions; he is an inspired hierophant whose poetic frenzy is a mark of his divine calling. This Orpheus is the legendary priest-king of pre-Mosaic antiquity, founder of that esoteric mystery religion whose doctrines were thought to have formed the basis of the *Timaeus.* Identifying himself with the divinely possessed author of the so-called Hermetic tracts (actually composed by a number of unknown Egyptian writers in the second or third century AD), Ficino set out to recapture the Orphic ideal of inspired communication. By imparting something of his own poetic frenzy, an inspired singer could, Ficino believed, transmit to his audiences those cosmic mysteries that he had been specially chosen to reveal. Fundamental to Ficino's theory of inspired communication was the belief that the singer must begin by liberating his listeners' spirits from the world of sensible objects. The way to do this was to imitate the music of the spheres. The first stage in this process was to supplicate the appropriate planetary influence. In his commentary on Plotinus Ficino writes:

Our spirit is consonant with the heavenly rays which, occult or manifest, penetrate everything. We can make it still more consonant, if we vehemently direct our affections towards the star from which we wish to receive a certain benefit ... above all, if we apply the song and light suitable to the astral deity and also the odour, as in the hymns of Orpheus addressed to cosmic deities ... For when our spirit is made more consonant to a planetary deity by means of our emotions, the song, the odour and the light, it breathes in more copiously the influx which comes from this deity.[12]

The procedures involved in achieving this state of spiritual harmony are naturally not simple, and the rules that Ficino gives for capturing the appropriate planetary emanations in music involve complex astrological calculations. Ficino summarizes the process in the following passage from the *De vita coelitus comparanda*:

From tones chosen by the rule of stars, and then combined in accordance with the stars' mutual correspondences, a sort of common form can be made, and in this a certain celestial virtue will arise. It is indeed very difficult to judge what kind of tones will best fit what kind of stars, and what combinations of tones agree best with what stars and their aspects. But, partly by our own diligence, partly by divine destiny ... we have been able to accomplish this.[13]

Astrology, then, forms an essential part of Ficino's theory of musical inspiration. Possibly because he himself was of a melancholic temperament, and because melancholy, when tempered by other humours, was considered to be conducive to intense and profound contemplation,[14] Ficino believed that the influence of Saturn was of particular significance to the student of occult philosophy. Whereas the Middle Ages saw Saturn, the melancholy planet, as a baleful and malign influence,[15] Ficino sees him as potentially beneficial. By supplicating Saturn through talismanic songs the melancholy man could learn to withdraw from the sensible world and achieve a state of spiritual sublimity. If we bear in mind that in Neoplatonic lore melancholy was traditionally believed to be the consequence of man's longing for his celestial origins, we can see how Ficino was able to persuade himelf that the melancholy man was uniquely suited to perform the talismanic incantations that he believed were capable of liberating the spirit from the world of appearances.

Such, in brief, is Ficino's theory of musical inspiration. Though he was never professionally employed by a university, his influence as a teacher was considerable. The academy he established in his native Florence in 1462 through the munificence of Cosimo de' Medici became a centre of European intellectual life. But it was his translations of Plato and Plotinus and other Neoplatonic sources and of the *Corpus Hermeticum*, together with his own philosophical writings, that had such a radical effect on the course of Renaissance thought. Florentine Neoplatonism spread far beyond its place of origin and by the end of the sixteenth century there were few major European poets who did not show some awareness of fundamental Neoplatonic ideas in however diluted a form. However, it is not the aesthetic Neoplatonism – often the object of satire – that is familiar to readers of Sidney, Spenser and Greville to which Rooley refers, but the esoteric body of mystical doctrine that Ficino taught and practised in his Academy. If it could be shown that Dowland was 'steeped in' Hermetic Neoplatonism,[16] this could profoundly modify our misunderstanding of his music.

In considering the evidence for this claim we must turn first to the question of the currency of Hermetic thought in Elizabethan England.[17] There can be little doubt that mystical Neoplatonism acquired a certain fashionable appeal in England towards the end of Elizabeth's reign. The poet who illustrates this most clearly is George Chapman. Chapman's fondness for arcane philosophy is best seen in his early poem *The Shadow of Night*, where he adopts the pose of platonic mystagogue appealing, not to the 'prophane multitude', but to 'those serching spirits, whom learning hath made noble and nobilitie sacred'.[18] *The Shadow of Night* is a remarkable poem. Eschewing conventional notions of poetic decorum, it deals in 'huge spirits, and outragious passions' (397). With its violent emotions, its cataclysmic imagery, its mangled syntax and its gothic terrors, the poem is in effect a manifesto of Hermeticism. Chapman is quite explicit about his intentions. In consecrating his life to 'black shades and desolation' (270) he hopes that the spirit of Night will inspire in him that state of tortured frenzy which alone is capable of allowing man access to nature's hidden secrets. 'No pen can anything eternal wright', he says with characteristic hyperbole. 'That is not steept in humor of the Night' (376–7).

As poetry, *The Shadow of Night* is not generally considered to be a success.[19] Although it did inspire some imitations, the authors of these did not constitute a school, much less an academy. Indeed, Chapman was something of an isolated figure, and we must treat with some caution Frances Yates' claim that 'there was a group of noblemen-scientists and their friends, pursuing deep philosophical and mathematical studies, and that Chapman was a member of this group'.[20] Yates' claim is, as she herself admits, no more than a supposition. That part of *The Occult Philosophy in The Elizabethan Age* that deals specifically with England consists largely of the author's own readings of works by Spenser, Marlowe, Shakespeare and Chapman himself. These interpretations rely heavily on conjecture. For example, in discussing *The Merchant of Venice* Yates writes:

> the actual context in which Shakespeare makes his supreme formulation of the theme [of music's affective power] is the Venice of Francesco Giorgi, visited in Shakespeare's Venetian play. Thus, it may be suggested that the immediate inspiration for this outburst [Lorenzo's speech on the harmony of the spheres] was the universal harmony of the Friar of Venice ... Think of Giorgi's poetic expositions of the theme through canticles and tones in his vast volume ... surely the influence of the Friar of Venice lies behind this scene.[21]

In fact, as James Hutton showed many years ago, not only Lorenzo's ideas, but even their arrangement, was traditional.[22] So well rehearsed was the *laudes musicae topos* that verbal and structural similarities between different expressions of it are unlikely to have had any special significance.

Yates makes similar suppositions in her chapter on Spenser. 'Seeking for a contemporary philosophy on which to base his panegyric of the queen', she writes, 'Spenser might well have been drawn to the work on world harmony by the Friar of Venice.'[23]

When her argument is based on evidence of this nature it is not surprising that Yates' claims for the existence of a caucus of Elizabethan poets and dramatists devoted to occult studies have not received strong support from specialists in this field. The most recent research on the subject suggests that in sixteenth-century England occult studies were largely confined to the universities.[24] What prestige they did have was seriously damaged when the true provenance of the Hermetic texts became known. In 1614 Isaac Casaubon demonstrated in his *De rebus sacris et ecclesiasticis exercitationes* that the works of 'Hermes Trismegistus' were actually written and compiled in the early Christian era. However, it has recently been shown that forty years earlier than this there was already a widespread scholarly opinion that rejected the traditional dating.[25] With their status as divinely communicated sources of ancient wisdom demolished, the *Hermetica* no longer enjoyed the same authority. G. J. Parry argues that in neglecting these facts, modern students of Hermeticism have 'over-simplified and distorted the intellectual currents of the sixteenth century and ... inflated the importance [of Hermetic thought] for contemporaries'.[26]

In the absence of evidence indicating a wider commitment among major writers and intellectuals to Hermetic studies we must conclude with Wayne Shumaker that 'theological Hermeticism was never a powerful intellectual force in England ... Certainly there was awareness of the newly recovered *Corpus* in England, and frequent references were made to its supposed pedigree. In the present state of our knowledge, however, the Hermetic influence on thought would seem to have been small.'[27] Shumaker argues that what is at issue here is not simply a question of factual information, but of methodology. 'It is essential', he writes, 'not to exaggerate, not to find in a new idea – particularly if it is esoteric, surprising, and so freshly discovered or re-emphasised that as yet little use has been made of it – a key to virtually every unsolved problem and a means to the re-interpretation of what is already accurately understood.'[28]

However, the fact that Hermeticism did not occupy a central position in English Renaissance thought after the 1570s does not rule out the possibility that Dowland may have taken an interest in occult philosophy. If Chapman was serious in his claim that melancholy, 'bred vnder sorrowes wings' may raise the spirit to heaven (366–7), there is no reason in principle why Dowland should not have entertained similar beliefs. Rooley claims that Dowland's work is imbued with Hermetic principles. He argues that his interest in 'abstruse philosophy' may be seen most clearly in his use of the six-note descending chromatic motif in the *Forlorne Hope Fancye* and in the opening motif of the *Lachrimae* tune. These figures form 'a musical image of the Fall of Man from his pristine high estate to his present woeful condition' and represent the 'corner-stone of our understanding of the fundamental nature of his music as a means of divine gnosis'.[29]

Since the Fall is a central fact of human experience for the Christian – an experience that can scarcely be called gnostic – it does not seem at all implausible that a Renaissance composer setting such words as 'down, down, down I fall' (*Sorow stay, Second Booke of Songs*, no. 3) should intend some specific allusion to that universal fact in his music. Such obvious and conventional symbolism cannot be described as esoteric.

Following Yates, Rooley claims that 'there was a wide circle of artists, poets and musicians who ... persevered with the notion of inspired melancholy' and that 'by the end of the 16th century [Hermetic] ideas had become woven into art, music and poetry to varying degrees'.[30] Proof of Dowland's membership of this putative circle, he argues, may be seen in his manifest penchant for melancholy and by the fact that he dedicates his *Second Booke of Songs* to the Countess of Bedford, who 'may be ... more central to the poetic cult of darkness than has hitherto been supposed'.[31]

That there existed a cult of melancholy in Elizabethan England, and perhaps even a 'School of Night',[32] cannot be denied. However, the only notable Englishmen in this period who seem to have shown any interest in or awareness of 'inspired' melancholy in the Ficinian sense were Chapman, and possibly Dee. But Dee, far from being 'the characteristic philosopher of the age' as Yates claims,[33] was in many respects at odds with the Protestant-humanistic ethos of his time, as would seem to be confirmed by the sad events of his latter years, when, rejected by the king, and persecuted by the mob, he returned to Mortlake to die in poverty. Those Elizabethans who gave serious thought to the subject of melancholy – as opposed, that is, to adopting it as a theme for lyrical development – tended on the whole to take a traditionally negative view of it.[34] Typical of this traditional attitude to melancholy is John Gower, writing at the end of the fourteenth century. Gower sees one of the primary functions of music as being to banish this, 'the most ungoodlich and the werste' of all the humours.[35] At the end of the Prologue to his encyclopaedic *Confessio Amantis* he prays that a new Arion might restore harmony to a discordant world and 'putte awey malencholie' (1053–69). Elizabethans, too, tend on the whole to view melancholy as a malignant passion. The astrologer John Maplet describes the ill-favoured characteristics of those born under the melancholy planet:

Such as are born vnder *Saturne* commonly called Saturnystes, are lumpish, heauy and sad, dull witted, full of melancholy, hard & strange, a long time to receiue vnderstandinge and learninge ... Their Phisiognomy is altogether blockish, their countenaunce cruell and stronge, theyr head hanging downe, theyr eyes euer bent and caste vpon the ground ... They are also very ready and prone to ciuill dissention and discorde. They be also for the most part shorte lifed, because the exceeding cold in them is a shortner of their Dayes, as we see it cometh to passe in old men, which through coldnes of nature are chopte up of a sodaine: for olde men as they grow on towards death becom very colde and dry, all heate and moysture whych are the preseruatiues of Lyfe then forsakyng them and bidding them farewel.[36]

Where humanists regard excessive melancholy as an abrogation of man's essential humanity, Christians see it as one of the cardinal sins. This is why in Dowland's own *In this trembling shadow cast (A Pilgrimes Solace*, no.12) the singer implores God to purge his mind of melancholy so that he may receive the light of divine grace:

> Darknesse from my minde then take,
> For thy rites none may begin
> Till they feele thy light within.

Based, as it is, on conjecture, the external evidence for Dowland's alleged commitment to 'deep philosophical studies' must be considered to be inconclusive. Nor is the internal evidence any more convincing. In my brief discussion of Ficino's theory of musical inspiration I noted the emphasis he laid on the judicious consultation of the heavenly bodies. In his rules for the composition of magic songs Ficino says that the singer must first identify his own particular ruling star. He must then adapt the text of his song so as to harmonize with the temperament of the planet he is addressing. From this it will be clear that for Ficino the text was of paramount importance. As D. P. Walker writes, 'A song [according to Ficino] works on body, mind, and on whatever intermediate faculties may be between; but it is the text alone that can carry an intellectual content and thus influence the mind.'[37]

It is true that by appealing to Orpheus in the dedication to the *First Booke of Songs*, Dowland acknowledges the 'higher authority and power' that has traditionally been accorded to song, compared with instrumental music, as a means of 'stirring vp the mindes of the hearers to admiration and delight'. But he makes no mention of the Platonic *furor poeticus* that is such an important aspect of Ficino's theory of musical inspiration. Dowland's Orpheus is no frenzied hierophant, but the sober moralist of humanist tradition, 'expressing', as he writes in his dedication, 'some worthy sentence or excellent Poeme'. Although Dowland rehearses the humanist commonplace concerning the importance of words, there is no evidence to suggest that he ever attempted to choose lyrics that possessed the kind of talismanic astrological significance that is fundamental to Ficino's theory of magic song. Had he been seriously interested in making a declaration of his Hermetic affiliations he need have gone no further than Chapman's *Shadow of Night* in his search for suitable philosophical material to set. As it is, the verses he does choose tend on the whole to be insignificant in proportion as the emotional impact of the music is profound. What is remarkable about the lyrics of songs like *Flow my teares* or *In darknesse let me dwell* is precisely the absence of any specific intellectual content, manifest or occult. These lyrics are in the broad tradition of late medieval and Renaissance complaint where the primary function of the words is to provide a generalized mood that the composer can express in musical terms. They do not make any reference to the astrological principles that form such an essential element in Ficino's theories, but instead versify a conventional pathology of melancholy.[38]

II

Why should a composer of Dowland's stature ignore the more serious verses of his age and choose instead to set lyrics that are to all intents and purposes devoid of intellectual interest? One answer is simply that 'Humor is inuencions foode.'[39] Of the four humours, it is melancholy that offers invention the greatest challenge. The lyrical treatment of melancholy that is such a characteristic feature of late Elizabethan music and poetry was not a new phenomenon. It became fashionable in the 1580s when poets and composers were re-discovering the possibilities of affective writing. In medieval and Renaissance England there was an extensive and continuous tradition of complaint, with composers and poets co-operating in their deprecation of fortune's treachery. This tradition can be seen in its purest form in the dramatic laments from the children's plays.[40] But these stylized consort songs of the 1560s and 1570s with their formulaic supplications to death are still a far cry from the affective ideal proclaimed by Sir Thomas More in the early years of the century. 'All their musike', wrote More in his fictional account of life in Utopia,

bothe that they playe upon instrumentes, and that they singe with mannes voyce dothe so resemble and expresse naturall affections, that it dothe ... wonderfullye move, stirre, pearce, and enflame the hearers myndes.[41]

In describing the musical culture of his imaginary commonwealth More was articulating an ideal that inspired humanists throughout Renaissance Europe. But it was well over half a century before that ideal was realized. Not until the publication of Spenser's *Shepheardes Calender* in 1579 and Nicholas Yonge's *Musica Transalpina* nine years later in 1588 can the Renaissance as an artistic movement truly be said to have arrived in England. In the following years Sidney and Spenser and, slightly later, Morley and Dowland transformed the character of English poetry and music. Late though they were in arriving in England, it was the Petrarchan sonnet sequence and the madrigal that provided English poets and composers with the means of realizing that affective ideal that is fundamental to Renaissance art. It is no coincidence that it is precisely at this time that melancholy begins to acquire a fashionable appeal.

The primary source of inspiration for Elizabethan poets and composers was Italy, either in the immediate form of Italian models or of humanist theories. English diplomats, Italian expatriates and cultural tourists all helped to transmit foreign ideas. But in the absence of formal musical and literary academies in Elizabethan England, one of the most important mediums for the dissemination of humanist theories was rhetoric books. Although these manuals of style cannot explain the artistic renaissance of the final years of Elizabeth's reign, they do provide some insight into the affective ideals that informed it.

Until the middle of the century rhetoric books were frankly utilitarian in their conception.[42] The most important book of the period is Erasmus' *De Copia* (1512). Erasmus' object was to impart those skills necessary for mastering the abundant style and his work was quickly adopted as a textbook of rhetoric in schools and universities throughout northern Europe. Erasmus' pragmatic approach to style is reflected in the work of English writers of the early and mid-century. Richard Sherry, for example, in his *Treatise of Schemes and Tropes* (1550) tells the reader that his object is to frame a new English style that would be 'apt and mete elegantly to declare our myndes in al kindes of Sciences'.[43] Laudable as its aims were, Sherry's treatise is a dull affair and has none of the enthusiasm and eloquence we find only three years later in Thomas Wilson's *Arte of Rhetorique* (1553). Here for the first time you can glimpse something of the excitement at the magical possibilities of language that fired the imaginations of Elizabethan poets and dramatists. 'If the worthinesse of Eloquence maie moove us', asks Wilson anticipating Marlowe's Tamburlaine, 'What worthier thing can there bee, then with a word to winne Cities and whole Countries?'[44]

When Henry Peacham takes up the same theme in his *Garden of Eloquence* (1577), it is clear that his interest in rhetoric is not simply that of the pedagogue. What excites Peacham, like Wilson, is the affective potential of eloquent language. For him, the orator is like a magician with powers as great as those of Marlowe's Faustus or the 'philosophre' in Chaucer's *Franklin's Tale*. 'The Oratour', writes Peacham,

> may leade his hearers which way he list, and draw them to what affection he will: he may make them to be angry, to be pleased, to laugh, to weepe, and lament: to loue, to abhorre, and loath: to hope, to feare, to couet, to be satisfyed, to enuye . . . and briefly to be moued with any affection that shall serue best for his purpose. By fygures he may make his speech as cleare as the noone day: or contrary wyse, as it were with cloudes and foggy mistes, he may couer it with darknesse, he may stirre vp stormes, & troublesome tempestes, or contrariwyse, cause and procure, a quyet and sylent calmnesse, he may set forth any matter with a goodly perspecuitie, and paynt out any person, deede, or thing, so cunninglye with these couloures, that it shall seeme rather a lyuely Image paynted in tables, then a report expressed with the tongue.[45]

What Peacham is saying here is of great significance. His book marks a transition from a purely utilitarian conception of language to one that sees poets as, in Puttenham's words, 'creating gods' invested with the power 'To deuise and make ... things of them selues, without any subject of veritie.'[46]

The Arte of English Poesie (1589) is much the most important of the sixteenth-century English rhetoric books. By now any pedagogic pretence has been dropped. Puttenham is writing not for schoolboys, but for courtiers. His aim is to devise 'a new and strange' art of rhetoric that will rather 'please the Court than the schoole'.[47] Like Wilson and Peacham, Puttenham speaks of the power of rhetoric to 'inueigle and appassionate the mind'.[48] But it is poetry rather than oratory that concerns him. And not only didactic poetry. Puttenham is particularly interested in love poetry because, he says, 'loue is of all other humane affections the most puissant and passionate' and requires 'a forme of Poesie variable, inconstant, affected, curious and most witty of any others'.[49] In short, Puttenham is interested in love poetry because of the affective opportunities it offers the rhetorician. Through poetry the passions of love may 'throughly ... be discouered', he writes,

> the poore soules sometimes praying, beseeching, sometime honouring, auancing, praising: an other while railing, reuiling, and cursing: then sorrowing, weeping, lamenting: in the ende laughing, reioysing & solacing

the beloued againe, with a thousand delicate deuises, odes, songs, elegies, ballads, sonets and other ditties, moouing one way and another to great compassion.[50]

By the time *The Arte of English Poesie* was published in 1589 a substantial volume of 'New' poetry had already been written: Spenser, Sidney, Lyly, Kyd and Marlowe had all produced major works testifying to the affective possibilities of rhetorically patterned language. What Wilson and Peacham had foreseen was now a reality, and for a relatively brief period Elizabethan poetry – both dramatic and non-dramatic – is filled with highly patterned, emotionally expressive language. There is in this period a sense of excitement, an awareness on the part of poets and dramatists that what they are doing is new. When Marlowe introduces the first part of his great epic hymn to the power of eloquence with a contemptuous gibe at the 'jygging vaines of riming mother wits'[51] he is speaking for a generation that had been made aware of the magical power of words.

The self-conscious nature of so much writing in the 1580s and 1590s, with its conspicuously stylized rhetorical devices deployed with the object of wringing the last drop of emotion from the situation, has its counterpart in the music of the period. With the advent of the Italian madrigal in the 1580s we see not just a new interest in pictorialism, but a new set of techniques for the realization of emotionally expressive effects. Just as Puttenham, England's first truly descriptive critic, gives close and detailed analyses of actual examples of the rhetorical schemes he lists, so Thomas Morley offers precise technical advice on how to achieve particular emotional effects. 'When you would express a lamentable passion', he writes in a well-known passage from the *Plaine and Easy Introduction to Practical Music* (1597), 'then must you use motions proceeding by halfe notes. Flat thirdes, and flat sixes, which of their nature are sweet, speciallie being taken in the true tune and naturall aire with discretion and iudgement.' And he goes on in the same passage to explain how the use of accidentals 'may fitlie express the passions of griefe, weeping, sighes, sorrowes, sobbes, and such like'.[52]

What Morley is saying here of the madrigal applies equally to the lute song, and examples of the effects he describes can be found everywhere in the repertory of the period. In madrigals like Ward's *Come sable night* and in songs like Dowland's *In darknesse let me dwell* dissonance and chromaticism are used to exploit to the full not the didactic, but the dramatic and emotional possibilities of the text.

It is no coincidence that the examples I have cited in illustration of the new affective techniques that had been made available to both poets and composers express grief, mourning or despair. One reason for this is simply that grief and despair, being the most intense emotions that human beings normally experience, naturally demand the most powerfully affective language or music. Nor is there any reason to assume that the feelings expressed are those of the writer. So familiar is the praise of melancholy as a debating *topos*,[53] and so alien in this period is the notion of giving 'transparent access to the represented',[54] that a composer could safely exploit to the full the emotional possibilities of a text without the risk of seeming morbid. If you compare what poets and composers have to say on the subject of the artistic representation of melancholy you find a general agreement that, provided you do not confuse life with art, dolour can safely be welcomed as a 'passion full of great delite'.[55] Puttenham writes: 'Lamenting is altogether contrary to rejoicing, every man saith so, and yet is it a piece of ioy to be able to lament with ease.'[56] Dowland says much the same thing in his dedication of the *Lachrimae* pavans to Queen Anne:

pleasant are the teares which Musicke weepes, neither are teares shed alwas in sorrowe, but sometime in joy and gladnesse. Vouchsafe then ... your Gracious protection to these showers of Harmonie, least if you frowne on them, they bee Metamorphosed into true teares.[57]

Puttenham's and Dowland's statements are significant because they confirm what contemporary poetic and musical texts suggest, namely, that the most intense emotions were valued as an end in themselves. The point may be seen most clearly in the following two exceptional cases cited by Bruce Pattison.[58] The first is from Byrd's *Psalmes, songes, and sonnets* (1611), the second from Danyel's book of lute songs of 1606:

> Come wofull Orpheus with thy charming Lyre,
> And tune my voyce unto thy skilfull wyre,
> Some strange Cromatique Notes doe you devise,
> That best with mournefull accents sympathize,
> Of sowrest Sharps and uncouth Flats make choise,
> And Ile thereto compassionate my voyce.   (no. 19)
>
> Can dolefull Notes to measur'd accents set,
> Expresse unmeasur'd griefes that tyme forget?

No, let Chromatique Tunes harsh without ground,
Be sullayne Musique for a Tuneless hart:
Chromatique Tunes most lyke my passions sound,
As if combyned to beare their falling part.
Uncertaine certaine turnes, of thoughts forecast,
Bring backe the same, then dye and dying last.   (nos. 13–15)

These two songs are exceptional only in their self-reflexive concern
with technique. Though the fact is not usually remarked on by poets
themselves in this explicit way, the principle they illustrate holds
good for many Elizabethan and Jacobean composers: literary texts
were often chosen for purely technical reasons. The final couplet of
Dowland's *Sorow stay* ('But down, down, down, down I fall, / And
arise I never shall') with its open invitation to musical pictorialism is
an obvious example.

At a time when humanists were becoming increasingly interested
in the problems of affective writing, grief, melancholy and despair
were welcomed as 'inuencions food'. If Elizabethan composers
tended to choose lyrics that express simple, stylized emotions this is
because they were more interested in writing about feelings than
ideas. And, as Pattison rightly says, this was only possible within the
framework of a familiar poetic convention in which emotions were
not complex, but followed well-worn paths.[59] Dowland's songs are
no exception to this rule.

III

The group of airs printed at the beginning of the *Second Booke of Songs*
contains some of Dowland's most powerful expressions of melancholy. The traditional Marxist explanation for music of this kind
would be to say that its dissonances are 'symbolic enactments of
social antagonisms'.[60] Although this approach is potentially illuminating, it can too easily lead to a reductive categorization of composers into two groups – those who 'establish order' and those who
'resist it'.[61] Potentially more responsive to the feelings that are, after
all, the subject of these songs is the biographical approach. But this
too has its limitations. Writing of *In darknesse let me dwell* (*A Musicall
Banquet*, no. 10), a song whose imagery links it thematically with
Flow my teares and *Mourne, day is with darknesse fled*, Diana Poulton
remarks: 'The hearer is left with the conviction that this is the
expression of a profoundly tragic experience.'[62] This may well have
been the case. But even if it were true it would not tell us very much

about Dowland's art. We should not forget that Dowland was the product of an age that did not expect to find in a poet's or composer's work an intimate record of his emotional life. Sidney's quasi-autobiographical *Astrophil and Stella* was described as 'a tragicommody of loue';[63] Spenser's *Amoretti* was praised for its 'rare inuention bewtified by skill'.[64] Both of these sonnet sequences contain overt reference to the poet's own courtship, either real or imaginary. Yet in neither case does the contemporary critic show any interest in the ostensibly autobiographical element of the poetry. What concerns the Elizabethan reader is not emotional truth-to-life, but rhetorical skill. 'The chief prayse and cunning of our Poet', writes Puttenham, 'is in the discreet vsing of his figures, as the skilfull painters is in the good conueyance of his coulours and shadowing traits of his pensill.'[65] In his advice to the aspiring poet, George Gascoigne emphasizes not emotions, but the power of invention: 'The first and most necessarie poynt that ever I founde meete to be considered in making of a delectable poeme is this, to ground it upon some invention [that is to say] some good and fine devise, shewing the quicke capacitie of a writer.'[66] When Elizabeth Barrett Browning writes of the pangs of love her tears 'come falling hot and real';[67] but for Gascoigne a lyric poem is not a personal document, but an artefact that is to be judged in accordance with the rules of its genre. 'If I should undertake to wryte in prayse of a gentlewoman', he continues,

I would neither praise hir christal eye, nor hir cherrie lippe, &c. For these things are *trita & obvia*. But I would either find some supernaturall cause wherby my penne might walke in the superlative degree, or els I would undertake to aunswere for any imperfection that shee hath, and thereupon rayse the prayse of hir commendacion. Like-wise if I should disclose my pretence in love, I would eyther make a straunge discourse of some intollerable passion, or finde occasion to pleade by the example of some historie, or discover my disquiet in shadows *per Allegoriam*, or use the covertest meane that I could to avoyde the uncomely customes of common writers.[68]

The first song in Dowland's *Second Booke* is a good example of what Gascoigne is talking about. The subject of *I saw my Lady weepe* – the magnetic power of female beauty – is a familiar one in Elizabethan poetry. But instead of cataloguing his mistress's charms in the form of a conventional blazon, the poet presents us with a paradox. Although grief is normally felt to be inimical to beauty, in this case

the poet's mistress appears even more charming in her sorrow.
Indeed her grief *becomes* her in the same way that in Shakespeare's
Cleopatra vices seem, inexplicably, like virtues. 'Fye wrangling
Queene' says Antony in the play's opening scene

> Whom euery thing becomes, to chide, to laugh,
> To weepe: whose euery passion fully striues
> To make it selfe (in Thee) faire and admir'd.   (*Ant.*, 1.i.48–51)

Just as Cleopatra's anger – normally an ugly passion – paradoxically
becomes her, so in Dowland's song 'Sorow was there made faire, /
And passion wise, teares a delightful thing'. In short, the poet's
mistress is an enigma.

This apparent defiance of convention should not be taken at its
face value. In enumerating his lover's paradoxical charms and, in
Gascoigne's phrase, answering 'for any imperfection that she hath'
the poet is simply drawing on convention of another kind: the
flouting of convention. Well-known contemporary examples of this
inverted form of *laus* are Sidney's *Astrophil and Stella*, no. 7 (*When
Nature made her chiefe worke, Stella's eyes*) and Shakespeare's sonnet no.
130 (*My Mistres eyes are nothing like the Sunne*). In both cases a
carefully contrived effect of ingenuousness is created by the listing of
qualities that are the antithesis of what custom dictates. *I saw my
Lady weepe* is a variation on this *topos*. And, like most examples of its
type, it ends with an ironic admission of the power of love to conquer
reason. Moving as he finds her sadness, the singer recognizes its
dangers, for, in the rarified world of Petrarchan love where beauty
can enslave, sorrow is potentially lethal: 'Teares kills the heart
believe', says the poet; or, as Donne puts it even more succinctly in *A
Valediction: Of Weeping* when he warns his lover: 'Weep me not
dead'.

What the poet is doing in these verses is precisely what Gascoigne
advises. As a true Elizabethan he relies for poetic effect, not on
naturalism, but on 'some good and fine devise'. *I saw my Lady weepe* is
not exceptional in this respect. *Flow my teares*, the next song in the
book, makes similar use of poetic conceit.[69] Once again the emotion
expressed in the lyrics is uncomplicated. Following a tradition that
goes back from Surrey, through Petrarch to Horace,[70] the poet
evokes a physical setting appropriate to his mood: 'Where nights
black bird hir sad infamy sings, / There let mee live forlorn'. The
night bird, which Rooley interprets as a Hermetic symbol,[71] is an

ancient and familiar figure of folly or vice. Ovid, for example, tells
how on the night of Tereus' ill-fated marriage to Procne, the cursed
screech-owl sat brooding ominously on the roof of their marriage
chamber ('tectoque profanus incubuit bubo thalamique in culmine
sedit').[72] Shakespeare similarly uses the owl to portend evil in *Julius
Caesar*. Shortly before Caesar's murder Casca reports how 'the Bird
of Night did sit, / Euen at Noone-day, vpon the Market place, /
Howting, and shreeking' (1.iii.26–8). From Anglo–Saxon times the
owl is conflated with members of the crow family as a bird of evil
omen. As he is about to be murdered, Shakespeare's Henry VI
recalls how 'The Owl shriek'd at thy birth, an euill signe, / The
Night-Crow cry'ed, aboding lucklesse time' (*3H6*, v.vi.44–5). The
night-bird can still be heard singing its ill-favoured song in Milton's
L'Allegro.

For an age that saw a natural symbolic opposition between 'Good
things of Day' and 'Night's black Agents' (*Mac.*, iii.ii.52–3), the
night-bird, with its nocturnal habits and its cacophonous song, was
an obvious symbol for the discords of hell. In one of Hieronymus
Bosch's eschatological paintings – *The Last Judgment* in the Groeningemuseum, Bruges – an owl perched in the rose of a monstrous lute
forms an essential part of the iconography of damnation (see chapter
3, illus. 3). If, as the ancients taught, 'in music consists the agreement of all things, and aristocracy of the universe',[73] then the
meaning of Bosch's composite symbol is plain enough: to pervert
music from its true function as an inspirer of virtue is to invite chaos.
In other paintings, too, Bosch consistently links the owl with the
debasement of music (e.g. *The Temptation of St Anthony*). The same
symbolic association is made by Robert Burton. In consecutive
panels of the title-page illustration of the *Anatomy of Melancholy* can
be seen (in the words of the 3rd edition of 1628) 'Owles which o'er
the shady bowers over / In melancholy darkness hover' juxtaposed
with the satiric figure of the Inamorato with his lute and books 'as
symptoms of his vanity'.

Bizarre as these surrealistic collocations of images may look to the
modern eye, they are based on a familiar tradition of symbolism that
survived to the end of the Renaissance. As Shakespeare uses it in
Julius Caesar and *Henry VI*, or Sidney in *Astrophil and Stella* (no. 71) or
Dowland himself in *Cleare or Cloudie* (*Second Booke of Songs*, no. 21),
night's black bird has no occult meaning. Nor is there anything to
suggest that it is being used in a significantly different way in *Flow my*

teares. With its songs of 'sad infamy' the night-bird is simply a standard feature of the literary landscape of melancholy. Having exhausted his litany of hyperboles the poet concludes this musical *pathopoeia* with a conceit (*pathopoeia* is a rhetorical figure in which the speaker 'by declaring some lamentable cause, moueth his hearers to pitie and compassion [through] the liuely descriptions of wofull sufferings, and pitiful miseries ... artificially expressed').[74] Console yourselves, he tells the souls of the dead, that however terrible the pains of hell may be, they cannot be as excruciating as the torments I am experiencing:

> Harke you shadowes that in darknesse dwell,
>   Learne to contemne light,
> Happie, happie they that in hell
>   Feele not the worlds despite.

Although he does not explain the cause of his grief, there is no need: a tradition going back at least as far as Andreas Capellanus in the twelfth century had catalogued in such wealth of detail the conventional pathology of love that for a contemporary audience there could be no doubt about the reason for the singer's 'teares, and sighs, and grones'. But while that audience praised Dowland for his ability to 'ravish humaine sense',[75] it is significant that it attributed the affective power of his music not to his philosophical ideas, but to his 'depth of skill and richnesse of conceipt'.[76]

To describe these lyrics as unexceptional expressions of stereotyped *topoi* is not to belittle Dowland's musical achievement: the fact that his verses lack any serious intellectual content confirms the impression that, in his melancholy songs at least, it is emotions rather than ideas that interest him. As an illustration of the truth of the old tag *est quaedam flere voluptas* – there is in weeping a certain pleasure – Dowland's songs are without parallel in this or any other period.

CHAPTER 9

'Ydle shallowe things': love and song in 'Twelfth Night'

Man is in love and loves what vanishes,
What more is there to say?
(W. B. Yeats, *Nineteen Hundred and Nineteen*)

I

If there is a tutelary deity in *Twelfth Night* she is *Venus vulgaris*, the goddess who speaks to men, like Viola, 'in many sorts of Musicke' (1.ii.58). Associated not only with the melody of the flesh,[1] but also with the caprices of fortune,[2] Venus is a goddess of various parts. Among the less well known of her many liaisons was her affair with the symbolically named Antigamus. The offspring of this union was Jocus, the bastard god whose nature was to make light of love.[3] It is the spirit of his mother Venus, 'music of the World',[4] that informs this, the most playful and also the saddest of Shakespeare's romantic comedies. The link between music and love is made in the frequently quoted first line of the play: 'If Musicke be the food of Loue, play on.' Music is part of the fabric of *Twelfth Night*: the play's opening mood of self-indulgent melancholy is established by instrumental music; the brittle joy of its conclusion is qualified by a ballad of ingenuous pessimism; and its action is punctuated by a series of art songs that serve both to flesh out the characters of the players and also to hint at the darker motifs that lie beneath its glittering surface.

Because the action of *Twelfth Night*, like that of all Shakespeare's comedies, is one of confusion resolved into order, it is natural enough to see the music of the play as a symbolic reflection of its themes of sexual discord and harmony. Wilson Knight finds in the play 'a pattern of music [and] love ... threaded by the sombre strands of a sea tempest'; he sees *Twelfth Night* as 'the most harmonious of Shakespeare's human romances'.[5] Wilson Knight's metaphors are repeated by countless critics of the play. John Hollander even goes so far as to claim that 'the general concern of *Twelfth Night* ... is *musica humana*, the Boethian application of abstract order and proportion to human behaviour'.[6] Though no one, to my knowledge, has taken up Hollander's suggestion, many critics whose primary concern is not with music inevitably use images of harmony and discord in discussing the play's action. Clifford Leech writes: 'We leave the theatre with a tune in our ears, and the harmony of *Twelfth Night* is after a fashion maintained';[7] Leo Salingar notes that 'there are discordant strains ... in the harmony of *Twelfth Night*';[8] Nevill Coghill concludes that Shakespeare's comic vision is 'the firm assertion of basic harmony'.[9]

So powerful is the ancient association of music with cosmic order that the image survived as a metaphor for social well-being long after the body of ideas that gave birth to it had been forgotten. The metaphor may be a dead one for modern audiences, but for Shakespeare's contemporaries it expressed a metaphysical reality. When Sir William Ingpen, in 1624, describes the universe as 'an harmonious body, containing number, order, beauty, and proportion, in all the parts thereof',[10] he is writing not figuratively, but literally. But although this quasi-scientific view of the universe continued to generate live metaphors for some decades after Shakespeare's death,[11] Renaissance composers had begun to treat music as a symbol, not simply of the universal harmony that it was believed was the underlying principle of social order, but of fortune's rule. The mutability of the natural world is a commonplace of medieval and Renaissance thought. Fundamental to the great medieval theodicies is the belief that change is part of nature's purpose. No matter how harsh fate might seem to be there was, it was believed, a beneficent, unchanging order behind the seemingly random flux of events in the world. However, as the medieval cosmos began gradually to disintegrate, this was an argument that was increasingly difficult to sustain. In the politically unstable world of Renaissance and Reformation Europe, signs of an underlying pattern of universal order began to seem less obvious than those of inexorable change.

As traditional ideas of world order began slowly to be abandoned, so too the medieval modal system was beginning to be replaced by the harmonic tonality that dominated musical composition from the seventeenth to the twentieth centuries. Edward E. Lowinsky has argued that, in the new possibilities for modulation made available by the modern key system, Renaissance theorists saw an analogy with fortune's mutability: 'Modulation is change; its name in Renaissance terminology was the same term used for the activities of *Fortuna: mutatio* ... Renaissance composers were activated by the desire to create an image in tones of the Goddess Fortuna.'[12]

Twelfth Night is no opera, and in the absence of surviving contemporary scores for the play's instrumental music it would be fruitless to look for symbolism of the kind that Lowinsky finds in the tonal modulations of a composer like Josquin. All the same, Shakespeare does make extensive use of music for symbolic purposes. I shall argue that, insofar as music performs a symbolic role in *Twelfth Night* (in addition to its functions of providing atmosphere, character amplification and, of course, simply entertainment), it reflects the idea not of social harmony and discord, but of mutability.

II

Like Shakespeare's other romantic comedies, *Twelfth Night* portrays a world apparently dominated by fortune. In a play about anything as capricious as romantic love this is natural enough. As Orsino says in his opening speech, 'so full of shapes is fancie / That it alone, is high fantasticall' (I.i.14–15). It is because, as Bottom says, 'reason and loue keepe little company together' (*MND*, III.i.132) that lovers are so vulnerable to fortune. The moral to be drawn – no less clear for being seemingly impossible to follow – is repeated in play after play. Hermia's reply to Lysander's complaint at the cruelty of fortune sums up that lesson:

> If then true louers haue bin euer crost,
> It stands as an edict, in destiny.
> Then let vs teach our triall patience:
> Because it is a customary crosse,
> As dewe to loue, as thoughts, and dreames, and sighes,
> Wishes, and teares; poore Fancies followers.   (I.i.150–5)

It is the folly and at the same time the irresistibility of romantic love that is Shakespeare's great comic theme.

Twelfth Night differs from the other romantic comedies in two respects; first, because it conspicuously lacks the kind of moralizing judgments that are normally found in the comedies and love tragedies; and second, because of its emphasis on the brevity of youth, and therefore of romantic love. But if love is sad in *Twelfth Night* it is not because 'Warre, death, or sicknesse, did lay siege to it' (*MND*, I.i.142), or even because of parental interference. In fact there are no parents in the play. Unlike most of the other comedies, which divide their time between two worlds – a holiday world of romance and laughter, and a contrasting world of harsh domestic, political or commercial realities – *Twelfth Night* has only one location. If that world is not exactly an Elysium for the characters who inhabit it, it sounds close enough when Viola mentions the two names in the same breath (I.i.3–4). Like Homer's mythical land of revelry, feasting and song where the living is easy,[13] Illyria contains no natural obstacles to impede the course of love. The romantic confusions in this land of Cockaigne are all self-generated. Moreover, despite the widely held view that they are self-deceivers,[14] the major characters know exactly what they are doing. They are playing a game. That game is called romantic Love.

It might be thought that the most essential characteristic of romantic love is its spontaneity. When played as a game, however, it is the reverse. Romantic love has two features that are common to all successful games; it is of compelling interest to the players; and its rules are both complex and very precise. Those rules had been codified by many writers including, most notably, Ovid in the ancient world, and Andreas Capellanus and Guillaume de Lorris in the Middle Ages. The Elizabethans knew them by heart. Sentimental recreation of an ideal of courtly love is just as typical a characteristic of the age as Spenser's epic celebration of chivalric honour in *The Faerie Queene*, or the factitious splendours of the royal progresses, or the extravagantly anachronistic costumes and armorial symbolism of the court tournaments. All are essential aspects of that self-conscious medievalism that is such a distinctive feature of late Elizabethan culture. They are the expressions of an age that responded to the contradictions of the present by moulding for itself an image of chivalry, love and honour based on an idealized image of the past. No less than the preposterous rituals of the Accession Day tilts, the love sonnets of writers like Sidney or Drayton are a kind of stylized game, combining sentimentality and self-parody in a form that, if it can be said to avoid the charge of escapism does so only by virtue of its extreme self-consciousness. It is in this respect that such poets differ most radically from the spirit of their ostensible model. In place of Petrarch's anguished self-torture is a playful

self-mockery that has more in common with Ovid's *Amores* or
Andreas' ironically titled *De arte honeste amandi* than with the *Can-
zioneri*. But most influential of all the medieval treatises on the art of
love is the thirteenth-century *Roman de la Rose*.

When Guillaume's dreamer pledges his loyalty to the god of love
he is instructed by his master in the rules of the game of love. These
rules are, of course, purely a matter of convention, like those of any
game, for, as Chaucer remarks in *Troilus and Criseyde*, far from being a
matter of blind instinct, love is no less subject to changes in fashion
than language itself:

> Ye knowe ek that in forme of speche is chaunge
> Withinne a thousand yeer, and wordes tho
> That hadden pris, now wonder nyce and straunge
> Us thinketh hem, and yet thei spake hem so,
> And spedde as wel in love as men now do;
> Ek for to wynnen love in sondry ages
> In sondry londes, sondry ben usages.   (II.22–8)[15]

In his catechism of the dreamer Guillaume's god of love explains
that he must devote himself exclusively to his lady's service. Indeed,
he must never cease to think of love; it must occupy his thoughts
night and day. His entire being must be given over to love, 'hool and
quyt'.[16] At the same time he must not neglect his own appearance or
manners, but must at all times act with courtesy and grace and take
great pains to ensure that he is always fashionably dressed. As a
social accomplishment, the ability to sing or play a musical instrument is a great advantage to the lover. But while he should thus 'hym
contene jolily' (2248) and 'hym disgysen in quentise' (2250), he must
never succumb to the temptations of pride, for pride, says the god of
love, is altogether 'Contrarie unto loves art' (2246).

The fact that rules are essential to games of every kind does not
mean that powerful emotions may not be involved: as any poker-
player knows, in many games the ability to conceal strong feelings is
one of the marks of a skilful player. Like the successful gambler, the
player in the game of love must adopt an 'aquentable' social manner.
But inwardly he will be tormented by the vicissitudes of his passion:

> For now the lover [is] joyous,
> Now can he pleyne, now can he grone,
> Now can he syngen, now maken mone.
> To-day he pleyneth for hevynesse,
> To-morowe he pleyeth for jolynesse.   (*Romaunt*, 2298–302)

In short, the lover is a type and example of mutability; like fortune itself, 'The lyf of love is full contrarie' (2303).

The vicissitudes of love catalogued at such length by Guillaume are the result of unrequited passion. The anguish, the torment, the bitter-sweet joy experienced by the lover are all the consequence of unfulfilled desire. When the thirst for passion is slaked, all these emotions disappear and are replaced by different ones. Love may blossom or it may wither; but once the conditions essential for its existence have been removed, it will no longer be romantic love. That can only flourish when desire is met by impossible obstacles. As Sidney's Astrophil puts it in sonnet 108, 'in my woes for thee thou art my joy, / And in my joyes for thee my only annoy'.[17] The most succinct definition of this kind of love is in Marvell's poem of that title:

> My love is of a birth as rare
> As 'tis for object strange and high:
> It was begotten by despair
> Upon Impossibility.   (*The Definition of Love*, 1–4)[18]

The love described by Marvell may be in earnest or it may be a game. If the obstacles that call it into being are unlooked for then it will probably be the former; if they are consciously invented, then it will be the latter. But, either way, romantic love cannot survive without them.

Though not so essential, certain other conditions are also necessary if the game of love is to approximate to the level of the high art described by Guillaume. Medieval representations of the court of Venus[19] describe the romantic setting of her temple with flowers, music and sweet odours augmenting the aphrodisiac effects of food and wine. Among her courtiers are not only Youth, Grace, Nobility and Charm, but also Elegance, Affability, Courtesy and Patience. But the most illustrious of them is Wealth,[20] for only a monied society can afford the leisure that can free the mind from other distractions and allow it to devote itself exclusively to the business of passion. This is why the allegorical figure of Ydleness (*Romaunt*, 593ff), or in Spenser's case Ease (*Faerie Queene*, III.xii.4), plays such a prominent role in medieval and Renaissance pantomimes of love. Leisure is also necessary for the development of the arts of poetry, music and conversation – all of them, as Guillaume explains, essential accomplishments of the skilful player of the game of love.

Romantic love is above all a social art, relying partly on gesture and performance, but also on the written, spoken and sung word. Although, as the beautifully constructed wooing scenes in *Sir Gawain and the Green Knight* show so well, the game of love can be played perfectly satisfactorily by two players in private, it is obvious that far greater scope is offered to skilful performers if there is a knowledgeable audience to appreciate their art. Finally, it is money alone that can provide the costumes, the professionally produced music and the food that create a sympathetic environment in which to act out the rituals of love.[21]

III

The opening scene of *Twelfth Night* immediately establishes Orsino's court as a neo-medieval temple of Venus waiting for its goddess to emerge, like Viola, from the sea. With its music, its ease, its luxury, its canopies of flowers and its poetic grace, Illyria's ducal palace is dedicated to one purpose alone: homage to the goddess of love. As the master of so much wealth Orsino can take his pick from among the fairest ladies in Illyria. However, he must choose carefully, for the game of love cannot progress beyond the first move if the lady is not unattainable. But Orsino is an experienced player. He chooses someone who fits his purpose beautifully, a lady who has vowed to immure herself for seven years in memory of her brother's death. The situation is the reverse of that in Boccaccio's *Teseida* and Chaucer's *Knight's Tale*: instead of the lover literally incarcerated in a gaol that is symbolic of his own imprisoning passion, it is the lady in this play who has sequestered herself from the world. But the result is the same and provides the perfect scenario for the enactment of love 'begotten by despair upon impossibility'. A hedonist Orsino may be, but he cannot be accused of self-deception when he shows so clearly that he knows exactly what he is doing. Declaring his passion for Olivia 'with fertill teares, / With groanes that thunder loue, with sighes of fire' (1.v.256–7), he is every inch the correct lover described by Guillaume. When his servant informs him that Olivia is unavailable, he does not collapse in hysterics, like Romeo. But then why should he? It is, after all, only a game. Instead, he asks Valentine to lead him away 'to sweet beds of Flowres' to plan his next move, for 'Loue-thoughts lye rich, when canopy'd with bowres' (1.i.41–2). His is a polished and knowing performance.

With the arrival of Viola at Illyria's court of Venus a new dimension is added to the game of love: Orsino now has a go-between to 'act his woes' (1.iv.26) to Olivia. But, more important, he also has a willing and sympathetic audience at the spectacle of his passion. The nature of that passion is epitomized in the song he arranges to be performed for Viola in act 11 scene iv:

> Come away, come away, death;
> And in sad cypresse let me be laide;
>   Fye away, fie away, breath,
> I am slaine by a faire cruell maide:
> My shrowde of white, stuck all with Ew,
>   O, prepare it.
> My part of death no one so true
>   Did share it.
>
>   Not a flower, not a flower sweete,
> On my blacke coffin, let there be strewne;
>   Not a friend, not a friend greet
> My poor corpes, where my bones shall be throwne;
> A thousand thousand sighes to saue,
>   Lay me o where
> Sad true louer neuer find my graue,
>   To weepe there.

Though no contemporary setting of Shakespeare's lyrics has been identified, there are numberless analogues in the contemporary lute song repertory testifying to the irresistible appeal for the Eliza-bethans of this kind of melancholy song. As it lingers self-indulgently over the funeral arrangements for a death we know to be feigned, Feste's romantic dirge serves both a mimetic and an affective function: it is intended not only to mirror in music the feelings that are its subject, but also to evoke in Viola a sympathetic response to Orsino's chosen plight. When it is over she is silent. But this should not be read as the disillusioned reaction of one who perceives that the man she loves is no more than an idle voluptuary.[22] Viola, no less than Orsino, is addicted to the 'sweet pangs' of unrequited love. It is her song as much as his. If Viola's disguise prevents Orsino from seeing in her a possible opponent for him in the game of love, he does recognize her skill as a player. In a series of ironic exchanges that owe much to Lyly's comic example, he tries to draw her out and persuade her to reveal something of her true self. But Viola is only too aware of the dangers of unguarded self-revelation and counters his moves with such skill that he is moved to compliment her on her game: 'Thou dost speake masterly', he tells her (II.iv.21).

Viola's successful performance is testimony both to her talent as a player and also to her knowledge of the rules of the game of love. That knowledge is perhaps best revealed in her exchanges with Olivia, where it is she who now has the upper hand. Her reply to Olivia's question at I.v.251 regarding the correct presentation of love is a model catechist's response. Guillaume's god of love advises his pupil 'all pryvyly' to go by night and take up a position at his lady's gate and there appeal to her pity:

> Go putte thiself in jupartie,
> To aske grace, and thee bimene,
> That she may wite, withouten wene,
> That thou [a-] nyght no rest hast had,
> So sore for hir thou were bystad.
> Wommen wel ought pite take
> Of hem that sorwen for her sake. (2666–72)

In urging Olivia to do the same Viola gently parodies this conventional prescription:

> VIO: If I did loue you in my masters flame,
> With such a suffring, such a deadly life,
> In your deniall I would finde no sence,
> I would not vnderstand it.
> OLI: Why, what would you?
> VIO: Make me a willow Cabine at your gate,
> And call vpon my soule within the house,
> Write loyall Cantons of contemned loue
> And sing them lowd euen in the dead of night:
> Hallow your name to the reuerberate hilles,
> And make the babling Gossip of the aire
> Cry out *Olivia*: O you should not rest
> Betweene the elements of ayre, and earth
> But you should pittie me. (I.v.248–60)

Viola's words are, of course, full of irony. Not only is she inviting Olivia to make a fool of herself by adopting a masculine role in the game of love, and thereby violating one of its most fundamental rules, but she is herself acting a part. Moreover, she relishes that part, taking conscious pleasure in her talent, and sufficiently confident of her own performance to be able to laugh at its absurdity.

The ability to laugh at your own performance is a valuable asset to the player of a game as essentially absurd as romantic love. Another important quality that Viola possesses is patience. In his gloss on the Temple of Venus in the *Teseida* Boccaccio explains that, without patience, success in love is impossible. The reason why the temple figure of Patience is portrayed as being pale is that she 'has no place except where there are pains and torments, which, as we see from experience, make the one who endures them grow emaciated and pale'.[23] Viola's little allegory in act II scene iv shows that she is well versed in love's lore. But despite her archly histrionic representation of herself as Patience on a monument wanly smiling at grief (II.iv.109–14), she never relaxes her guard in her verbal sparring with Orsino. She may drop hints of her feelings towards the duke, but she does not lose her self-possession. The dangers of doing so are made clear in the second of her three private interviews with Olivia.

Like Orsino and Viola, Olivia is an experienced player who recognizes the importance of concealing one's true feelings. For all its romantic accoutrements, the game of love can be a harshly competitive affair. Beneath the surface talk of 'Roses of the Spring' (III.i.146) there may be lurking 'scorne', 'contempt' and 'anger' (142–3). Perceiving that she is in danger of falling 'prey' to her 'enemy' (125; 122), Olivia knows that ''tis time to smile agen' (123). But having wisely decided to save face by allowing Viola to leave, she then commits an unforgivable error: she asks Viola what her real feelings towards her are: 'I prethee tell me what thou thinkst of me?' (135). Blushing with embarrassment at such a *faux pas* (143–4), Viola tries to restore a sense of decorum to their game by shifting the exchange back to its proper level of equivocation. But the damage has been done and Olivia later regrets that

> There's something in me that reproues my fault:
> But such a head-strong potent fault it is,
> That it but mockes reproofe. (III.iv.193–5)

But if she lacks the self-possession that is the mark of the truly accomplished player, Olivia does at least know how to lose gracefully. Acknowledging her defeat, she turns loss into gain by making a joke of the whole affair:

> Well, come again to morrow: far-thee-well,
> A Fiend like thee might beare my soule to hell. (III.iv.206–7)

Twelfth Night portrays a sophisticated, elegant social world in which the major characters are all adept and skilful players in the game of love. Whether they lose or win they are alike in the pleasure they take in the verbal sparring that is really the essence of their game. But there is one character who does not enjoy the game of love. Malvolio's humiliation is due not to want of skill, but to ignorance of the game's most basic rules. Indeed, with his puritan sensibility he is antipathetic to the very idea of play. Little wonder that he is detested in Illyria.

Malvolio has presumably read his text-books and is aware that the way to a lady's heart may well begin with haberdashery. (As Guillaume remarks, 'fair clothyng / A man amendeth in myche thyng'.[24]) His error is to mistake game for earnest and to attribute to fortune (''Tis but Fortune, all is fortune' (II.v.21)) what is in fact the work of comic design. The gulf that divides the puritan from his adversaries is epitomized by the way each responds to music. Act II scene iii shows Sir Toby and Sir Andrew at their most convivial, cracking puerile jokes and singing drunken catches 'without any mitigation or remorse of voice'. Their merriment is interrupted by Malvolio. Reproving them for their irresponsibility, he demands of them with dour self-righteousness 'Is there no respect of place, persons, nor time in you?' (88). Feste and Sir Toby respond, not with a simple riposte, but by weaving a magic net of sound in which the helpless Malvolio can only flounder and gasp. In a buffoonish antiphony they sing alternate lines from a recently published popular song. The song is from Robert Jones' *First Booke of Songes and Ayres* (1600) and tells of a foolishly vacillating lover who cannot bring himself to leave his cruel-hearted mistress:

> Farewel dear love since thou wilt needs be gon,
> Mine eies do shew my life is almost done,
> > Nay I will never die,
> > So long as I can spie,
> > Ther by many mo
> > Though that she do go
> There be many mo I feare not,
> Why then let her goe I care not.
>
> Farewell, farewell, since this I finde is true,
> I will not spend more time in wooing you:
> > But I will seeke elswhere,
> > If I may find her there,

Shall I bid her goe,
What and if I doe?
Shall I bid her go and spare not,
Oh no no no no I dare not.

Ten thousand times farewell, yet stay a while,
Sweet kisse me once, sweet kisses time beguile:
      I have no power to move,
      How now, am I in love
      Wilt thou needs be gone?
      Go then, all is one,
Wilt thou needs be gone? oh hie thee,
Nay, stay and doe no more denie mee.

Once more farewell, I see loth to depart,
Bids oft adew to her that holdes my hart:
      But seeing I must loose,
      Thy love which I did chuse:
      Go thy waies for me,
      Since it may not be,
Go thy waies for me, but whither?
Go, oh but where I may come thither.

What shall I doe? my love is now departed,
Shee is as faire as shee is cruell harted:
      Shee would not be intreated,
      With praiers oft repeated:
      If shee come no more,
      Shall I die therefore,
If she come no more, what care I?
Faith, let her go, or come, or tarry.[25]

Olivia's arrogant admirer has probably never heard of Jones' song, and in any case, the script has not yet been written for the play in which he himself is to perform the role of foolish lover. But it is clear enough to Malvolio that Feste's and Sir Toby's innuendos refer to him in some way that is not favourable. With his natural suspicion of music and its powers of exciting the passions, the puritan is here symbolically trapped and caught by what he most deprecates. When he has gone Maria diagnoses his problem. 'Marrie sir', she tells Sir Toby, 'sometimes he is a kinde of Puritane' (131).

A distaste for puritan sanctimony is something that Maria shares with her mistress. Olivia's censure of Malvolio's dyspeptic puritanism is in effect a defence of social games-playing:

OLI: O, you are sicke of selfe-loue, *Maluolio*, and taste with a distemper'd appetite. To be generous, guiltlesse, and of free disposition, is to take those things for Birdbolts, that you deeme Cannon bullets: There is no slander in an allow'd foole, though he do nothing but rayle. (I.v.85–90)

But if we are expected to endorse Olivia's plea for a generous and free disposition that can laugh at raillery, there is more than a little truth in Malvolio's counter-attack on his tormenters. There is a real sense in which not only Maria, Sir Toby and Sir Andrew, but also Orsino, Olivia and Viola are 'ydle shallowe things' (III.iv.118). To speak, as one critic does, of Viola's being 'kept hard at work' throughout the play[26] is grotesquely to misrepresent the world of *Twelfth Night*. In that world servants must presumably work – though we do not see them doing very much of it – but their masters and mistresses most emphatically do not. It is precisely because they do not need to work for a living that they are able to commit themselves so exclusively to the service of their goddess. Theirs is a life dedicated, no less than Sir Toby's, to play. Where he and his companions are content with a buffoonery that requires few rules, their play is of a different order. They have raised the game of love to a sophisticated art. Their lives are a performance. But, like any performance, it is an essentially transitory one. Critics of *Twelfth Night* often remind us that this is a play whose title hints not only at the festive origins of its mood, but also at the fact that holidays presuppose a workaday world to which we must all sooner or later return. But there is a larger sense in which the aristocratic world of Illyria is overshadowed by change.

The theme of mutability pervades *Twelfth Night*. But it is expressed most poignantly in Feste's beautiful song in act II scene iii:

> O Mistris mine where are you roming?
> O stay and heare, your true loues coming,
>   That can sing both high and low.
> Trip no further prettie sweeting.
> Iourneys end in louers meeting,
>   Euery wise mans sonne doth knowe.
>
> What is loue, tis not heerafter,
> Present mirth, hath present laughter:
>   What's to come, is still vnsure.
> In delay there lies no plentie,
> Then come kisse me, sweet and twentie:
>   Youths a stuffe will not endure.

In Thomas Morley's eloquently simple setting *O Mistress Mine* evokes the sweetness and the delight of courtship and anticipates the happy conclusion of love's journey, suggesting idealistically that such unions always receive the blessing of age and wisdom. But the facile optimism of the first stanza is qualified by the radically different tone of the second. Despite the assertion that 'Journeys end in louers meeting', it insists on the impermanence of 'present laughter' and concludes with the commonplace reminder that 'Youths a stuffe will not endure'. The irony of the song's double view of love is underlined by the circumstances in which it is performed. As J. R. Moore so well puts it, 'There is something pathetically human about the gross old knight and his withered dupe, sitting in the drunken gravity of midnight to hear the clown sing of the fresh love of youth.'[27]

The themes implicit in *O Mistress Mine* are rehearsed for the last time in Feste's valedictory song. The world evoked in this balladeer's version of the ancient *topos* of the four ages of man is a bleak and loveless world in which human beings do not gain wisdom with age and in which the only principle of constancy is the rain that raineth every day.

With its emphasis on the ephermerality of youth, its repeated allusions to the passing of time, and its suggestion that 'pleasure will be paide one time, or another' (ii.iv.69–70), *Twelfth Night* anticipates the melancholy beauty of the royalist love lyrics of the 1630s and 1640s. When Carew, for example, writes,

> Beauty's sweet, but beauty's frail,
> 'Tis sooner past, 'tis sooner done,
> Than summer's rain, or winter's sun;
> Most fleeting, when it is most dear,
> 'Tis gone, while we but say 'tis here
>
> (*To A. L. Persuasions To Love*)[28]

he is expressing not simply the time-honoured commonplaces of the *carpe diem* tradition, but the feelings of a generation about to witness the death of an old order.

Though Shakespeare could not have known how true the puritan's curse, 'Ile be reueng'd on the whole packe of you!' (v.i.364) was eventually to prove for England's aristocrats and their culture, he was as aware as any of his contemporaries of the sense of a civilization passing 'like courts removing, or like ended playes'.[29] As *Twelfth Night* reminds us of how 'the whirlegigge of time, brings in its reuenges' we are brought back from the world of self-indulgent games to the reality not of work, but of mutability. When Orsino tells Viola that 'women are as Roses, whose faire flowre, / Being once displaid, doth fall that verie howre', she caps his maxim with an equally sententious couplet:

> And so they are: alas, that they are so:
> To die, euen when they to perfection grow. (II.iv.37–40)

Although she is talking, like him, simply of youth and love, there lies behind her words that sense of the transitoriness of civilization which the Elizabethans inherited from the late Middle Ages. It is a commonplace embodied in some of the age's greatest literature that not only flowers and women, but also civilizations, begin 'to die, even when they to perfection grow'. The idea is never explicitly articulated in the play. The most you can say is that, with its sense of sadness and dereliction, this play seems to reflect that sense of national decline that is such a characteristic feature of the period.

For the Cavalier lyricists writing on the eve of revolution romantic love was a uniquely appropriate theme because it embodied so vividly their sense of mutability. Like the societies that created it, romantic love is fragile, artificial and above all impermanent. For, paradoxically, no sooner are the lover's wishes fulfilled than romantic love must die. Andreas Capellanus' warning that love is violently put to flight when lovers marry[30] is not simply the worldly cynicism it might seem to be. For it is true that the kind of love he is describing, a love 'begotten by despair upon impossibility', can thrive, like arctic flowers, only on deprivation. If it surfeits, it dies, just as Orsino's appetite for music dies. This is why the happiness of *Twelfth Night*'s conclusion is tinged (as almost every critic of the play points out) with sadness. The multiple marriage, which in Elizabethan comedy conventionally symbolizes the restoration of social and personal harmony, here spells the death of romantic love. In the happiness of the marriage partners lies their sorrow. It is this paradox that *Twelfth Night*'s songs embody.

IV

In a general sense it is obvious that *Twelfth Night*'s music reflects its mood of self-indulgent melancholy: as Viola says, 'It giues a verie eccho to the seate / Where loue is thron'd' (II.iv.20–1). But there is a more important sense in which the play's music enacts its theme. Feste's art songs not only express but actually embody the paradoxical truth about romantic love that is the play's subject. Beautiful, brief and sad, they are like concrete symbols of the love they describe. They are not *carmina figurata*, like Herbert's *Easter Wings* or Quarles' *Behold how short a span*, both of which rely on the conceit of visual mimesis, or 'ocular representation', as Puttenham terms this kind of concrete poetry.[31] They are more like Ezra Pound's *Fanpiece, for her Imperial Lord* (another courtly trifle that encapsulates a sense of the sad impermanence of things): they are poems, that is, which enact aesthetically not the visual but the abstract nature of their subject.

As lyrics on the printed page these songs are not much more than pretty clichés, stereotyped variations on the conventional commonplaces of a literary tradition. But when set to music and performed on the stage they take on a different meaning. Unlike the reader, who can return to the words on the page as many times as he or she wishes, the audience in the theatre hears the songs only once. A fixed and permanent artefact is for the audience a transitory experience. The brevity of these songs is part of their meaning: like the love they describe, they are not only beautiful and sad, but also ephemeral. They illustrate perfectly the truth of the analogy made by the author of the thirteenth-century *Owl and the Nightingale* between love and song:

> Þat maide wot, hwanne ich swike,
> Þat luue is mine songes iliche:
> For hit nis bute a lutel breþ
> Þat sone kumeþ & sone geþ.
> Þat child bi me hit understond,
> An his unred to red vvend,
> An ise3þ wel bi mine songe
> Þat dusi luue ne last no3t longe.   (1459–66)[32]

Unlike the old ballad that Orsino recalls at ii.iv.41–7 with its 'silly sooth' of love's innocence, Feste's songs are self-conscious artefacts: elegant and contrived, they are also essentially trivial, like the court society for which they are intended. Despite the hint contained in Orsino's opening speech that *Twelfth Night* is to be a variation on the conventional theme of the moral dangers of excess, the play does not approve or condemn that society. It shows its beauty and also its emptiness, but it does not pass judgment on the 'ydle shallowe things' whose lives it portrays. The sober moralist may condemn their world for its spiritual and intellectual bankruptcy, but only the puritan can be happy to see it pass.

Coda: 'floreat Orpheus'

If Musique and sweet Poetrie agree,
As they must needes (the Sister and the Brother)
Then must the Love be great, twixt thee and mee,
   Because thou lov'st the one, and I the other.
   Dowland to thee is deare; whose heavenly tuch
Upon the Lute, doeth ravish humaine sense:
Spenser to mee; whose deepe Conceit is such,
   As passing all Conceit, needs no defence.
   Thou lov'st to hear the sweete melodious sound,
That *Phoebus* Lute (the Queene of Musique) makes:
And I in deepe Delight am chiefly drownd,
   When as himselfe to singing he betakes.
     One God is God of Both (as Poets faigne)
     One Knight loves Both, and Both in thee remaine.
          Richard Barnfield, To His Friend Maister R.L.

When Renaissance humanists interpreted the Orpheus story as an allegory of the birth of civilization they did so because they recognized in the arts in which Orpheus excelled an instrument of social control so powerful that with it you could 'winne Cities and whole Countries'. Fundamental to Renaissance poetics is a belief in the transforming power of music and poetry: for the lover it is a means of access to his mistress's (or in Barnfield's case, master's) heart; for the Neoplatonist it is a way to heaven; for the puritan it leads to damnation; for the mythographer it is the origin and basis of social order. But though poets may claim, in Puttenham's words, a 'dignitie and preheminence aboue all other artificers', few are blest with the inspiration that 'the Platonicks call *furor*'.[1] As Puttenham explains, a poet is someone exceptionally endowed, either with 'some diuine instinct ... or by excellencie of nature and complexion: or by great subtiltie of the spirits & wit, or by much experience and obseruation of the world, and course of kinde, or peraduenture by all or most part of them'.[2] He goes on to argue that just as a poet is someone of exceptional ability, so the language he employs is different in kind from that of everyday usage:

So as the Poets were also from the beginning the best perswaders and their eloquence the first Rethoricke of the world. Euen so it became that the high mysteries of the gods should be reuealed & taught, by a maner of vtterance and language of extraordinarie phrase, and briefe and compendious, and aboue al others sweet and ciuill as the Metricall is.[3]

Such a theory of poetry is a function of an essentialist view of human nature. While the artist who 'contriues out of his owne braine, both the verse and matter of his poeme',[4] is an individual who exceeds the human norm, his art addresses humanity's inherent potential for purposive change. Where the anti-essentialist, or atomist, admits of no defining human characteristic, and sees human society simply as an aggregate of individuals all constructed differently according to the contingent discourses that impinge on them, the essentialist sees humankind as a species with its own unique propensities and potentialities.[5] For the Elizabethan puritan this essence included humanity's innate corruption; for the human-ist it meant our ability to transform our fallen nature and achieve our *telos*, or full potential as human beings. Sidney's well-known account of poetry's function – 'to lead and draw us to as high a perfection as our degenerate soules ... can be capable of' – is an attempt to reconcile both views. In our struggle to realize our human *telos* we may be assisted by the arts, or we may be impeded by them. But whether we choose, in Pico's words, 'to degenerate into the lower forms of life which are brutish', or strive 'to be reborn into the higher forms, which are divine', the inherent potential for change exists in everyone, or so the Elizabethan humanist believes. It was the transforming power of the arts, and of music and poetry in particular, that interested the *rhétoriqueurs* of the sixteenth century, and it was this that they tried to codify and analyse. In doing so they established the groundwork for a criticism that undertook, in John-son's words, 'to improve opinion into knowledge'.[6]

When post-structuralist historicism claims that one of the defining features of the renaissance *épistème* is a radical anti-essentialism, it is, in effect, denying this whole ensemble of theories. Abandon the human subject and you have to abandon any notions of artistic genius, of intentionality and finally of literature itself. As Catherine Belsey explains, once you have shown that the author, like any other human subject, is merely a discursive construct with no capacity for generating original meaning, what you are left with is simply text conceived as having an infinite plurality of meaning.[7] That is why for Terence Hawkes a Shakespeare play, having no intrinsic meaning of its own, can mean literally whatever we like it to mean.[8]

Obliteration of the distinction between the arts and other forms of discourse is an objective that post-structuralist historicism has taken over from older forms of Marxist criticism. In 1973 Raymond Williams wrote: 'We cannot separate literature and art from other kinds of social practice, in such a way as to make them subject to quite specific and distinct laws'.[9] His words have been echoed by virtually every practitioner of the new post-structuralist historicism: 'refusal' to discriminate between literature and non-literary writing is a mark of affiliation to the movement. 'Materialist criticism refuses to privilege "literature" in the way that literary criticism has done hitherto', writes Dollimore in the introduction to *Political Shakespeare*;[10] Louis Montrose makes the same point in his own policy statement: 'the newer historical criticism is *new* in its refusal of unproblematized distinctions between "literature" and "history", between "text" and "context"'.[11]

But although post-structuralist historicism argues that the category 'literature', together with any false notions of canonicity, should be dispensed with, in practice it continues to make use of it. It has been noted that the great bulk of books published in the sixteenth century would be classified by a modern bookseller as non-fiction.[12] Despite the wealth of such material – available on microfilm in any university library – post-structuralist historicism has so far confined itself largely to reinterpretation of the traditional Renaissance canon. Its attempts to appear to be doing otherwise are not always convincing. 'I do not want to seem to privilege drama', writes Catherine Belsey in an essay on Renaissance tragedy;[13] 'I refuse to discriminate' between literary and non-literary materials, says Leonard Tennenhouse in the introduction to *Power on Display*, explaining that he has 'tried not to hierarchize symbolic practices in this way'.[14] Try though he may, this is exactly what both he and Belsey are doing – giving special prominence to drama and adducing a small number of non-dramatic texts for illustrative purposes. It was no doubt the frustration of seeing the promise to de-privilege literature so regularly broken by post-structuralist historicists who continue to write books about Shakespeare and other major authors that led Jean Howard, in a sympathetic critique of New Historicist practice, to call for a radical shift of emphasis. Noting that literature is merely one form of discursive practice that happens arbitrarily to have been privileged by the academic establishment, she puts the case for a criticism that is 'increasingly less literature-centered'.[15]

Whether or not there is any such thing as 'literature' is an issue that will no doubt continue to be debated by literary critics. Certainly the question of what constitutes its canon is unlikely ever to be resolved, though the latter debate is in itself no grounds for rejecting literature as a category. (The fact that no two people can agree exactly where to draw the line between the literary and the non-literary does not mean that they are one and the same thing; on the contrary, as John Searle point out, 'it is a condition of the adequacy of a precise theory of an indeterminate phenomenon that it should precisely characterize that phenomenon as indeterminate; and a distinction is no less a distinction for allowing for a family of related, marginal, diverging cases').[16]

Ultimately, our answer to the question of whether it is meaningful to talk about 'literature' as a special category of writing will probably depend on whether we incline to an atomist or an essentialist interpretation of reality. But that is a philosophical problem that lies beyond the scope of this book.[17] However, one thing is clear, namely, that there is little evidence to support the claim that there is a significant body of atomist theory in Renaissance England. It is true that by asking new questions about Renaissance culture, post-structuralist historicism has shown us that Elizabethan poetry, drama and even song is far more political than traditional academic criticism has generally allowed. But in replacing what Dollimore calls 'the grid of essentialist humanism' with a grid of atomist constructivism, the new criticism has painted a picture of Elizabethan culture that is no less distorted than Tillyard's.

Post-structuralist historicism insists on the folly of attempting 'falsely to unify history and social process in the name of the collective mind of the people'.[18] Why it should feel that it is necessary repeatedly to emphasize the dangers of such a model is something of a puzzle when scholars have been saying much the same thing for the last forty years. In 1950 Hiram Haydn complained that the trouble with the *Elizabethan World Picture* was that it left out everything that subverted or contradicted those Christian humanist principles which Tillyard took to be representative of the true spirit of the age. 'No one', he wrote, 'who approaches intellectual history (or any other kind) from an established doctrinaire point of view is ever going to give us the full picture.'[19] A few years later Helen Gardner similarly warned of the dangers of attempting to interpret Elizabethan literature in terms of a monolithic 'world picture':

The 'Elizabethan World Picture' tidily presented to us as a system of thought cannot tell us how much of that picture had truth and meaning for any Elizabethan. And even if we could discover a kind of highest common factor of contemporary beliefs and attitudes, it could not tell us what an individual believed, and certainly not what Shakespeare believed.[20]

Not only must you be wary of allowing your sense of period to harden into a 'fixed background', says Gardner, but you must constantly remind yourself that, when you reinterpret the literature of the past, it is in part your own age that you are describing. Post-structuralist historicism similarly emphasizes the importance of critical self-consciousness. Jean Howard writes: 'it seems to me that the historically-minded critic must increasingly be willing to acknowledge the non-objectivity of his or her own stance'.[21] Gardner would have agreed: 'the historical imagination', she writes, 'is itself historically conditioned'.[22] However, the fact that our view of the past is unavoidably coloured by our own prejudices does not invalidate the historical project. Howard argues that 'since objectivity is not in any pure form a possibility, let us acknowledge that fact and acknowledge as well that any move into history is an . . . attempt to reach from the present moment into the past'.[23] Again, Gardner would agree: 'That the answers we find are conditioned by our own circumstances does not destroy their value'.[24] This kind of historicism inevitably involved what Howard calls 'a revisioning of both the past and the present'.[25] Indeed, one of the chief reasons for studying history has always been the light it throws on the present. But as Samuel Johnson said, 'to judge rightly on the present we must oppose it to the past'.[26] If, instead of *opposing* past and present, you attempt to bring them into conformity, then any sense of historical perspective vanishes.

In place of Tillyard's homogeneous, conformist picture of Elizabethan intellectual life, Haydn evoked a period characterized above all by its contrariety; if there is a ruling principle in Elizabethan writing it is paradox: 'inconsistency runs through all their work'.[27] But vigorous as intellectual debate is in this period, its parameters are not identical with those of our own post-Nietzschean world.

Elizabethan theology, anthropology, psychology, historiography and social theory may all be sites of energetic debate, but those debates take place within an essentialist framework. Anchored in those same principles, Elizabethan poetics articulates a clear sense of literature as a distinct category with its own history, laws, objectives and taxonomy. It has an equally clear sense of genius, both individual and national. If historical scholarship, old or new, is going to engage in any meaningful dialogue with the past it has to begin with a recognition of these facts. In practice, this is what the best post-structuralist (and traditionalist) historicism has done. Despite repeated calls for an abandonment of the notion of 'literature', the most illuminating criticism of the past decade has a very clear sense of literature as a special category. One of the refreshing aspects of Stephen Greenblatt's work, for example, is his continuing and unrepentant interest in 'great art'.[28] Though his account of the circulation of what he calls 'social energy' – those cultural practices through which works of art apparently acquire their compelling force – may not match in clarity Harvey's account of the circulation of the blood, his analyses always manage to capture something of the irreducible complexity of great art. It is this, and not his excursions into theory, that make him worth reading. In a period like that of the late sixteenth and early seventeenth centuries, when established myths gradually cease to command unconditional assent and begin to be seen for the fictions they are,[29] the arts are unique in their ability to provide the cultural historian with insight into the intellectual tensions of the age. It is one reason, among many others, why the category 'art' is worth preserving. *Floreat Orpheus.*

Notes

PREFACE

1 Terence Hawkes, 'Bardbiz', review article, *LRB*, 22 February 1990, p. 13.
2 Heather Dubrow and Richard Strier point out that post-structuralist historicism 'is not primarily an archival movement; its triumphs are not discoveries of new documents but ... reinterpretations and reconfigurations of existing materials, of materials that the "old" historicism discovered' (Introduction to *The Historical Renaissance: New Essays in Tudor and Stuart Literature and Culture*, ed. Dubrow and Strier (Chicago and London: University of Chicago Press, 1988), p. 4).
3 John Drakakis, Introduction to *Alternative Shakespeares*, ed. Drakakis, Methuen New Accents (London: Methuen, 1985), pp. 24–5.
4 Kiernan Ryan, *Shakespeare*, Harvester New Readings (Hemel Hempstead: Harvester Wheatsheaf, 1989), p. 1.
5 Susan McClary writes: 'The ways in which one composes, performs, listens, or interprets are heavily influenced by the need either to establish order or resist it' ('The Blasphemy of Talking Politics during the Bach Year' in *Music and Society: the Politics of Composition, Performance and Reception*, ed. Richard Leppert and Susan McClary (Cambridge University Press, 1987), p. 18).

INTRODUCTION

1 Raymond Williams, 'Literature and Sociology' in *Problems in Materialism and Culture* (London: Verso, 1980), p. 24.
2 Coincidentally, it was a junior lecturer in Tillyard's own college who was the first to challenge the Master of Jesus. Where Tillyard found intellectual certainty and moral conviction, A. P. Rossiter saw ambivalence. To him the supposedly orthodox Elizabethan doctrine of order and degree seemed 'too rigid, too black-and-white, too doctrinaire and narrowly moral' ('Ambivalence: The Dialectic of the Histories', paper delivered at the Shakespeare Summer School, Stratford, 1951, first published in *Talking of Shakespeare*, ed. John Garrett (London: Hodder

& Stoughton, 1954), repr. in *Angel with Horns*, ed. Graham Storey (1961; repr. London: Longman, 1970), p. 43). Taking their cue from Rossiter, a number of Shakespeare critics in the 1960s and 1970s emphasized the dialectical nature of the plays. See Ernest William Talbert, *The Problem of Order: Elizabethan Political Commonplaces and an Example of Shakespeare's Art* (Chapel Hill: University of North Carolina Press, 1962); Norman Rabkin, *Shakespeare and the Problem of Meaning* (New York: Free Press, 1967); Bernard McElroy, *Shakespeare's Mature Tragedies* (Princeton University Press, 1973); Robert Grudin, *Mighty Opposites: Shakespeare and Renaissance Contrariety* (Berkeley and London: University of California Press, 1979). I am indebted to Tom McAlindon for pointing out to me A. P. Rossiter's influence on this line of criticism.

3 The Elizabethan world view had already been the subject of a number of scholarly studies before Tillyard published his own book. See in particular Ruth Leila Anderson, *Elizabethan Psychology and Shakespeare's Plays* (1927; repr. New York: Haskell House, 1964); Hardin Craig, *The Enchanted Glass: The Elizabethan Mind in Literature* (New York: Oxford University Press, 1936); James Emerson Phillips, *The State in Shakespeare's Greek and Roman Plays* (New York: Columbia University Press, 1940); Theodore Spencer, *Shakespeare and the Nature of Man* (Cambridge University Press, 1942).

Notable among the many books on this subject published in the 1950s and 1960s are Hiram Haydn, *The Counter-Renaissance* (New York: Grove, 1950); Marjorie Hope Nicolson, *The Breaking of the Circle: Studies in the Effect of the 'New Science' upon Seventeenth-Century Poetry* (Evanston, Ill.: Northwestern University Press, 1950); Herschel Baker, *The Wars of Truth: Studies in the Decay of Christian Humanism in the Earlier Seventeenth Century* (Cambridge, Mass.: Harvard University Press, 1952); Christopher Morris, *Political Thought in England: Tyndale to Hooker* (Oxford University Press, 1953); James Winny, *The Frame of Order: An Outline of Elizabethan Belief Taken from Treatises of the Late Sixteenth Century* (London: Allen & Unwin, 1957); John F. Danby, *Shakespeare's Doctrine of Nature: A Study of King Lear* (London: Faber, 1961); Ernest William Talbert, *The Problem of Order: Elizabethan Political Commonplaces and an Example of Shakespeare's Art* (Chapel Hill, NC: University of North Carolina Press, 1962); George W. Keeton, *Shakespeare's Legal and Political Background* (London: Pitman, 1967).

In the next decade the most outstanding contributions to the history of ideas in Renaissance England were S. K. Heninger, Jr, *Touches of Sweet Harmony: Pythagorean Cosmology and Renaissance Poetics* (San Marino: Huntington Library, 1974) and James Daly, 'Cosmic Harmony and Political Thinking in Early Stuart England', *TAPS*, 69 (1979), 1–40.

For a recent discussion of changing conceptions of order in this period see Stephen L. Collins, *From Divine Cosmos to Sovereign State: An Intellectual History of Consciousness and the Idea of Order in Renaissance England* (New York and Oxford: Oxford University Press, 1989). Collins rehearses a familiar view when he argues that 'traditionally order was founded upon the belief that rest was natural' (p. 28). However, as T. McAlindon points out in *English Renaissance Tragedy* (Houndmills and London: Macmillan, 1986), hierarchical order was only one aspect of the pre-modern cosmology that the Elizabethans inherited from the Middle Ages and the Greeks. At least as important was the notion of polarity. In the Heraclitean principle of *discordia concors* the Renaissance found an essentially dynamic conception of the universe that accommodated not only order but also strife (pp. 5–6). See also McAlindon, *Shakespeare's Tragic Cosmos* (Cambridge University Press, 1991), chap. 1.

4 Frederic Jameson, *The Political Unconscious: Narrative as a Socially Symbolic Act* (London: Methuen, 1981), pp. 53–4 and *passim*.

5 Roland Barthes, *Mythologies*, selected and trans. Annette Lavers (London: Cape, 1972), p. 143. Barthes is speaking here of myth in the sense of a body of popular lore that offers a falsely reductive version of reality. The great classical deities, most of whom had by the Renaissance assimilated other traditions and cults, are of course anything but simple or unitary. See Jean Seznec, *The Survival of the Pagan Gods: The Mythological Tradition and its Place in Renaissance Humanism and Art*, trans. Barbara F. Sessions (New York: Pantheon, 1953), pp. 179–83 and *passim*.

6 *Hero and Leander*, 1.304, *The Complete Works of Christopher Marlowe*, ed. Fredson Bowers, 2 vols., 2nd edn (Cambridge University Press, 1981), II, 453.

7 Marlowe does not give Herse's name, nor does he mention Minerva's cruel vengeance on Aglauros for her part in helping Mercury to win her sister. For his most likely source for the story (Musaeus does not include it in his poem) see Ovid, *Metamorphoses*, II.752–832.

8 On Mercury's thieving habits, his trickery, and his cunning see the Homeric *Hymn to Hermes*; see also Ovid, *Metamorphoses*, II.685ff; II.815ff. It is these qualities, as well as his love of song, that Shakespeare's Autolycus inherits from his father (*Wint.*, IV.iii.25). By contrast, an emblem in George Wither's *Collection of Emblemes, Ancient and Moderne* (1635) appeals to Mercury as a representative of responsible intelligence and diligent study (no. 9). On the paradoxical combination of silence and eloquence attributed to him in Florentine Neoplatonic mythography see Edgar Wind, *Pagan Mysteries in the Renaissance* (London: Faber, 1958), p. 20 n.3; see also ibid. pp. 106–7 and Douglas Brooks-Davies, *The Mercurian Monarch: Magical Politics from Spenser to Pope* (Manchester University Press, 1983), p. 2.

9 *Odes*, I.x.1–3.

10 See Kirsty Cochrane, 'Orpheus Applied: Some Instances of his Importance in the Humanist View of Language', *RES*, n.s. 19 (1968), 1–13.
The myth of the musician-king originates in the shepherd-kings and
singers of the ancient Near East such as Tammuz, Enkidu and David
(see Charles Segal, *Orpheus: The Myth of the Poet* (Baltimore and
London: John Hopkins University Press, 1989), p. 4). In the Middle
Ages both Orpheus and David are seen as a type of Christ, the 'king of
kings' (1 Tim. 6:15) who maintains the harmony of the universe (see
Eleanor Irwin, 'The Songs of Orpheus and the New Song of Christ' in
John Warden, ed., *Orpheus: The Metamorphosis of a Myth* (University of
Toronto Press, 1982), pp. 51–62). See also Emile Mâle, *The Gothic
Image: Religious Art in France of the Thirteenth Century*, 3rd edn, trans. Dora
Nussey (1913; repr. New York: Harper & Row, 1972), p. 157; Frances
Yates, *The French Academies of the Sixteenth Century* (London: Warburg
Institute, 1947), pp. 38, 64; D. P. Walker, 'Orpheus the Theologian
and Renaissance Platonists', *JWCI*, 16 (1953), 101; John Block Fried-
man, *Orpheus in the Middle Ages* (Cambridge, Mass.: Harvard University
Press, 1970), pp. 147–55.
   On the transmission of allegorized versions of the Orpheus myth from
antiquity through the Middle Ages to the Renaissance see Elizabeth A.
Newby, *A Portrait of the Artist: The Legends of Orpheus and their Use in
Medieval and Renaissance Aesthetics* (New York: Garland, 1987),
pp. 73–107. However, Newby seems unaware of Orpheus' central role
in Elizabethan poetics.

11 Thomas Wilson, *The Arte of Rhetorique* (1560) ed. G. H. Mair (Oxford:
Clarendon Press, 1909), Preface, Sig. Avii.

12 *The Testament of Cresseid*, II.240–3, *The Poems of Robert Henryson*, ed.
Denton Fox (Oxford: Clarendon Press, 1981), pp. 118–19.

13 *Timber or Discoveries*, *Ben Jonson*, ed. C. H. Herford and Percy and
Evelyn Simpson, 11 vols. (Oxford: Clarendon Press, 1925–52), VIII
(1947), 620–1.

14 Wilson, *The Arte of Rhetorique*, Preface, Sig. Avii.

15 The nearest Gramsci gets to defining hegemony is probably the following passage from *The Prison Notebooks* where he writes of 'The "spontaneous" consent given by the great masses of the population to the
general direction imposed on social life by the dominant fundamental
group; this consent is "historically" caused by the prestige (and con-
sequent confidence) which the dominant group enjoys because of its
position and function in the world of production' (*Selections from the
Prison Notebooks*, ed. and trans. Quintin Hoare and Geoffrey Nowell
Smith (London: Lawrence and Wishart, 1971), p. 12).

16 Wilson, *The Arte of Rhetorique*, dedicatory epistle, Sig. Aii^v.

17 See Brooks-Davies, *The Mercurian Monarch*, p. 2; see also Wind, *Pagan
Mysteries*, p. 91n2.

18 Pierre de La Primaudaye, *The French Academie* (London, 1586), p. 744.

New editions of *The French Academie* were issued in 1589, 1594, 1602, 1611, and 1618. It enjoyed wide popularity as a source book for English poets and moralists in the late sixteenth and early seventeenth centuries. See Louis I. Bredvold, 'The Sources Used by Davies in *Nosce Teipsum*', *PMLA*, 38 (1923), 745–69; Ruth L. Anderson, 'A French Source for John Davies of Hereford's System of Psychology', *PQ*, 6 (1927), 57–66; D. T. Starnes, '*The French Academie* and *Wits Commonwealth*', *PQ*, 13 (1934), 211–20.

19 See Leo Spitzer, 'Classical and Christian Ideas of World Harmony; Prolegomenon to an Interpretation of the Word "Stimmung"', *Traditio*, 2 (1944), 409–69; 3 (1945), 307–64; James Hutton, 'Some English Poems in Praise of Music', *EngM*, 2 (1951), 1–63; Gretchen Ludke Finney, *Musical Backgrounds for English Literature: 1580–1650* (New Brunswick: Rutgers University Press, 1961); John Hollander, *The Untuning of the Sky: Ideas of Music in English Poetry, 1500–1700* (1961; repr. New York: Norton, 1970); Heninger, *Touches of Sweet Harmony*; Daly, 'Cosmic Harmony and Political Thinking in Early Stuart England', 1–40.

20 La Primaudaye, *The French Academie*, p. 743.

21 Ibid., p. 19.

22 John Case, *The Praise of Mvsique* (Oxford, 1586), p. 2.

23 Stephen Gosson, *Plays confuted in fiue actions* (London, 1582), Sig. G7^v.

24 Sydney Anglo, *Spectacle, Pageantry, and Early Tudor Policy* (Oxford: Clarendon Press, 1969), pp. 261–5.

25 *Euphues Glass for Europe*, *The Complete Works of John Lyly*, ed. R. Warwick Bond, 3 vols. (Oxford: Clarendon Press, 1902), II, 205.

26 Peter McClure and Robin Headlam Wells, 'Elizabeth I as a Second Virgin Mary', *RS*, 4 (1990), 38–70. Although Henry VIII is naturally portrayed in government propaganda as defender of the true imperial religion against Pope-Antichrist (see Frances Yates, 'Queen Elizabeth as Astraea', *JWCI*, 10 (1947), 42–3), it is not until the end of the century that monarchists begin seriously to develop the idea of an elect nation chosen by God to fulfil a unique apocalyptic purpose. According to William Haller (*Foxe's Book of Martyrs and the Elect Nation* (London: Cape, 1963)) it was Foxe's *Actes and Monuments* that was responsible for disseminating the idea of England as an elect nation. Although Foxe undoubtedly saw Elizabeth as playing a crucial role in liberating the true church in England, identifying her in the 1563 edition of the *Actes and Monuments* with Constantine, there is little evidence to support Haller's general thesis. Paul Christianson (*Reformers and Babylon: English Apocalyptic Visions from the Reformation to the Eve of the Civil War* (Toronto University Press, 1978)) argues that it was later writers like Thomas Brightman who transformed Foxe's international outlook into the more narrowly nationalistic concept of an elect nation (p. 41). See also Richard Bauckham, *Tudor Apocalypse: Sixteenth-Century Apocalypticism*,

Millenarianism and the English Reformation (Appleford: Sutton Courtenay Press, 1978), p. 87; Katherine R. Firth, *The Apocalyptic Tradition in Reformation Britain, 1530–1645* (Oxford University Press, 1979), p. 106; G. J. R. Parry, *A Protestant Vision: William Harrison and the Reformation of Elizabethan England* (Cambridge University Press, 1987), pp. 73, 236.

27 See Elkin Calhoun Wilson, *England's Eliza* (Cambridge, Mass.: Harvard University Press, 1939); Yates, 'Queen Elizabeth as Astraea'; Roy Strong, *The Cult of Elizabeth: Elizabethan Portraiture and Pageantry* (London: Thames & Hudson, 1977); Robin Headlam Wells, *Spenser's 'Faerie Queene' and the Cult of Elizabeth* (London: Croom Helm, 1983); McClure and Headlam Wells, 'Elizabeth I'.

28 Greenblatt, *Renaissance Self-Fashioning: from More to Shakespeare* (University of Chicago Press, 1980), p. 174.

29 See F. J. Levy, *Tudor Historical Thought* (San Marino: Huntington Library, 1968), pp. 237–85.

30 See Bauckham, *Tudor Apocalypse*; Christianson, *Reformers and Babylon*; Parry, *A Protestant Vision*; Firth, *The Apocalyptic Tradition in Reformation Britain*; Achsah Guibbory, *The Map of Time: Seventeenth-Century English Literature and Ideas of Pattern in History* (Urbana and Chicago: University of Illinois Press, 1986).

31 *Renaissance Self-Fashioning*, p. 179.

32 See Friedman, *Orpheus in the Middle Ages* and Irwin, 'The Songs of Orpheus and the New Song of Christ'.

33 There has been much dispute on the question of how far literature is capable of distancing itself from the ideology in which it is imbricated. Inevitably, the answer will vary according to the terms in which it is put. If you define ideology as coextensive with consciousness itself, then obviously it is no more possible for the poet or the critic to escape its jurisdiction than it is for any other sentient being (though this does not prevent philosophers like Althusser and Foucault, who subscribe to a panoptic theory of ideology, from deconstructing its strategems). However, if you are prepared to settle for something less commodious than a fully furnished metaphysics of power – in an empirical world we have no other option – then there is no reason why literature should not, in principle, be capable of exposing to critical scrutiny the myths that form the basis of our sense of political reality.

The two classic texts on this question are Pierre Macherey, 'Lenin, Critic of Tolstoy' (1964) in *A Theory of Literary Production*, trans. Geoffrey Wall (Routledge: London, 1978), pp. 105–35, and Louis Althusser, 'A Letter on Art' in *Lenin and Philosophy and Other Essays*, trans. Ben Brewster (London: NLB, 1971), pp. 203–4. Macherey's claim – endorsed by Althusser – that 'literature establishes myth and illusion as visible objects' (p. 133) was to prove highly influential. However, in an essay entitled 'On Literature as an Ideological Form: Some Marxist Propositions', *OLR*, 3 (1978), 4–12, Macherey, together with Etienne Balibar, rejects the concept 'literature' as a nineteenth-century bourgeois invention, and with it any possibility of establishing a critical vantage point from which to view ideology.

The compromise position adopted by some feminist scholars on the question of how far it is possible to resist ideology has much to recommend it. In *Feminist Practice and Post-Structuralist Theory* (Oxford: Blackwell, 1987) Chris Weedon echoes Goffman's ideas of role-theory when she argues that, although discursively produced, the individual is still able to 'reflect upon the discursive relations which constitute her and the society in which she lives, and able to choose from the options available' (p. 125).

34 Graham Holderness reaches a similar conclusion in *Shakespeare's History* (Dublin: Gill and Macmillan, 1985), pp. 136ff.

35 In *The Sense of an Ending: Studies in the Theory of Fiction* (New York; Oxford University Press, 1967), Frank Kermode writes: 'Myths are the agents of stability, fictions the agents of change. Myths call for absolute, fictions for conditional assent' (p. 39).

36 Peter L. Berger, *Invitation to Sociology* (1963; repr. Harmondsworth: Penguin, 1975), p. 140.

37 Marx writes, '*just as* society itself produces *man* as *man*, so it is *produced* by him' (*Early Writings*, trans. Rodney Livingstone and Gregor Benton (1974; repr. Harmondsworth: Penguin, 1975), p. 34), or again, 'If man is formed by circumstances, these circumstances must be humanly formed' (*Selected Writings in Sociology and Social Philosophy*, ed. T. B. Bottomore and Maximilien Rubel, trans. Bottomore (London: C. A. Watts, 1956), p. 243).

38 The foundations of modern role theory were laid by George H. Mead in *Mind, Self, and Society*, ed. Charles W. Morris (1934; repr. University of Chicago Press, 1970). See also Hans H. Gerth and C. Wright Mills, *Character and Social Structure* (New York: Harcourt, Brace, 1953), Erving Goffman, *The Presentation of Self in Everyday Life* (Garden City, NY: Doubleday Anchor, 1959); Berger, *Invitation to Sociology*; Clifford Geertz, *The Interpretation of Cultures* (New York: Basic Books, 1973).

Traditional literary criticism has been widely accused by post-structuralists of mindless subscription to a rigidly essentialist view of man. But as long ago as 1942 C. S. Lewis wrote, 'It is better to study the changes in which the Human Heart largely consists than to amuse yourself with fictions about its immutability. For the truth is that when you have stripped off what the human heart actually was in this or that culture, you are left with a miserable abstraction totally unlike the life really lived by any human being' (*A Preface to Paradise Lost* (1942; repr. Oxford University Press, 1960), p. 64).

39 A seminal document in the development of modern Marxist thought is Althusser's *For Marx* (1965), trans. Ben Brewster (London: Allen Lane, 1969). Althusser argues that in 1845 Marx made a radical break with

his early theoretical position and came to see essentialist humanism for what it was, namely, a fiction promulgated by ideology: everything in his mature philosophy, says Althusser, depends on an understanding of the ideological nature of humanism (pp. 227–31). However, as many writers have pointed out, Marx's essentialism is not just a youthful aberration, but the very foundation of his mature philosophy of history. In *Essentialism in the Thought of Karl Marx* (London: Duckworth, 1985) Scott Meikle argues that the essentialist categories of law, form, and necessity are 'the powerhouse of his explanatory theories' (p. viii). See also Leslie Stevenson, *Seven Theories of Human Nature* (Oxford: Clarendon Press, 1974), pp. 4–5; Lucien Sève, *Man in Marxist Theory and the Psychology of Personality*, trans. John McGreal (Hassocks: Harvester, 1978), pp. 63–129; Roger Trigg, *Ideas of Human Nature: An Historical Introduction* (Oxford: Blackwell, 1988), pp. 101–16.

40 Michel Foucault, 'The Subject and Power', *CI*, 8 (1982), 792–3.

41 Jonathan Dollimore, *Radical Tragedy: Religion, Ideology and Power in the Drama of Shakespeare and his Contemporaries* (1984; repr. Brighton: Harvester, 1986), p. 169.

42 Ernst Cassirer, *The Individual and the Cosmos in Renaissance Philosophy*, trans. Mario Domandi (1927; repr. Oxford: Blackwell, 1963), p. 119.

43 Pico della Mirandola, *Oration on the Dignity of Man*, trans. Elizabeth Livermore in *The Renaissance Philosophy of Man*, ed. Ernst Cassirer, Paul Oskar Kristeller, and John Herman Randall, Jr (University of Chicago Press, 1948), p. 225, quoted by Dollimore, *Radical Tragedy*, p. 149.

44 The Middle Ages was well aware of this fallacy. St Augustine warns against those 'vain babblers' who 'because they have observed that there are two wills in the act of deliberating, affirm thereupon, that there are two kinds of natures ... the truth [is] ... that in the acts of one man's deliberation there is one soul distracted between two contrary wills' (*Confessions*, VIII.x, trans. William Watts (1631), Loeb Classical Library, 2 vols. (London: Heinemann, 1922–5), I (1922), 449–51).

45 Castiglione argues that, in adapting one's behaviour for political purposes 'it is meete eche man know him selfe, and his owne disposition, and apply him selfe thereto, and consider what thinges are meete for him to follow, and what are not' (*The Book of the Courtier*, trans. Sir Thomas Hoby (London: Dent, 1928), p. 110). Tom McAlindon points out to me that Castiglione is here following his Roman model. In that favourite handbook of humanist counsel, the *De Officiis*, Cicero emphasizes that, in promoting the public good, we 'must so act as not to oppose the universal laws of human nature, but while safeguarding those, to follow the bent of our own particular nature' (I.xxxi.110, trans. Walter Miller, Loeb Classical Library (London: Heinemann, 1913), p. 113).

46 Sir Thomas More, *Utopia*, trans. Raphe Robinson (1910; repr. London: Dent, 1918), p. 114.

47 Francis Bacon, *The Essayes or Counsels, Civill and Morall*, facsimile edn (Menston: Scolar Press, 1971), pp. 233, 227.

48 John Donne, *Biathanatos*, ed. Ernest W. Sullivan II (London and Toronto: Associated University Presses, 1984), p. 40.

49 Pierre Charron, *Of Wisdome* (1601), trans. Samson Lennard (London, 1606), p. 223.

50 Ibid.

51 John Dowland, *Shall I sue*, *The Second Booke of Songs* (London, 1600), Sig.Li^v.

52 John Gower, *Confessio Amantis*, Prol., 1053ff; Luis de Milan, *El Maestro*, frontispiece; Edmund Spenser, *The Faerie Queene*, iv.ii.1–2; John Dowland, *First Booke of Songes or Ayres*, dedicatory epistle. In the Middle Ages there is a long tradition among professional poets and singers of referring to themselves as another Orpheus (see Friedman, *Orpheus in the Middle Ages*, p. 158).

53 George Puttenham, *The Arte of English Poesie*, ed. Gladys Doidge Willcock and Alice Walker (Cambridge University Press, 1936), p. 6.

54 David Kalstone, *Sidney's Poetry: Contexts and Interpretations* (Cambridge, Mass.: Harvard University Press, 1965); Donald L. Guss, *John Donne, Petrarchist: Italianate Conceits and Love Theory in 'The Songs and Sonets'* (Detroit: Wayne State University Press, 1966). Both Kalstone (p. viii) and Guss (p. 14) acknowledge a debt to Tuve.

55 Antony Easthope, *Poetry as Discourse*, Methuen New Accents (London: Methuen, 1983), p. 95. There seems to be a widely held assumption among post-structuralists that, in Gary Waller's words, 'most modern criticism' takes it for granted that a literary text is 'a unified, organic creation which "reflects" or "expresses" its author's views or vision, or the dominant philosophical assumptions of its age' (*English Poetry in the Sixteenth Century* (London: Longman, 1986), p. 5). Waller's assumptions about 'modern criticism' of the Renaissance lyric are shared by Thomas Docherty, who also claims – though again without citing particular examples – that modern readers are still being taught to look for 'crude and often reductionist biographical correspondences between poems and persons or events' (*John Donne, Undone* (London and New York: Methuen, 1986), p. 1). Although it is true that the biographical-realist approach to Donne's lyrics still survives in the occasional critical throwback, such as William Zunder's *John Donne: Literature and Culture in the Elizabethan and Jacobean Periods* (Brighton: Harvester, 1982), it is as misleading to claim that 'contemporary [i.e. modern] criticism of Donne contrives to ignore the historical culture which informed his writings' (Docherty, p. 1) as it is to suggest that modern Shakespeare criticism would have continued doggedly to follow in Tillyard's footsteps had post-structuralist historicism not come along and woken it from its dogmatic slumbers.

56 Easthope, 'Poetry and the Politics of Reading' in *Re-Reading English*, ed.

Peter Widdowson, Methuen New Accents (London: Methuen, 1982), p. 142.

57 Rosemond Tuve, *Elizabethan and Metaphysical Imagery: Renaissance Poetics and Twentieth-Century Critics* (University of Chicago Press, 1947), p. 49.

58 Easthope, *Poetry as Discourse*, pp. 107–8.

59 Ibid., p. 67; cf. Easthope, 'Poetry and the Politics of Reading', pp. 136–49; *Poetry and Phantasy* (Cambridge University Press, 1989), p. 56.

60 *The Arte of English Poesie*, p. 302.

61 *Troilus and Criseyde*, v.1786–98, *The Works of Geoffrey Chaucer*, ed. F. N. Robinson, 2nd edn (London: Oxford University Press, 1957), p. 479.

62 Michel Foucault, *The Order of Things: An Archaeology of the Human Sciences*, English trans. (1970; repr. London: Tavistock, 1977), pp. 299–300. Foucault claims that the word 'literature' is 'of recent [i.e. nineteenth century] date' (p. 300). It was of course in use as early as the fourteenth century (see *OED*).

63 See, for example, Chaucer, *The Franklin's Prologue*, 8ff; Persius, Prologue to the *Satires*; Ovid, *Metamorphoses*, x.19–20. The classic example of the supremely gifted orator who claims to be unfamiliar with the art of rhetoric is of course Plato's Socrates (*The Apology of Socrates*, 1ff). There is extensive discussion in the classical rhetorics of techniques for disarming an audience by humorous means. See Aristotle, *Rhetoric*, i.iv.6–8; Cicero, *De Oratore*, ii.liv.217ff; [Cicero], *Rhetorica ad Herennium*, i.vi.9–10. Among the various devices recommended in the *Ad Herennium* for capturing an audience's attention through wit is the 'promise to speak otherwise than as we do; we shall briefly explain what the other speakers do and what we intend to do' (*Ad C. Herennium*, trans. Harry Caplan, Loeb Classical Library (London: Heinemann, 1954), i.vi.10, p. 21). Castiglione's Count Ludovico recalls 'some most excellent Orators, which among other their cares, enforced themselves to make everie man believe, that they had no sight in letters, and dissembling their cunning, made semblant their Orations to be made verie simply, and rather as nature and truth ledde them, than studie and arte' (*The Courtier*, p. 46).

64 *On the Life of Man, The Poems of Sir Walter Ralegh*, ed. Agnes M. C. Latham (London: Constable, 1929), p. 48.

I SPENSER AND THE POLITICS OF MUSIC

1 *Amoretti*, no. 29. On the *Amoretti* as a concealed tribute to Queen Elizabeth see Robin Headlam Wells, 'Poetic Decorum in Spenser's *Amoretti*', *CE*, 25 (1984), 9–21.

2 John Lyly, 'Euphues' Glass for Europe', *The Complete Works of John Lyly*, ed. R. Warwick Bond, 3 vols. (Oxford: Clarendon Press, 1902), ii, 205.

3 *Spenser*, Harvester New Readings (London: Harvester Wheatsheaf, 1989), p. 2.

4 Pierre de La Primaudaye, *The French Academie* (London, 1586), p. 743 (see Introduction, pp. 6–7).

5 Guillaume de la Perriere, *The Mirrour of Policie* (London, 1599), Sig. ci^v.

6 Sir Walter Ralegh, *The Historie of the World* (London, 1614), p. 382.

7 C. S. Lewis, *The Allegory of Love* (London: Oxford University Press, 1936), p. 326.

8 John Hollander, *The Untuning of the Sky: Ideas of Music in English Poetry, 1500–1700* (1961; repr. New York: Norton, 1970), p. 112. Strictly speaking, it is not true to say that there is no music in the Garden of Adonis, as I shall show below. Hollander later expanded his claim that the key to the Bower of Bliss' evil influence lay in its 'blending of natural and contrived musical sounds' (*Untuning*, p. 113). In 'Spenser and the Mingled Measure' (*ELR*, 1 (1971), 226–38) he writes: 'Conflated are: conventional pastoral antiphony and actual Renaissance instrumental consort as well as indoor and outdoor music, which in sixteenth-century practice, were two different modalities associated with different sorts of instrumentation and sometimes different concert pitches'. This 'jumbling of musical conditions', he argues, 'is morally unwholesome' (235, 230). This may well be true. However, its limitation as a comment on the Bower of Bliss is that it reduces allegory of some complexity to the level of satire on contemporary concert performance. My own interest is in the allegory – tropological, political and anagogical – rather than the topical satire.

9 A. Bartlett Giamatti, *The Earthly Paradise and the Renaissance Epic* (Princeton University Press, 1966), pp. 284, 256.

10 Millar MacLure, 'Nature and Art in *The Faerie Queene*', *ELH*, 28 (1961), 9.

11 R. Nevo, 'Spenser's "Bower of Bliss" and a Key Metaphor from Renaissance Poetic', in *Studies in Western Literature*, 10, ed. Daniel A. Fineman (Jerusalem: Hebrew University, 1962), p. 26.

12 N. S. Brooke, 'C. S. Lewis and Spenser: Nature, Art and the Bower of Bliss', *CJ*, 2 (1949), 434.

13 *Wilson's Arte of Rhetorique* (1560), ed. G. H. Mair (Oxford: Clarendon, 1909), Sig. Avii.

14 Nevo, 'Spenser's "Bower of Bliss"', p. 22.

15 Robert M. Durling, 'The Bower of Bliss and Armida's Palace', *CL*, 6 (1954), 335–47.

16 *Godfrey of Bulloigne: A Critical Edition of Edward Fairfax's Translation of Tasso's 'Gerusalemme Liberata'*, ed. Kathleen M. Lea and T. M. Gang (Oxford: Clarendon Press, 1981), pp. 450–1.

17 'A New yeeres Gift', *The Poetical Works*, ed. Smith and de Selincourt, p. 628.

18 *Roman de la Rose*, trans. Chaucer, *The Complete Works*, ed. F. N. Robinson, 2nd edn (London: Oxford University Press, 1957), p. 571.

19 Isidore of Seville, *Etymologiarum*, ed. W. M. Lindsay, 2 vols. (Oxford: Clarendon Press, 1911), xi.iii.30, cited by Beryl Rowland, *Birds with Human Souls: A Guide to Bird Symbolism* (Knoxville: University of Tennessee Press, 1978), p. 156.

20 Brunetto Latini, *Li Livres dou Tresor*, ed. Francis J. Carmody (Berkeley: University of California Press, 1948), pp. 131–2.

21 *Tutte le opere di Giovanni Boccaccio*, ed. Vittore Branca, 12 projected vols. (Milan: Mondadori, 1964–   ), ii, ed. Alberto Limentani (1964), 330–1.

22 *Parlement of Foules, Complete Works*, ed. Robinson, p. 312.

23 Ernst Robert Curtius, *European Literature and the Latin Middle ages*, trans. Willard R. Trask (London: Routledge & Kegan Paul, 1953), pp. 195–200; Giamatti, *The Earthly Paradise*, pp. 33ff.

24 Quotations from the Bible are from *The Geneva Bible*, facsimile of the 1560 edn, with an introduction by Lloyd E. Berry (Madison, Wis.: University of Wisconsin Press, 1969).

25 'Ut decursi vel adoriendi nocturni juxta ac diurni temporis laudes suo referant Creatori' (St Ambrose, *Hexaemeron*, v.xii.36, *Patrologia*, series latina, ed. J.-P. Migne (Paris, 1844ff), 14, 237). On birds and natural harmony in medieval iconography see D. W. Robertson, 'The Doctrine of Charity in Medieval Literary Gardens', *Spec*, 26 (1951), 31ff; Leo Spitzer, 'Classical and Christian Ideas of World Harmony: Prolegomena to an Interpretation of the Word "Stimmung"', *Traditio*, 2 (1944), 455–8.

26
        Unas tenien la quinta, e las otras doblavan,
        Otras tenien al punto, errar no las dexavan,
        Al posar, al mover todas se esperavan,
        Aves torpes nin roncas hi non acostavan.
(Gonzalo de Berceo, *Milagros de Nuestra Senora*, ed. A. G. Solalinde (Madrid: Espasa-Calpe, 1958), p. 3)

27 *The Harmony of Birds, Two Early Renaissance Bird Poems*, ed. Malcolm Andrew (London: Renaissance English Text Society, 1984), p. 45.

28 *The Poems of Sir Philip Sidney*, ed. William A. Ringler (Oxford: Clarendon Press, 1962), p. 219.

29 *Liber xii quaest.ii, Patrologia*, series latina, 172, 1179, quoted by Donald W. Rowe, *O Love O Charite! Contraries harmonized in Chaucer's 'Troilus'* (Carbondale: Southern Illinois University Press, 1976), p. 37.

30 *Donne's Sermons: Selected Passages*, ed. Logan Pearsall Smith (Oxford: Clarendon Press, 1920), p. 162.

31 George Wither, *A Preparation to the Psalter* (1619) (London, 1884), p. 12.

32 *The Minor Poems of John Lydgate*, ed. Henry Noble MacCracken, 2 vols. (London: EETS, 1911; 1934), ii, 410–18; i, 221–34.

33 Such arguments are summarized by Arlene N. Okerlund, 'Spenser's Wanton Maidens: Reader Psychology and the Bower of Bliss', *PMLA*, 88 (1973), 62–8. Okerlund's own response – 'the reader discovers

himself in an embarrassing confrontation with his innate and basic concupiscence' (p. 68) – is challenged by Harriett Hawkins on the grounds of reductive simplification ('Spenser's Wanton Maidens', *PMLA*, 88 (1973), 1185–7).

34 Alain de Lille, *The Plaint of Nature*, trans. James J. Sheridan (Toronto: Pontifical Institute of Medieval Studies, 1980), p. 119.

35 The complex genealogy of Genius is too extensive to summarize here. For Spenser's most likely sources for this figure see E. C. Knowlton, 'The Genii of Spenser', *SP*, 25 (1928), 439–56. See also D. T. Starnes, 'The Figure Genius in the Renaissance', *StudR*, 11 (1964), 234–44. On Alain's Genius see H. D. Brumble, 'The Role of Genius in the "De planctu Naturae" of Alanus de Insulis', *CM*, 31 (1970), 306–23.

36 Greenblatt, 'To Fashion a Gentleman: Spenser and the Destruction of the Bower of Bliss', *Renaissance Self-Fashioning: from More to Shakespeare* (University of Chicago Press, 1980), pp. 157–92.

37 Friedrich Nietzsche, *Twilight of the Idols*, trans. R. J. Hollingdale (1968; repr. Harmondsworth: Penguin, 1990), pp. 53–4.

38 Greenblatt, 'To Fashion a Gentleman', p. 177; cf. Louis Adrian Montrose, 'The Elizabethan Subject and the Spenserian Text', in *Literary Theory/Renaissance Texts*, ed. Patricia Parker and David Quint (Baltimore: Johns Hopkins University Press, 1986), pp. 303–40: 'What is being fashioned [in Guyon's violent destruction of the Bower] is not merely a civilized self, but a male subject, whose self-defining violence is enacted against an objectified other who is specifically female' (p. 329). See also Alan Sinfield, *Faultlines: Cultural Materialism and the Politics of Dissident Reading* (Oxford: Clarendon Press, 1992), who argues that the same incident shows Spenser's 'anxiety that the place of pagan ... and courtly culture, is not altogether settled' (pp. 196–7).

39 Greenblatt, 'To Fashion a Gentleman', p. 179.

40 Samuel Johnson, *The History of Rasselas, Prince of Abyssinia*, ed. Philip Henderson (1930; repr. London: Dent, 1961), p. 22.

41 See Introduction, n. 49.

42 A. C. Hamilton, '"Like race to Runne": The Parallel Structure of *The Faerie Queene*, Books I and II', *PMLA*, 73 (1958), 327–34.

43 In Thomas Bentley's *The monument of matrones* God says to Elizabeth: 'Thou art my Daughter in deede, this daie have I begotten thee, and espoused thee to thy king CHRIST, my Sonne' (*The monument of matrones* (London, 1582), p. 307).

44 Camden reports that when in 1559 parliament urged the young queen to marry she replied: 'yea, to satisfy you, I have already joyned my selfe in marriage to an husband, namely, the Kingdome of England' (*Annals*, 3rd edn, trans. R. Norton (London, 1635), p. 16).

45 *Variorum Spenser*, ed. Edwin Greenlaw, Charles Grosvenor Osgood, Frederick Morgan Padelford and Ray Heffner, 10 vols. (Baltimore: Johns Hopkins University Press, 1932–49), Book I, 310.

46 See *The Anchor Bible*, Revelation, trans. and ed. J. Massyngberde Ford (New York: Doubleday, 1975), p. 310, n. 7.

47 Richard Bauckham, *Tudor Apocalypse: Sixteenth-Century Apocalypticism, Millenarianism and the English Reformation* (Appleford: Sutton Courtnay, 1978), p. 101. See also Josephine Waters Bennett, *The Evolution of "The Faerie Queene"* (1942; repr. New York, 1960), pp. 110–11; Paul Christianson, *Reformers and Babylon: English Apocalyptic Visions from the Reformation to the End of the Civil War* (University of Toronto Press, 1978), *passim*; Katharine R. Firth, *The Apocalyptic Tradition in Reformation Britain 1530–1645* (Oxford University Press, 1979), *passim*.; Bernard Capp, 'The Political Dimension of Apocalyptic Thought' in *The Apocalypse in English Renaissance Thought and Literature*, ed. C. A. Patrides and Joseph Wittreich (Manchester University Press, 1984), pp. 93–124.

48 Henry Bullinger, *A Hundred Sermons upon the Apocalipse* (1561), 2nd edn (London, 1573), fol. 229ᵛ. It was Bullinger's commentary that provided the basis for the Geneva Bible's marginal annotation of St John (see F. F. Bruce, *The English Bible* (London: Lutterworth, 1961), p. 90). In this way Bullinger's apocalyptic message was transmitted to a whole generation of Elizabethan Bible-readers.

49 See Walter Lowrie, *Art in the Early Church* (New York: Pantheon Books, 1947), pl. 23b, where sirens on a fourth-century sarcophagus carving are represented as teachers, wearing the philosopher's mantle and scroll, leading the Christian astray with heretical doctrines.

50 William Pierce, *An Historical Introduction to the Marprelate Tracts* (London: Constable, 1908), viii, quoted by Christianson, *Reformers and Babylon*, p. 45. Christianson adds: 'A growing body of recent studies has confirmed Pierce's insight. One can no longer claim that an apocalyptic interpretation of the reformation was confined to "puritans" or "extremists" – unless, that is, one wants to render these terms meaningless' (pp. 45–6).

51 Capp, 'The Political Dimension of Apocalyptic Thought', pp. 93–124.

52 George Gifford, *Sermons upon the Whole Booke of the Revelation* (London, 1596), p. 346.

53 Ibid., p. 348.

54 Arthur Dent, *The ruine of Rome: or an Exposition upon the whole Revelation* (London, 1603), p. 240.

55 *Davison's Poetical Rhapsody* (1602), ed. A. H. Bullen, 2 vols. (London: Bell, 1890–1), II (1891), 98.

56 Ralegh, *Historie of the World*, p. 25.

57 Christianson, *Reformers and Babylon*, pp. 9, 21. Bale's doctrine of the two churches – the church of God and the church of Antichrist – has its origins in St Augustine's doctrine of the two cities, which in turn is based on the symbolic cities of Revelation (see Bauckham, *Tudor Apocalypse*, pp. 55–6).

58 Babylon is a symbol of political corruption in *The Spanish Tragedy*, *The*

Malcontent, Antonio's Revenge, The Maid's Tragedy and *The Revenger's Tragedy* (see T. McAlindon, *English Renaissance Tragedy* (London: Macmillan, 1986), p. 245, n. 101). On Langland's use of the symbolic antithesis between Babylon and Jerusalem see D. W. Robertson and Bernard F. Huppé, *'Piers Plowman' and Scriptural Tradition* (Princeton University Press, 1951), pp. 14–15, 17. For discussion of parallels between *Piers Plowman* and *The Faerie Queene* see A. C. Hamilton, 'Spenser and Langland', *SP*, 55 (1958), 533–48 and 'The Visions of *Piers Plowman* and *The Faerie Queene*' in *English Institute Essays* (New York: Columbia University Press, 1961), 1–34. Hamilton does not discuss the Babylon/Jerusalem antithesis.

2 FALSTAFF, PRINCE HAL AND THE NEW SONG

1 J. Dover Wilson, *The Fortunes of Falstaff* (1943; repr. Cambridge University Press, 1953), pp. 17–25. Though Wilson was not the first to notice the underlying morality-play structure of *Henry IV*, his has arguably been the most influential discussion of this aspect of the plays. For a conspectus of scholarly responses to and refinements of his thesis see J. Paul McRoberts, *Shakespeare and the Medieval Tradition: An Annotated Bibliography* (New York and London: Garland, 1985), pp. 134–43.

2 Dover Wilson, *Fortunes of Falstaff*, p. 22. See also E. M. W. Tillyard, *Shakespeare's History Plays* (1944: repr. Harmondsworth: Penguin, 1964), p. 291; M. M. Reese, *The Cease of Majesty: A Study of Shakespeare's History Plays* (London: Arnold, 1961), p. 304.

3 Justus Lipsius, *Six Bookes of Politickes or Civil Doctrine*, trans. William Jones (London, 1594), p. 114; cf. Niccolo Machiavelli, *The Prince*, trans. Edward Dacres (1640), Tudor Translations, 39 (London: David Nutt, 1905), pp. 321–3.

4 See John Danby, *Shakespeare's Doctrine of Nature: A Study of King Lear*, (London: Faber, 1961), pp. 91–100; cf. Stephen Greenblatt, 'Invisible Bullets: Renaissance Authority and Its Subversion, *Henry IV* and *Henry V*', in *Political Shakespeare: New Essays in Cultural Materialism*, ed. Jonathan Dollimore and Alan Sinfield (Manchester University Press, 1985), p. 20.

5 On the popularity of the prodigal son paradigm in Elizabethan homiletic fiction see J. Dover Wilson, 'Euphues and the Prodigal Son', *Lib*, 10 (1909), 337–61. See also Richard Helgerson, *The Elizabethan Prodigals* (Berkeley and London: University of California Press, 1976).

6 C. L. Barber, *Shakespeare's Festive Comedy* (Princeton University Press, 1959), p. 196.

7 Dover Wilson, *Fortunes of Falstaff*, p. 227.

8 Ibid., p. 127.

9 Ibid., pp. 127–8.

10 For a survey of modern criticism of Shakespeare's history plays from

1944 to 1984 see Robin Headlam Wells, 'The Fortunes of Tillyard: Twentieth-Century Critical Debate on Shakespeare's Historic Plays', *ES*, 66 (1985), 391–403.

11 St Thomas Aquinas, *On Kingship: To the King of Cyprus*, trans. Gerald B. Phelan, revised edn I. Th. Eschmann, OP (Toronto: Pontifical Institute of Medieval Studies, 1949), p. 27.

12 Louisa Desaussure Duls, '*Richard II' in the Early Chronicles* (The Hague and Paris: Mouton Press, 1975), pp. 112–17. Writing shortly after Richard's deposition the chronicler Henry Knighton argued that

> From ancient statute and a precedent of times not long past which might be invoked again, though it was a painful thing, the people have an established principle that if, because of evil counsel of any kind, or silly obstinacy, or contempt, or singularly impudent willfulness or irregular behavior, the king should alienate himself from his people and refuse, despite the sane advice of the lords and most celebrated men of the realm, to be governed and regulated by the laws, statutes, and praiseworthy ordinances of the realm, but would impudently exercise in his insane counsels his own singular willfulness, then it is allowable for them, with common assent and with the consensus of the people of the realm, to depose the king himself from the royal throne and to raise to that throne in his place someone near at hand from the royal family stock. (*Chronicon Henrici Knighton*, ed. Joseph Rawson Lumby (London, 1895), II, 219, quoted and trans. Russell A. Peck, *Kingship and Common Profit in Gower's 'Confessio Amantis'* (Carbondale: Southern Illinois University Press, 1978), p. 9).

13 Franklin le van Baumer, *The Early Tudor Theory of Kingship* (1940); repr. New York: Russell & Russell, 1966), p. 89.

14 *An Homilie Agaynst Disobedience and Wylful Rebellion* (London, 1570), Sig. Div^v.

15 Robert Parsons, *A Conference About the Next Succession to the Crown of England* (London, 1594), pp. 32–3.

16 William Baldwin, 'To the Reader', *The Mirror for Magistrates* (1563), ed. Lily B. Campbell (1938; repr. New York: Barnes & Noble, 1960), pp. 420–1.

17 Recording the events of 13 September, Holinshed explains how, after Richard has formally abdicated and voluntarily nominated Bolingbroke as his successor, the Archbishop of Canterbury first sounds out the Lords, then addresses the assembled Commons, asking them 'if they would assent to the lords, which in their minds thought the claime of the duke made, to be rightfull and necessarie for the wealth of the realme and them all: whereto the commons with one voice cried, Yea, yea, yea' (Raphael Holinshed, *Chronicles of England, Scotland, and Ireland* (1577) revised edn by John Hooker, 6 vols. (1587; repr. London, 1807), II, 865).

18 Sir Thomas Smith, *De Republica Anglorum* (1583), ed. Mary Dewar (Cambridge University Press, 1982), pp. 53, 51–2.

19 James Emerson Phillips Jr, *The State in Shakespeare's Greek and Roman Plays* (1940; repr. New York: Columbia University Press, 1972), p. 20.

20 *Shakespeare's History Plays*, p. 64.

21 Leonard Tennenhouse, 'Strategies of State and Political Plays: *A Midsummer Night's Dream, Henry IV, Henry V, Henry VIII*', in *Political Shakespeare*, ed. Dollimore and Sinfield, p. 111.

22 A. D. Nuttall, *A New Mimesis: Shakespeare and the Representation of Reality* (London and New York: Methuen, 1983), p. 159.

23 *Fortunes of Falstaff*, p. 20.

24 J. A. Bryant, Jr, 'Prince Hal and the Ephesians', *SewR*, 67 (1959), 204–19; D. J. Palmer, 'Casting off the Old Man: History and St Paul in *Henry IV*', *CQ*, 12 (1970), 267–83.

25 See J. S. Manifold, *The Music in English Drama: From Shakespeare to Purcell* (London: Rockliff, 1956); Lawrence J. Ross, 'Shakespeare's "Dull Clown" and Symbolic Music', *SQ*, 17 (1966), 107–28.

26 Emanuel Winternitz, *Musical Instruments and their Symbolism in Western Art* (London: Faber, 1967), pp. 150–2.

27 *The New Science of Giambattista Vico*, trans. Thomas Goddard Bergin and Max Harold Fisch (1948; revised edn Ithaca: Cornell University Press, 1968), p. 244.

28 A. J. Hipkins, *Musical Instruments: Historic, Rare and Unique* (1888; repr. London: A. and C. Black, 1921), p. 9.

29 For discussion of the symbolism of the bagpipe see G. Fenwick Jones, 'Wittenwiler's *Becki* and the Medieval Bagpipe', *JEGP*, 48 (1949), 209–28; Edward A. Block, 'Chaucer's Millers and their Bagpipes', *Spec*, 29 (1954), 239–43; Ross, 'Shakespeare's "Dull Clown"'. The bagpipe is consistently linked with the sins of the flesh in English medieval church carvings. Pig bagpipers may be seen at Manchester Cathedral and Ripon Minster. A carving at Beverley Minster, where the bag of the pipes forms the piper's belly, points to the possible origin of the association of the bagpipe with gluttony.

30 George Wither, *A Collection of Emblemes, Ancient and Moderne* (1635; repr. in facsimile, Columbia: University of South Carolina Press, 1975), II.xx; I.xxii.

31 'The harp, and the chord stretched on its wooden frame, signifies the flesh of Christ linked with the wood of the passion' (St Victorinus, *Commentary on the Apocalypse of the Blessed John*, trans. Robert Ernest Wallis, in *The Writings of Quintus Sept. Flor. Tertullianus with the Extant Works of Victorinus and Commodianus*, ed. Alexander Roberts and James Donaldson, 3 vols. (Edinburgh: T. and T. Clark, 1869–70), III, 410).

32 John Robert Moore, 'The Tradition of Angelic Singing in English Drama', *JEGP*, 22 (1923), 89–99 (p. 96).

33 Clement of Alexandria, *The Exhortation to the Greeks*, in *Clement of Alexandria*, trans. G. W. Butterworth (London: Heinemann, 1919), pp. 7, 11.

34 Victorinus, in *Tertullianus*, III, 409–10.

35 'Uetus enim homo est, et uetus homo canticum uetus potest cantare, non nouum. Vt autem cantet canticum nouum, sit nouus homo. Quomodo autem possit esse nouus homo, audi, non me, sed apostolum dicentem: "Exuite uos ueterem hominem, et induite nouum"' (*Sermones de uetere testamento*, ed. Cyrillus Lambot, Corpus Christianorum, series latina, 41 (Turnholt: Brepols, 1961), 122–3). St Augustine also associates the Old and New Men with the Old and New Songs in *De eo quod scriptum est in psalmo deus canticum novum cantabo tibi* (pp. 413–16) and in *Sermo habitus carthagine ad maiores de responsorio Psalmi CXLIX cantate domino canticum novum* (pp. 424–7).

36 Wither, *Collection of Emblemes*, ii.iii.

37 D. W. Robertson, Jr, *A Preface to Chaucer: Studies in Medieval Perspectives* (Princeton University Press, 1963), pp. 127–8.

38 Danby writes: 'The rejection of Falstaff is an allegory ... In the rejection scene Hal and my Lord Chief Justice stand for Authority; Falstaff is Appetite' (*Shakespeare's Doctrine of Nature*, pp. 94–5).

39 Graham Holderness, *Shakespeare's History* (Dublin: Gill and Macmillan, 1985), p. 130.

40 See Jean Wilson, Introduction to *Entertainments for Elizabeth I* (Woodbridge and Totowa: D. S. Brewer, 1980), pp. 1–60 *passim*. See also Sydney Anglo, *Spectacle, Pageantry, and Early Tudor Policy* (Oxford: Clarendon Press, 1969).

41 See, for example, the entertainment at Bisham in 1592 (Wilson, *Entertainments for Elizabeth I*, pp. 43–7).

42 In his Introduction to the New Arden edition of *Henry V* (London: Methuen, 1954), J. H. Walter compares the archbishop's words with the Baptismal Service from the *Book of Common Prayer* (1560): 'graunt that the olde Adam in this child may be so buryed, that the new man may be raised up in him' (p. xix). Walter notes that the phrase 'to put on the new man' had become proverbial in the sixteenth century (p. xxi), but does not mention its source in St Paul.

43 Henry Bullinger, *A Hundred Sermons on the Apocalipse* (1561), 2nd edn (London, 1573), fol. 201ᵛ.

44 David Bevington, *Tudor Drama and Politics: A Critical Approach to Topical Meaning* (Cambridge, Mass.: Harvard University Press, 1968), p. 301.

45 See Bernard Capp, 'The Political Dimension of Apocalyptic Thought' in *The Apocalypse in English Renaissance Thought and Literature*, ed. C. A. Patrides and Joseph Wittreich (Manchester University Press, 1984), pp. 97–8.

46 See John Guy, *Tudor England* (Oxford University Press, 1988), p. 354.

47 *The Chronicle of John Hardyng* (London, 1543), fol. cc8; Edward Halle, *The Union of the Two Noble Families of Lancaster and York* (1550; repr. in facsimile, Menston: Scolar Press, 1970); *The Victorious Actes of Kyng Henry the Fifth*, fol. 1; *The Chronicle of Fabian* (London, 1559), p. 389.

48 *Holinshed's Chronicles*, iii, 61 (italics mine).

49 The refusal to privilege 'literature' over other forms of discursive practice is essential to both Cultural Materialist and New Historicist programmes. See Coda, pp. 227–8.

50 Pierre Macherey, 'Lenin, Critic of Tolstoy', in *A Theory of Literary Production*, trans. Geoffrey Wall (London: Routledge, 1978), p. 133. Cf. Louis Althusser: 'What [great] art makes us *see*, and therefore gives to us in the form of *"seeing"*, *"perceiving"*, and *"feeling"* ... is the *ideology* from which it is born, in which it bathes, from which it detaches itself as art, and to which it alludes' ('A Letter on Art' in *Lenin and Philosophy and Other Essays*, trans. Ben Brewster (London: NLB, 1971), p. 204). For Macherey's qualification of his earlier views see Etienne Balibar and Pierre Macherey, 'On Literature as an Ideological Form: Some Marxist Propositions', *OLR*, 3 (1978), 4–12.

51 This is a view also taken by Graham Holderness in *Shakespeare: the Play of History* by Graham Holderness, Nick Potter and John Turner (London: Macmillan, 1988), p. 58. Holderness sees the *Henry IV* plays not as oblique commentaries on the political problems of Shakespeare's own time, but as 'conscious acts of historiography: reconstructions of a feudal society analysed in the process of dissolution' (*Shakespeare's History*, p. 131). Well supported though it is, Holderness' approach runs the risk of stripping the plays of that contemporary relevance which Elizabethan audiences clearly found in the history plays.

3 PROSPERO, KING JAMES AND THE MYTH OF THE MUSICIAN-KING

1 *Hymn on the Morning of Christ's Nativity*, line 143, *The Poetical Works of John Milton*, ed. Helen Darbishire, 2 vols. (Oxford: Clarendon Press, 1952–5), II (1955), 117.

2 'Ultima Cumaei venit iam carminis aetas; / magnus ab integro saeclorum nascitur ordo. / iam redit et Virgo, redeunt Saturnia regna; / iam nova progenies caelo demittitur alto' (Eclogue IV. 4–7, Loeb Classical Library edn with trans. by H. Rushton Fairclough, revised edn, 2 vols. (London: Heinemann, 1935), I, 28).

3 'On the Harmony of the Spheres', trans. Phyllis B. Tillyard, *The Complete Prose Works of John Milton*, general ed. Douglas Bush and others, 8 vols. (New Haven: Yale University Press and Oxford University Press, 1953–82), I (1953), 239.

4 George Puttenham, *The Arte of English Poesie*, ed. Gladys Doidge Willcock and Alice Walker (Cambridge University Press, 1936), p. 154.

5 On the supposition motif in *As You Like It* see Maura Slattery Kuhn, 'Much Virtue in *If*', *SQ*, 28 (1977), 40–50.

6 Carol Thomas Neely, 'Constructing the Subject: Feminist Practice and the New Renaissance Discourses', *ELR*, 18 (1988), 6; H. Aram Veeser, Introduction to *The New Historicism*, ed. Veeser (New York and London: Routledge, 1989), p. xiii.

7 Francis Barker and Peter Hulme, '"Nymphs and reapers heavily vanish": the Discursive Con-texts of *The Tempest*' in *Alternative Shakespeares*, ed. John Drakakis (London: Methuen, 1985), p. 198. See also Paul Brown, '"This thing of darkness I acknowledge mine": *The Tempest* and the Discourse of Colonialism' in *Political Shakespeare: New Essays in Cultural Materialism*, ed. Jonathan Dollimore and Alan Sinfield (Manchester University Press, 1985), pp. 48–71; Malcolm Evans, *Signifying Nothing: Truth's True Contents in Shakespeare's Texts* (Brighton: Harvester, 1986), pp. 74–9. For a brief survey of modern treatments (before 1978) of the play's connections with colonialism see Stephen Orgel, ed., *The Tempest*, The Oxford Shakespeare (Oxford: Clarendon Press, 1987), p. 24, n.1.

8 The Revels Accounts for 1611 record that 'at Hallomas nyght was presented at Whitehall before the kinges Maiestie a play called the Tempest' (E. K. Chambers, *William Shakespeare: A Study of Facts and Problems*, 2 vols. (Oxford: Clarendon Press, 1930), II, 342). For a recent discussion of the play's early performance history see Orgel's Oxford edn, pp. 1–4.

9 See Patrick Grant, 'The Magic of Charity: A Background to Charity', *RES*, ns 27 (1976), 1–16.

10 *Preface to Shakespeare*, *The Works of Samuel Johnson*, Yale edn, 15 vols. (New Haven, Conn.: Yale University Press and Oxford University Press, 1958–85), VII, ed. Arthur Sherbo (1968), 88.

11 In *Shakespeare and the Popular Voice* (Oxford: Blackwell, 1989) Annabel Patterson writes: 'Common sense suggests ... that a popular dramatist, himself the son of a country glover ... was unlikely to have unquestioningly adopted anti-popular myth as his own' (p. 1). Kiernan Ryan goes further, arguing that Prospero forfeits our moral sympathy and respect because he epitomizes a hierarchical principle that denies any true social harmony (*Shakespeare* (New York and London: Harvester Wheatsheaf, 1989), p. 103).

12 On natural law see John Neville Figgis, *Studies of Political Thought: from Gerson to Grotius 1414–1625* (Cambridge University Press, 1907), pp. 84–6; Otto Gierke, *Political Theories of the Middle Age*, trans. and ed. Frederick William Maitland (Cambridge University Press, 1922); Gierke, *Natural Law and the Theory of Society 1500–1800*, trans. and ed. Ernest Barker, 2 vols. (Cambridge University Press, 1934); A. P. d'Entrèves, *Natural Law: An Introduction to Legal Philosophy* (London: Hutchinson, 1951). On changing theories of natural law in the Renaissance see Hiram Haydn, *The Counter-Renaissance* (New York: Grove, 1950).

13 Ryan, *Shakespeare*, p. 99.

14 *Biathanatos*, ed. Ernest W. Sullivan II (London and Toronto: Associated University Presses, 1984), p. 40.

15 'An Apologie of Raymond Sebond', *The Essayes of Montaigne*, trans. John Florio, 3 vols. (1910; repr. London: Dent, 1928), II, 229.

16 Margaret Attwood Judson, *The Crisis of the Constitution: An Essay in Constitutional and Political Thought in England 1603–1645* (1949; repr. New York, Octagon Books, 1964), pp. 17–43.

17 *Of the Lawes of Ecclesiastical Politie, The Works of Richard Hooker*, Folger Library edn, ed. W. Speed Hill, 4 vols. (Cambridge, Mass.: Harvard University Press, 1977–82), IV (1981), p. 342.

18 Baldassare Castiglione, *The Book of the Courtier*, trans. Sir Thomas Hoby (London: Dent, 1928), p. 75.

19 *Confessio Amantis*, Prologue, 1072–5, *The Complete Works of John Gower*, ed. G. C. Macaulay, 4 vols. (Oxford: Clarendon Press, 1899–1902), II (1901), 34.

20 *Ars poetica*, 391–401. See also Cicero, *De Oratore*, I.xxxi–v; *De Officiis*, I.l–li; *De Inventione*, I.v; Quintilian, *Institutio Oratoria*, I.x.7, II.xvi.9–19.

21 On the origins and transmission of the myth of the musician-king see Introduction, note 10.

22 St Ambrose, *Enarrationes in psalmos*, cited by Frances Yates, *The French Academies of the Sixteenth Century* (London: Warburg Institute, 1947), pp. 38–9.

23 Anthony Cope, *Godly meditacion upon xx ... psalmes* (London, 1547), Preface, quoted by Anne Lake Prescott, 'King David as a "Right Poet": Sidney and the Psalmist', *ELR*, 19 (1989), 132.

24 *The Arte of English Poesie*, pp. 6, 9.

25 William Strachy, *A true reportory of the wracke and redemption of Sir Thomas Gates*, in Samuel Purchas, *Purchas His Pilgrimes*, 20 vols. (Glasgow: MacLehose, 1905–7), XIX (1906), p. 67.

26 See John P. Cutts, 'Music and the Supernatural in *The Tempest*: A Study in Interpretation', *ML*, 39 (1958), 348ff. On music in the Late Romances and *The Tempest* in particular see also J. M. Nosworthy, 'Music and its Function in the Romances of Shakespeare', *ShS*, 11 (1958), 60–9; John H. Long, *Shakespeare's Use of Music: The Final Comedies* (Gainesville, Fla.: University of Florida Press, 1961); Catherine M. Dunn, 'The Function of Music in Shakespeare's Romances', *SQ*, 20 (1969), 391–405; Mary Chan, *Music in the Theatre of Ben Jonson* (Oxford: Clarendon Press, 1980), pp. 318–31; David Lindley, 'Music, Masque and Meaning in *The Tempest*' in *The Court Masque*, ed. Lindley (Manchester University Press, 1984), pp. 47–59.

27 Stephen Gosson, *The School of Abuse Containing a Pleasant Invective Against Poets, Pipers, Players, Jesters, &c.* (London: The Shakespeare Society, 1841), p. 16.

28 In the *Symposium* Plato explains how 'Music, by implanting mutual love and sympathy, causes agreement between [the] elements ... and music in its turn may be called a knowledge of the principles of love in the realm of harmony and rhythm' (trans. W. Hamilton (1951; repr. Harmondsworth: Penguin, 1961), p. 55).

29 *Boethius' Consolation of Philosophy*, trans. George Colville, ed. Ernest Belfort Bax, The Tudor Library (London: Nutt, 1897), p. 52.

30 Ibid.
31 Ibid.
32 *Convivium*, III.iii., quoted by John Warden, 'Orpheus and Ficino' in *Orpheus: the Metamorphosis of a Myth* (Toronto University Press, 1982), p. 102.
33 The commendatory sonnets appended to James' *Essayes of a Prentice* (1584) represent him as a poet-prince descended from the gods (*The Poems of James VI of Scotland*, ed. James Craigie, 2 vols. (Edinburgh: Blackwood, 1955–8), I (1955), 3–5.
34 George Marcelline, *The Triumphs of James the First* (London, 1610), p. 35.
35 On this aspect of the play see Stephen Orgel, *The Illusion of Power: Political Theater in the English Renaissance* (Berkeley and Los Angeles: University of California Press, 1975), pp. 44ff.
36 Jonathan Dollimore, 'Critical Developments: Cultural Materialism, Feminism and Gender Critique, and New Historicism' in *Shakespeare: A Bibliographical Guide*, ed. Stanley Wells (Oxford: Clarendon Press, 1990), p. 414.
37 In 1607 the Venetian ambassador to London noted James' 'neglect of affairs of state' (cited by Robert Ashton, ed., *James I By His Contemporaries* (London: Hutchinson, 1969), p. 8).
38 See, for example, the lines (167–8) from James' 'Answere to the Libell called the Comons teares' in which he threatens that 'If I once bend my angrie browe / Your ruyne comes though not as nowe' (*Poems*, ed. Craigie, II, 190).
39 See Greg Walker, *Plays of Persuasion: Drama and Politics at the Court of Henry VIII* (Cambridge University Press, 1991). See also O. B. Hardison, Jr, *The Enduring Monument: A Study of the Idea of Praise in Renaissance Literary Theory and Practice* (Westport, Conn.: University of North Carolina Press, 1962). The assumption, central to most New Historicist and Cultural Materialist Shakespeare criticism, that the drama was a potent political force in early modern England has recently been challenged by Paul Yachnin, who argues that the theatre was acknowledged by both playwrights and authorities to be politically powerless. Such powerlessness was, he argues, the price players paid for their liberty to address topical issues ('The Powerless Theater', *ELR*, 21 (1991), 49–74. On censorship, see also Annabel Patterson, *Censorship and Interpretation: The Conditions of Writing and Reading in Early Modern England* (Madison, Wis.: University of Wisconsin Press, 1984) and Janet Clare, '*Art made tongue-tied by authority': Elizabethan and Jacobean Dramatic Censorship* (Manchester University Press, 1990).
40 Patterson argues that Caliban's eloquence and his love of music are difficult to square with the critical convention of bestializing him and idealizing Prospero (*Shakespeare and the Popular Voice*, p. 155).
41 Thomas Starkey, *Dialogue Between Cardinal Pole and Thomas Lupset* in

England in the Reign of King Henry the Eighth, ed. J. M. Cowper (1878; repr. London: EETS, 1927), p. 180.

42 See James Daly, 'Cosmic Harmony and Political Thinking in Early Stuart England', *TAPS*, 69 (1979), 23.

43 *Campaspe*, v.iv.150–1, *The Complete Works of John Lyly*, ed. R. Warwick Bond, 3 vols. (Oxford: Clarendon Press, 1902), ii, 357–8.

44 Ryan, *Shakespeare*, p. 108.

45 Paul Brown writes, 'we should note a general analogy between text and context; specifically between Ireland and Prospero's island ... Both locations are subject to powerful organising narratives which recount the beleaguerments, loss and recovery – the ravelling and unravelling – of colonising subjects' ('"This thing of darkness"', pp. 57–8).

46 Lynne A. Magnusson, 'Interruptions in *The Tempest*', *SQ*, 37 (1986), 52–65.

47 See Allan H. Gilbert, '*The Tempest*: Parallelism in Characters and Situations', *JEGP*, 14 (1915), 63–74.

48 Robert Egan, *Drama Within Drama: Shakespeare's Sense of His Art* (New York: Columbia University Press, 1975), p. 108.

49 Lindley, 'Music, Masque and Meaning', p. 53.

50 'A Tale of Two Magicians' (Peter Greenaway in conversation with Adam Barker), *SS*, ns 1 (1991), p. 29.

51 In *Shakespeare and the Idea of the Play* (1962; repr. Harmondsworth: Penguin, 1967) Anne Righter argues that in the Last Plays Shakespeare 'turns the world itself into a theatre, blurring the distinctions between art and life ... he creates a world in which illusion and reality are indistinguishable and the same' (p. 172).

52 Gary Schmidgall compares the two episodes in *Shakespeare and the Courtly Aesthetic* (Berkeley, Los Angeles and London: University of California Press, 1981), pp. 173ff. Schmidgall interprets the cancellation of the masques as evidence of the poets' frustration: 'Both actions are signs of the artist's frustration and the artist's sense of the limitations of his art and of human nature' (p. 206).

53 Sir Philip Sidney, *The Defence of Poesie*, *The Complete Works of Sir Philip Sidney*, ed. Albert Feuillerat, 4 vols. (Cambridge University Press, 1912–26), iii (1923), 10.

54 Michel de Montaigne, 'Of the Caniballes', *The Essayes*, trans. John Florio, i, 220.

55 *Dialogue Between Cardinal Pole and Thomas Lupset*, p. 163.

56 On the myth of the noble savage in the ancient world, see Arthur O. Lovejoy and George Boas, *Primitivism and Related Ideas in Antiquity* (1935; repr. New York: Octagon Books, 1973), pp. 287–367.

57 See the excellent discussion of Ceres in Orgel's edition of *The Tempest*, p. 48.

58 *Shakespeare's Ovid: Being Arthur Golding's Translation of the Metamorphoses*, v.434–6, ed. W. H. D. Rouse (London: Centaur Press, 1961), p. 110.

59 See Introduction, note 37.
60 *L'Idea de' pittori, scultori et archetetti* (1607), quoted and trans. Geoffrey Shepherd (ed.), Sir Philip Sidney, *An Apology for Poetry* (London: Nelson, 1965), p. 65.
61 See S. K. Heninger, Jr, *Touches of Sweet Harmony: Pythagorean Cosmology and Renaissance Poetics* (San Marino: Huntington Library, 1974), pp. 287–324. See also E. N. Tigerstedt, 'The Poet as Creator: Origins of a Metaphor', *CLS*, 5 (1968), 456.
62 *The Arte of English Poesie*, p. 4.
63 *The Defence of Poesie*, p. 10.
64 Ibid., p. 8.
65 On theories of poetry implicit in Shakespeare's plays see Ekbert Faas, *Shakespeare's Poetics* (Cambridge University Press, 1986); see also Harriett Hawkins, 'Fabulous Counterfeits: Dramatic Construction and Dramatic Perspectives in *The Spanish Tragedy*, *A Midsummer Night's Dream*, and *The Tempest*', *SStud*, 6 (1970), 51–65; Anthony B. Dawson, *Indirections: Shakespeare and the Art of Illusion* (Toronto University Press, 1978).
66 Steiner, *Real Presences* (London: Faber, 1989), p. 229.
67 Writing of the marvellous which is such an essential ingredient in tragic drama, Joel Altman comments: 'We are not simply surprised by the unexpected; we are stirred by the dramatist's artful disposition of events to infer a larger rational pattern lying behind them' (*The Tudor Play of Mind* (Berkeley, Los Angeles and London: University of California Press, 1978), p. 1).
68 *The Grounds of Criticism in Poetry*, *The Critical Works of John Dennis*, ed. Edward Niles Hooker, 2 vols. (Baltimore: Johns Hopkins University Press, 1939–43), 1 (1939), 336.
69 Evans, *Signifying Nothing*, p. 76.
70 As George Lamming attests in *The Pleasures of Exile* (London: Michael Joseph, 1960) it is difficult for a modern West Indian reader to divorce the play from its colonial context (p. 13 and *passim.*).
71 Woolf, *A Room of One's Own* (1929; repr. London: Hogarth Press, 1949), pp. 52–3.
72 *Signifying Nothing*, p. 74.
73 Ibid.
74 Neely, 'Constructing the Subject', p. 15.
75 *Shakespeare*, p. 106.
76 See above, note 11.

4 THE LADDER OF LOVE: VERBAL AND MUSICAL RHETORIC IN THE ELIZABETHAN LUTE SONG

1 *The Second Booke of Songs or Ayres* (London, 1600), Sig. L^v.
2 See A. J. Smith, *The Metaphysics of Love: Studies in Renaissance Love Poetry from Dante to Milton* (Cambridge University Press, 1985).

3 *A Plaine and Easie Introduction to Practicall Musicke* (London, 1597), p. 178.

4 *The Garden of Eloquence*, facsimile reproduction of 1593 edn with an introduction by William G. Crane (Gainesville, Fla.: Scholars' Facsimiles and Reprints, 1954), pp. 106–7.

5 I first considered the relation between rhetoric and music in the Elizabethan lute song in 1974 ('The Art of Persuasion', *LSJ*, 16 (1974), 67–9). Despite the pioneering work of John Stevens (*Music and Poetry in the Early Tudor Court* (1961; repr. Cambridge University Press, 1979), pp. 6–7) and Claude V. Palisca ('*Ut Oratoria Musica*: the Rhetorical Basis of Musical Mannerism', in *The Meaning of Mannerism*, ed. Franklin W. Robinson and Stephen G. Nichols, Jr (Hanover, NH: University of New England Press, 1972), pp. 37–65) English-speaking scholars had given little attention to the subject at that time. Germany has been the pioneer in modern as well as Renaissance studies of rhetoric and music. A survey of the latter will be found in Gregory G. Butler, 'Fugue and Rhetoric', *JMT*, 21 (1977), 49–104. Further studies include Butler, 'Music and Rhetoric in Early Seventeenth-Century English Sources', *MQ*, 66 (1980), 53–64; George G. Buelow, 'Rhetoric and Musick', *The New Grove Dictionary of Music and Musicians*, ed. Stanley Sadie, 20 vols. (London: Macmillan, 1980); Brian Vickers, 'Figures of Rhetoric/Figures of Music?' *Rhet.*, 2 (1984), 1–44; Robert Toft, '"Musicke a sister to Poetrie": Rhetorical Artifice in the Passionate Airs of John Dowland', *EM*, 12 (1984), 191–9.

6 In an unpublished doctoral thesis H. R. Woudhuysen argues that while the name Areopagus may never have been more than a joke on the part of Harvey and Spenser, the philosophic and moral concerns of the Leicester circle were probably very close to those of the French academies ('Leicester's Literary Patronage: A Study of the English Court 1578–1582', Oxford University D. Phil. thesis, 1980, pp. 97–8).

7 *Two Bookes of Ayres* (London, *c.* 1613), 'To the Reader'.

8 This paragraph owes much to Kirsty Cochrane, 'Orpheus Applied: Some Instances of his Importance in the Humanist View of Language', *RES*, ns 19 (1968), 1–13.

9 'The Description of the Lords Maske', *Campion's Works*, ed. Percival Vivian (Oxford: Clarendon Press, 1909), p. 96.

10 Clement, *The Petie Schole* (1587), facsimile reproduction (Menston: Scolar Press, 1967), p. 45.

11 D. P. Walker writes '*Musica reservata*, the protestant and counter-reformation insistence on the audibility of the text, the vivid expressionism of the late madrigalists, the Pléiade's attempt to bring lyric verse and music closer together, *musique mesurée*, the Florentine *camerata* – in all these one can see more or less successful efforts to realize the same aesthetic ideal, namely, that the text should become an integral part of any composition' ('Musical Humanism in the 16th and early 17th Centuries', *MR*, 2 (1941), 8).

12 Vickers, 'Figures of Rhetoric/Figures of Music?', 1–44 *passim.*

13 *Peacham's Compleat Gentleman,* 2nd enlarged edn (1634), ed. G. S. Gordon (Oxford: Clarendon Press, 1906), p. 103.

14 *Sylva Sylvarum: or, A Naturall Historie* (London, 1627), p. 38.

15 *Institutio Oratoria,* II.xv.34, trans. H. E. Butler, Loeb Classical Library, 4 vols. (London: Heinemann, 1920–2), I (1920), 315.

16 See Sister Miriam Joseph, *Shakespeare's Use of the Arts of Language* (1947; repr. New York: Columbia University Press, 1949), pp. 8–13.

17 *Dialogue Between Cardinal Pole and Thomas Lupset,* in *England in the Reign of King Henry the Eighth,* ed. J. M. Cowper (1878; repr. London: EETS, 1927), p. 53. Cf. Cicero, *De inventione,* I.ii.2–3.

18 *The Arte of Rhetorique,* 2nd edn (1560), ed. G. H. Mair (Oxford: Clarendon Press, 1909), Sig. Avii.

19 In *The Seasons* (1726–30) James Thomson gives an account of the origin of civilization that corresponds in all its essential features to Wilson's version (see 'Summer', lines 1753ff).

20 *The Grounds of Criticism in Poetry, The Critical Works of John Dennis,* ed. Edward Niles Hooker, 2 vols. (Baltimore: John Hopkins University Press, 1939–43), I (1939), 336.

21 *Paradise Lost,* II.943–50, *The Poetical Works of John Milton,* ed. Helen Darbishire, 2 vols. (Oxford: Clarendon Press, 1952–5), I (1952), 50.

22 *The Arte of English Poesie,* ed. Gladys Doidge Willcock and Alice Walker (Cambridge University Press, 1936), p. 208.

23 Julius Caesar Scaliger, *Poetices libri septem* (Heidelburg, 1581), IV.xxxi, cit. and trans. Lee A. Sonnino, *A Handbook to Sixteenth-Century Rhetoric* (London: Routledge, 1968), p. 102.

24 *Oration on the Dignity of Man,* trans. Elizabeth Livermore Forbes in *The Renaissance Philosophy of Man,* ed. Ernst Cassirer, Paul Oskar Kristeller and John Herman Randall, Jr (Chicago: University of Chicago Press, 1948), p. 225.

25 *The Defence of Poesie, The Complete Works of Sir Philip Sidney,* ed. Albert Feuillerat, 4 vols. (Cambridge University Press, 1912–26), III (1923), 11.

26 *The Boke Named the Governour,* ed. Foster Watson (London: Dent, 1907), p. 4.

27 *Religio Medici and Other Writings,* ed. Halliday Sutherland (1906; repr. London: Dent, 1962), p. 37.

28 See Arthur O. Lovejoy, *The Great Chain of Being* (1936; repr. New York: Harper, 1960), pp. 55–8; S. K. Heninger, *Touches of Sweet Harmony: Pythagorean Cosmology and Renaissance Poetics* (San Marino: Huntington Library, 1974), p. 328.

29 *Commentary on the Dream of Scipio,* ed. and trans. William Harris Stahl (New York: Columbia University Press, 1952), p. 145.

30 See C. A. Patrides, *Premises and Motifs in Renaissance Thought and Literature* (Princeton University Press, 1982), pp. 34–5. I am indebted to Patrides for this and the following paragraph.

31 *A Discourse of the Freedom of the Will* (London, 1675), p. 30.

32 *De musica*, I.ii, in *Patrologia*, series latina, ed. J.-P. Migne (Paris, 1844ff), 63, 1171.

33 *In Joannem Homilia*, LXXXIII.v in *Nicene and Post-Nicene Fathers*, 1st series (New York, 1892–90), 14, 312, cit. and trans. Patrides, *Premises and Motifs*, p. 43.

34 See Kallistos Ware, Introduction to John Climacus, *The Ladder of Divine Ascent*, trans. Colm Luibheid and Norman Russell (London: SPCK, 1982), p. 11.

35 See John Rupert Martin, *The Illustration of the Heavenly Ladder of John Climacus* (Princeton University Press, 1954), p. 7.

36 *Consolation of Philosophy*, I.i. George Colville's translation (1556) reads: 'Her vestures or cloths were perfyt of the fynyste thredes, & subtyll workemanshyp ... In the lower parte ... was read the greke letter .P. wouen whych signifyeth practise or actyffe, and in the hygher part of the vestures the greke letter .T. whyche standeth for theorica, that signifieth speculacion or contemplation. And betwene both the sayd letters were sene cetayne degrees, wrought after the maner of ladders, wherin was as it were a passage or waye in steppes or degrees from the lower part wher the letter .P. was which is vnderstood from practys or actyf, vnto the hygher parte wher the letter .T. was whych is vnderstood speculacion or contemplacion' (ed. Ernest Belfort Bax (London: Nutt, 1897), p. 12).

37 See Emile Mâle, *The Gothic Image: Religious Art in France of the Thirteenth Century*, 3rd edn, trans. Dora Nussey (1913; repr. New York: Harper & Row, 1972), pp. 90–1; Painton Cowen, *Rose Windows* (London: Thames & Hudson, 1979), p. 82.

38 Kallistos Ware, Introduction to *The Ladder of Divine Ascent*, pp. 1ff.

39 Ibid., p. 11; Martin, *The Illustration of the Heavenly Ladder, passim*.; Adolf Katzenellenbogen, *Allegories of the Virtues and Vices in Medieval Art*, trans. Alan J. P. Crick (1939; repr. New York: Norton, 1964), pp. 22–6.

40 See Kathi Meyer-Baer, *Music of the Spheres and the Dance of Death: Studies in Musical Iconology* (Princeton University Press, 1970), pp. 209–10.

41 Erwin Panofsky, *The Life and Art of Albrecht Dürer*, 4th edn (Princeton University Press, 1955), pp. 156–71.

42 *The Occult Philosophy in the Elizabethan Age* (London, Boston and Henley: 1979), p. 56.

43 *Second Booke of Songs and Ayres* (London, 1601), Sig. M^v.

44 *Religio Medici*, ed. Sutherland, p. 39.

45 *Symposium*, 211 C, trans. W. R. M. Lamb, Loeb Classical Library (London: Heinemann, 1946), p. 207.

46 See Bojan Bujić, 'Josquin, Leonardo, and the *Scala Peccatorum*', *IRASM*, 4 (1973), 145–61.

47 *The Book of the Courtier*, trans. Sir Thomas Hoby (London: Dent, 1928), p. 318.

48 *Discours philosophiques* (Paris, 1587), pp. 9–10, cit. and trans. Frances A. Yates, *The French Academies of the Sixteenth Century* (London: Warburg Institute, 1947), p. 80.
49 *A Booke of Ayres* (London, 1601), Sig. Hi^v.
50 See Peter J. Ammann, 'The Musical Theory and Philosophy of Robert Fludd', *JWCI*, 30 (1967), 210.
51 *The Arte of Rhetorique*, p. 206.
52 *Directions for Speech and Style*, ed. Hoyt H. Hudson (Princeton University Press, 1935), p. 26.
53 Thomas Morley offers the following advice on the use of rests to represent sighs: 'when you would express sighes, you may vse the crotchet or minime rest at the most, but a longer then a minime rest you may not vse, because it will rather seeme a breth taking then a sigh' (*A Plaine and Easie Introduction*, p. 178).
54 *A Musicall Dreame: or The Fourth Booke of Ayres* (London, 1609), Sig. F2^v.
55 *The First Booke of Songes or Ayres* (London, 1597), Sig. B2^v.
56 Puttenham, *The Arte of English Poesie*, p. 302.
57 *The First Booke of Songes*, Sig. I^v.
58 See Allan H. Gilbert, 'The Ladder of Lechery, *The Faerie Queene*, III.i.45', *MLN*, 56 (1941), 594–7; James Hutton, 'Spenser and the "*Cinque Points en Amours*"', *MLN*, 57 (1942), 657–61.
59 'Les nobles Poetes disent, que cinq lignes y ha en amours, cestadire, cinq poincts ou cinq degrez especiaux, Cestasauoir le regard, le parler, lattouchement, le baiser: Et le dernier que est le plus desire, et auquel tous les autres tendent, pour finale resolution, ces celuy quon nomme par honnestete Le don de mercy', Jean Lemaire de Belges, *Les Illustrations de Gaule et singularitez de Troye, Œuvres*, ed. J. Stecher, 4 vols. (Geneva: Slatkine Reprints, 1969), I, 182–3.
60 See Lionel J. Friedman, 'Gradus amoris', *RP*, 19 (1966), 167–77.
61 *The Arte of English Poesie*, p. 154.
62 *Songs for the Lute Viol and Voice* (London, 1606), Sigs. E^v–Fii.
63 Peacham, *The Garden of Eloquence*, dedicatory epistle to 1593 edn, Sig. ABiii^v.
64 'The Description of the Lords Maske', *Campion's Works*, ed. Vivian, p. 89.
65 *A Plaine and Easie Introduction*, p. 178.
66 'scalas gradibus distinctas in celum erigunt' (*Genealogia Deorum Gentilium*, XIV.vii), trans. Charles G. Osgood in *Boccaccio on Poetry* (Books fourteen and fifteen of the *Genealogia*) (1930; repr. Indianapolis and New York: Bobbs Merrill, 1956), pp. 41–2.

5 MICROCOSMOS: SYMBOLIC GEOMETRY IN THE RENAISSANCE LUTE ROSE

1 Sir John Hayward, *An Answer to the First Part of a Certaine Conference Concerning Succession* (London, 1603), Sig. Bi^v.

2 In 'Poetry and the Politics of Reading' (*Re-Reading English*, ed. Peter Widdowson, Methuen New Accents (London: Methuen, 1982)) Antony Easthope writes, 'It is well known that [the transcendent subject] did not exist in the ancient world, nor in any developed form in the feudal period' (p. 142).

3 Catherine Belsey, *The Subject of Tragedy: Identity and Difference in Renaissance Drama* (London and New York: Methuen, 1985), p. 18.

4 Ibid., p. 33.

5 In *Radical Tragedy: Religion, Ideology and Power in the Drama of Shakespeare and his Contemporaries* (1984; repr. Brighton: Harvester, 1986) Jonathan Dollimore argues that the early seventeenth century saw 'a developing awareness of ideology in both its material and cognitive forms' (p. 11).

6 Ibid., p. 155.

7 Helkanah Crooke, *Microcosmographia* (London, 1615), p., 2.

8 Friedemann Hellwig first suggested that the lute rose might have symbolic meaning in an article in the Galpin Society journal in 1974 ('Lute Construction in the Renaissance and Baroque', *GSJ*, 27 (1974), 21–30). My article, 'Number Symbolism in the Renaissance Lute Rose' (*EM*, 9 (1981), 32–42) was the first to consider the subject in detail and to discuss the Pythagorean traditions on which the geometry of the lute rose is based. The present chapter is a completely revised and considerably expanded version of that article.

9 *Campion's Works*, ed. Percival Vivian (Oxford: Clarendon Press, 1909), pp. 50–1.

10 Ibid., p. 50.

11 Gretchen Ludke Finney, *Musical Backgrounds for English Literature: 1580–1650* (New Brunswick: Rutgers University Press, 1961), pp. 1–3; Kathi Meyer-Baer, *Music of the Spheres and the Dance of Death: Studies in Musical Iconology* (Princeton University Press, 1970), pp. 68–9.

12 'A Lent-Sermon Preached at White-hall, February 12, 1618', *Sermons*, ed. George R. Potter and Evelyn M. Simpson, 10 vols. (Berkeley and Los Angeles: University of California Press, 1953–62), II (1955), 170.

13 *The Poetical Works of William Drummond of Hawthornden*, ed. I. E. Kastner, 2 vols. (Edinburgh: Scottish Text Society, 1913), II, 165.

14 Baldassare Castiglione, *The Book of the Courtier*, trans. Sir Thomas Hoby (London: Dent, 1928), p. 75.

15 'Lute Construction in the Renaissance and Baroque', p. 25.

16 See Keith Critchlow, *Islamic Patterns: An Analytical and Cosmological Approach* (New York and London: Thames & Hudson, 1976).

17 See Ernst J. Grube, *The World of Islam* (London: Hamlyn, 1966), p. 11, 67–8; see also Oleg Grabar, *The Formation of Islamic Art* (New Haven, Conn. and London: Yale University Press, 1973), pp. 196ff.

18 *Metaphysics*, 985B–986A, trans. Hugh Tredennick, Loeb Classical Library (London: Heinemann, 1933), p. 33.

19 *Il Saggiatore*, trans. A. C. Crombie, *Augustine to Galileo: The History of Science AD 400–1650* (London: Falcon Press, 1952), p. 295.

20 *Timaeus*, 47D, trans. R. G. Bury, Loeb Classical Library (London: Heinemann, 1929), p. 109.

21 David Knowles, *The Evolution of Medieval Thought* (London: Longman, 1962), p. 197. See also Norman Daniel, *The Arabs and Medieval Europe* (London: Longman, 1975), pp. 263ff.

22 Henry George Farmer, 'The Influence of Music: From Arabic Sources', *PLMA*, 1925–6 (1926), 103; see also Farmer, *A History of Arabian Music to the XIIIth Century* (London: Luzac, 1973), p. 110; Titus Burckhardt, *Moorish Culture in Spain*, trans. Alisa Jaffa (London: Allen & Unwin, 1972), p. 71.

23 Quoted and trans. Eric Werner and Isaiah Sonne, 'The Philosophy and Theory of Music in Judaeo-Arabic Literature', *HUCA*, 16 (1941), 276.

24 Farmer, 'The Influence of Music: From Arabic Sources', pp. 97–8 and *passim*.

25 See Amnon Shiloah, *The Theory of Music in Arabic Writings (c. 900–1900)* (Munich: Henle, 1979), p. 258.

26 Farmer, 'The Influence of Music: From Arabic Sources', p. 101.

27 See Frederick Copleston, SJ, *A History of Philosophy*, 9 vols. (London: Burns Oates, 1946–75), II (1950), 196–9; Knowles, *The Evolution of Medieval Thought*, p. 199.

28 See Charles Homer Haskins, *The Renaissance of the Twelfth Century* (1927; repr. New York: Meridian, 1957), pp. 278–337; Copleston, *A History of Philosophy*, II, 186–200; A. C. Crombie, *Augustine to Galileo: The History of Science AD 400–1650* (London: Falcon Press, 1952), pp. 19–43; Knowles, *The Evolution of Medieval Thought*, pp. 193–205.

29 Winthrop Wetherbee, *Platonism and Poetry in the Twelfth Century: The Literary Influence of the School of Chartres* (Princeton University Press, 1972), pp. 11–73; see also Russell Peck, 'Number as Cosmic Language', in *By Things Seen: Reference and Recognition in Medieval Thought*, ed. David L. Jeffrey (University of Ottawa Press, 1979), p. 48.

30 See Vincent Foster Hopper, *Medieval Number Symbolism* (New York: Cooper Square, 1969); see also Peck, 'Number as Cosmic Language', pp. 47–80.

31 *The Secrets of Numbers According to Theologicall, Arithmeticall, Geometricall and Harmonicall Computation* (London, 1624), p. 2.

32 Robert M. Jordan, *Chaucer and the Shape of Creation* (Cambridge, Mass.: Harvard University Press, 1967), p. 47.

33 *Rose Windows* (London: Thames & Hudson, 1979), p. 8; see also Otto von Simson, *The Gothic Cathedral: The Origins of Gothic Architecture and the Medieval Concept of Order* (London: Routledge & Kegan Paul, 1956), pp. 21–61.

34 Otto von Simson writes; 'Gothic art would not have come into exist-

ence without the Platonic cosmology cultivated at Chartres' (*The Gothic Cathedral*, p. 26).

35 Wetherbee, *Platonism and Poetry*, pp. 21–2. Though it is not thought that Adelhard had any direct connection with the School of Chartres, his ideas anticipate the fundamentals of Chartrian thought.

36 The 'Vitruvian' figure represented in the Reims diagram is identified as the *spiritus aereus*, or 'Aer'. According to Neoplatonic doctrine this fifth element permeated the whole sensible universe. Neither wholly physical nor wholly spiritual (hence the human form with angel's wings), it formed an intermediary between microcosm and macrocosm (see D. P. Walker, 'Ficino's *Spiritus* and Music', *AM*, 1 (1953), 131–50).

37 *Rose Windows*, pp. 124–5. Cowan's book appeared when I had just prepared a first draft of the article on which this chapter is based. It seemed to confirm my belief that the geometry of the lute rose was based on Pythagorean principles.

38 *The Plaint of Nature*, trans. with a commentary by James J. Sheridan (Toronto: Pontifical Institute of Medieval Studies, 1980), pp. 118–19.

39 Rudolf Wittkower, *Architectural Principles in the Age of Humanism*, 3rd edn (1962; repr. London: Tiranti, 1967).

40 Quoted ibid., p. 15.

41 Among the most outstanding modern studies of Elizabethan number symbolism are A. Kent Hiett, *Short Time's Endless Monument: the Symbolism of Numbers in Spenser's 'Epithalamion'* (New York: Columbia University Press, 1960); Alastair Fowler, *Spenser and the Numbers of Time* (London: Routledge & Kegan Paul, 1964), Christopher Butler, *Number Symbolism* (London: Routledge & Kegan Paul, 1970), pp. 106ff; Fowler, *Triumphal Forms: Structural Patterns in Elizabethan Poetry* (Cambridge University Press, 1970).

For a discussion of the Globe theatre as a Vitruvian 'theatre of the world' see John Orrell, *The Quest for Shakespeare's Globe* (Cambridge University Press, 1983), pp. 139–49.

42 On the number symbolism of this canto see Vincent Foster Hopper, 'Spenser's "House of Temperance"', *PMLA*, 55 (1940), 958–67; Fowler, *Spenser and the Numbers of Time*, pp. 260–88; R. M. Cummings, 'A Note on the Arithmological Stanza: *The Faerie Queene*, II.ix.22', *JWCI*, 30 (1967), 410–14; Jerry Leath Mills, 'Spenser's Castle of Alma and the Number 22', *NQ*, 212 (1967), 456–7.

43 Kevin Coates, *Geometry, Proportion and the Art of Lutherie* (Oxford: Clarendon Press, 1985).

44 *The Secrets of Numbers*, p. 44.

45 *The French Academie*, trans. T. Bowes (London, 1586), p. 177.

46 Thomas Docherty believes that when Regan speaks of the 'precious square of sence' she is referring to her clitoris (*On Modern Authority: The Theory and Condition of Writing 1500 to the Present Day* (Brighton: Harvester, 1987), p. 112). However, it seems more probable that she is referring

to the 'soule *sensibilis*'. On the quadrangular nature of the sensible soul, see Stephen Batman: '[Bartholomaeus Anglicus] lykeneth the soule *Sensibilis* to a quadrangle square, and foure cornered. For in a Quadrangle is a line drawne from one corner to another, before it maketh two Triangles, and the soule sensible maketh two triangles of vertues' (*Batman uppon Bartholome, his Booke 'De Proprietatibus Rerum'* (London, 1582), fol. 14). Tom McAlindon has pointed out to me that there is a discussion of the latter point in John Erskine Hankins, *Backgrounds of Shakespeare's Thought* (Hassocks: Harvester, 1978), pp. 70–5.

47 *Commentary on the Dream of Scipio*, ed. and trans. William Harris Stahl (New York: Columbia University Press, 1952), p. 105.

48 *Vicissitudo Rerum* (1600), Shakespeare Association Facsimiles, 4, with an introduction by D. C. Collins (London: Shakespeare Association, 1931), Sig. D2ᵛ.

49 Ibid., Sig. A4.

50 *Religio Medici*, ed. Halliday Sutherland (1906); repr. London: Dent, 1962), p. 80.

51 *Batman uppon Bartholome*, fol. 14.

52 *Confessio Amantis*, III.689–90, *The Complete Works of John Gower*, 4 vols., ed. G. C. Macaulay (Oxford: Clarendon Press, 1899–1902), II (1901), 252.

53 *Batman uppon Bartholome*, fol. 14.

54 See Heninger, *Touches of Sweet Harmony: Pythagorean Cosmology and Renaissance Poetics* (San Marino: Huntington Library, 1974), pp. 151–2.

55 *The Life of Sir Philip Sidney, The Works of Fulke Greville*, 4 vols., ed. Alexander B. Grosart (London: Fuller Worthies' Library, 1868–70), IV, 139. There is a modern-spelling edn of *The Life of Sidney (A Dedication to Sir Philip Sidney)* by John Gouws, *The Prose Works of Fulke Greville, Lord Brooke* (Oxford: Clarendon Press, 1986).

56 In *Utriusque cosmi . . . historia* (1617–19) Fludd attempted to provide geometric proof of the relationship between macrocosm and microcosm (see Allen G. Debus, *Man and Nature in the Renaissance* (Cambridge University Press, 1978), p. 11).

57 Edwin Arthur Burtt, *The Metaphysical Foundations of Modern Physical Science*, revised edn (1932; repr. London: Routledge & Kegan Paul, 1949), pp. 23–73.

58 Eric Werner, 'The Last Pythagorean Musician: Johannes Kepler' in *Aspects of Medieval and Renaissance Music*, ed. Jan LaRue (Oxford University Press, 1967), p. 868. See also Burtt, *Metaphysical Foundations of Modern Science*, p. 52.

59 Gasparo Contarini, *The Commonwealth and Government of Venice*, trans. Lewes Lewkenor (London, 1599), pp. 64–5. On the use of music as state propaganda in Venice, see Ellen Rosand, 'Music in the Myth of Venice', *RenQ*, 30, (1977), 511–37.

60 Burtt, *Metaphysical Foundations of Modern Physical Science*, p. 42.

61 See Introduction, p. 14.

62 Pico della Mirandola, *Oration on the Dignity of Man*, trans. Elizabeth Livermore Forbes, in *The Renaissance Philosophy of Man*, ed. Ernst Cassirer, Paul Oskar Kristeller and John Herman Randall, Jr (University of Chicago Press, 1948), p. 225.

63 Ibid., p. 235.

64 Ibid.

65 This view was commonplace in criticism of the 1920s, 1930s and 1940s. However, as William G. Craven rightly remarks, 'the idea of man literally choosing his own nature, in a metaphysical sense, would have been nonsensical to Pico' (*Giovanni Pico della Mirandola: Symbol of his Age* (Geneva: Droz, 1981), p. 29). Dollimore's interpretation of Pico's anthropology is based on a misunderstanding of Cassirer's *The Individual and the Cosmos in Renaissance Philosophy*, first published in 1927 (see Introduction, p. 14).

66 *The Plaint of Nature*, pp. 118–19.

67 *Oration on the Dignity of Man*, p. 225.

68 Ibid., p. 234.

69 See, for example, Pierre de la Primaudaye, *The French Academie*, revised edn (London, 1618), p. 633; Sir Thomas Browne, *Religio Medici*, p. 39; Pope, *An Essay on Man*, 1.173–6: 11.1–18, *The Poems of Alexander Pope*, one-volume Twickenham edn, ed. John Butt (London: Methuen, 1963), 3.i (ed. Maynard Mack, 1950), pp. 511, 516.

70 *An Essay on Man*, one-volume Twickenham edn, pp. 502, 516.

71 St Augustine writes: 'love lifts us up [to heaven] ... Our body with its lumpishness strives towards it own place' (*Confessions*, XIII.ix, trans. William Watts (1631), Loeb Classical Library, 2 vols. (London: Heinemann, 1922–5), II (1925), 391; cf. *Confessions*, VIII.x. (I, 451–3).

72 Foucault, *The Order of Things: An Archaeology of the Human Sciences* (1966), unattributed English trans. (1970; repr. London: Tavistock Publications, 1977), p. xxiii. Cf. pp. 386, 387. J. G. Merchior describes Foucault's account of the Enlightenment *épistème* as 'a brazen historical caricature' (*Foucault* (London: Fontana Collins, 1985), p. 99).

73 See Antonio Poppi, 'Fate, Fortune, Providence and Human Freedom', in *The Cambridge History of Renaissance Philosophy*, ed. Charles B. Schmitt, Quentin Skinner and Eckhard Kessler (Cambridge University Press, 1988), pp. 641–67.

74 In his influential essay 'Of the Caniballes' Montaigne sees the South American Indian as an embodiment of the true essence of primitive human nature not yet bastardized by the corrupting influence of civilization: 'They are even savage, as we call those fruites wilde, which nature of hir selfe, and of hir ordinarie progresse hath produced ... The *lawes of nature do yet command them*, which are but little bastardized by ours' (*The Essayes*, trans. John Florio, 3 vols. (1910; repr., London: Dent, 1928), I, 220 (my italics).

75 *Critical Practice* (Methuen New Accents (London: Methuen, 1980), p. 87.

76 See Rudolf Allers, 'Microcosmus: from Anaximandros to Paracelsus', *Traditio*, 2 (1944), 364–5; see also Leonard Barkan, *Nature's Work of Art: The Human Body as Image of the World* (1975; repr. New Haven, Conn. and London: Yale University Press, 1977). Barkan's book is a valuable survey of microcosmic ideas in Renaissance England. However, Barkan does not make it clear that the image is used, not just by politically conservative writers like Sir Thomas Elyot, but also by the most radical opponents of the Tudor governments. One of Elizabeth's fiercest critics was the Jesuit Robert Parsons. Though Parsons argues for a radical curbing of royal power, he does not challenge the principle of monarchy itself. Like Contarini, and indeed like practically every other political writer in the period, he defends monarchy on analogical grounds: 'of all formes of gouernment the monarchy ... appeareth to be the most excellent and perfect ... this kind of gouernment resembleth most of al the gouernment of God, that is but one: it representeth the excellency of one sonne that lighteth al the planets, of one soule in the body that gouerneth al the powers and members therof, and finally [it doth] most conforme vnto nature' (*A Conference About the Next Svccession to the Crowne of Ingland* (Antwerp, 1594), pp. 15–16).

77 T. McAlindon, *Shakespeare's Tragic Cosmos* (Cambridge University Press, 1991), chaps. 4 and 8.

78 *Religio Medici*, p. 80.

6 THE ORPHARION: 'A BRITISH SHELL'

1 Among the Elizabethan composers who specify the orpharion on the title page of at least one of their collections are Barley, Bartlet, Campion, Dowland, Ford, Hume, Jones, Pilkington and Rosseter.

2 See Donald Gill, 'The Orpharion and Bandora', *GSJ*, 13 (1960), 14–25; Gill, *Wire-Strung Plucked Instruments Contemporary with the Lute*, Lute Society Booklets, 3 (London: The Lute Society, 1977), pp. 8–17; John Pringle, 'The Founder of English Viol-Making', *EM*, 6 (1978), 501–11.

3 Gill points out that 'it is not known who first used the name Orpharion, with its obvious allusions to "Orpheus and Arion, two famous in their time for their instruments ... " as Robert Greene wrote in his book *Greene's Orpharion* (1599)' (*Wire-Strung Plucked Instruments*, p. 17).

4 D. P. Walker, 'Musical Humanism in the 16th and Early 17th Centuries', *MR*, 2 (1941), 1–13, 111–21, 220–7, 288–308; Frances A. Yates, *The French Academies of the Sixteenth Century* (London: Warburg Institute, 1947), pp. 36–76; Bruce Pattison, *Music and Poetry of the English Renaissance*, 2nd edn (London: Methuen, 1970), pp. 122–7.

5 See Walker, 'Musical Humanism', pp. 4–8.

6 Giambattista Giraldi, *Tre dialoghi della vita civile* (1565), trans, and adapted by Lodowick Bryskett as *A Discourse of Civill Life: Containing the Ethike Part of Morall Philosophie* (London, 1606), pp. 147–8.

7 See John Blok Friedman, *Orpheus in the Middle Ages* (Cambridge, Mass.: Harvard University Press, 1970), p. 158.

8 John Dowland, *The First Booke of Songes or Ayres* (London, 1597), dedicatory letter to Sir George Carey.

9 Thomas Campion's address 'To the Reader' in Philip Rosseter, *A Booke of Ayres* (London, 1601).

10 'The Description . . . of the Lords Maske', *Campion's Works*, ed. Percival Vivian (Oxford: Clarendon Press, 1909), p. 89.

11 On Elizabethan antiquarianism see T. D. Kendrick, *British Antiquity* (London: Methuen, 1950); Stuart Piggot, *Ruins in a Landscape: Essays in Antiquarianism* (Edinburgh University Press, 1976). See also Jean Wilson, *Entertainments for Elizabeth I* (Woodbridge and Totowa: D. S. Brewer and Barnes & Noble, 1980), pp. 15–21; Michael Leslie, *Spenser's 'Fierce Warres and Faithfull Loves': Martial and Chivalric Symbolism in 'The Faerie Queene'* (Woodbridge and Totowa: Boydell & Brewer and Barnes & Noble, 1983), pp. 5–7. Paradoxically, fashionable obsession with England's mythical history coincides with the growing influence of a new historiography that recognized for the first time the importance of documentary evidence and criticized the romantic use of national legend for militantly patriotic purposes. On the new historiography see F. J. Levy, *Tudor Historical Thought* (San Marino: Huntington Library, 1967); Peter Burke, *The Renaissance Sense of the Past* (London: Arnold, 1969); Arthur B. Ferguson, *Clio Unbound: Perception of the Social and Cultural Past in Renaissance England* (Durham, NC: Duke University Press, 1979); Paul Avis, *Foundations of Modern Historical Thought: from Machiavelli to Vico* (London and Sydney: Croom Helm, 1986).

12 *The Arte of English Poesie*, ed. Gladys Doidge Willcock and Alice Walker (Cambridge University Press, 1936), p. 5.

13 See Mattie Swayne, 'The Progress Piece in the Seventeenth Century', *SE*, 16 (1936), 84–92. See also R. H. Griffeth, 'The Progress Pieces of the Eighteenth Century', *TR*, 5 (1920), 218–33; Aubrey L. Williams, *Pope's Dunciad: A Study of its Meaning* (London: Methuen, 1955), pp. 42–8. Sir John Denham's *Progress of Learning* (1668) is the first progress piece to use the term in its title. However, the seeds of the ideas that were to be developed in the progress poem proper lie in the sixteenth century. In *Orchestra* Sir John Davies combines elements of the British History (the action is set in Ithaca) with the idea of a continuous and purposeful development of the arts. Antinous' prophetic mirror reveals that the culmination of the plan that nature has been conceiving since the beginning of time will be a new golden age whose courtly arts far surpass those of antiquity (*Orchestra*, stanzas 120–6, *The*

Poems of Sir John Davies, ed. Robert Krueger (Oxford: Clarendon Press, 1975), pp. 122–3).

14 On the British History see Edwin Greenlaw, *Studies in Spenser's Historical Allegory* (Baltimore: Johns Hopkins University Press, 1932); Charles Bowie Millican, *Spenser and the Table Round* (Cambridge, Mass.: Harvard University Press, 1932); S. K. Heninger Jr, 'The Tudor Myth of Troy-novant', *SAQ*, 61 (1962), 378–87; Sydney Anglo, 'The British History in Early Tudor Propaganda', *BJRL*, 44 (1951), 17–48; Kendrick, *British Antiquity*.

15 In Thomas Hughes' *Misfortunes of Arthur* (1588) the ghost of Gorlois hails Elizabeth as a descendant of the royal house of Troy:

> That vertuous *Virgo* borne for *Brytaines* blisse:
> That pierelesse braunch of *Brute*: that sweete remaine
> Of *Priam's* state: that hope of springing *Troy*:
> Which time to come, and many ages hence
> Shall of all warres compound eternall peace.

Then, echoing Virgil, he expresses the hope that she will usher in a new golden age:

> Let her reduce the golden age againe,
> Religion, ease and health of former world.
> Yea, let that *Virgo* come and *Saturnes* raigne,
> And yeares oft ten times tolde expirde in peace.

(*The Misfortunes of Arthur* (v.i.18–26), ed. John W. Cunliffe, *Early English Classical Tragedies* (Oxford: Clarendon Press, 1912), pp. 290–1)

16 *Hero and Leander*, 1.55, *The Complete Works of Christopher Marlowe*, ed. Fredson Bowers, 2nd edn, 2 vols. (Cambridge University Press, 1981), II, 432.

17 *Pagan Mysteries in the Renaissance* (London: Faber, 1958), pp. 142–6. See also Bruce R. Smith, 'The Contest of Apollo and Marsyas: Ideas about Music in the Middle Ages' in *By Things Seen: Reference and Recognition in Medieval Thought*, ed. David L. Jeffrey (University of Ottawa Press, 1979), pp. 81–107.

18 *Metamorphoses*, VI.389–91, trans. Frank Justus Miller, Loeb Classical Library, 2 vols. (London: Heinemann, 1916), II, 315.

19 Tony Harrison, *The Trackers of Oxyrynchus* (London and Boston: Faber, 1990), p. 64.

20 'Today, those citterns made in Brescia are supposed to be of the highest repute. They are much used and appreciated among the nobility and, so it is said by their makers, perhaps a revival of the antique kithara' (*Dialogo della musica antica e della moderna* (1581); trans. James Tyler, quoted in David Munrow, *Instruments of the Middle Ages and Renaissance* (Oxford University Press, 1976), p. 81). Pierre Trichet, writing half a century later, similarly speaks of the cittern as 'une espèce de cithare, qui retient quelque ombrage ou désguisement de l'Antiquité' (*Traité des*

instruments de musique (*c.* 1640), ed. F. Lesure (Neuilly-sur-Seine: Société de Musique d'Autrefois, 1957), p. 157.

21 See Emmanuel Winternitz, *Musical Instruments and their Symbolism in Western Art* (London: Faber, 1967), pp. 57–65.

22 Percy Bysshe Shelley, *Hymn to Mercury* (translation of the Homeric *Hymn to Hermes*), lines 41–4, *Poetical Works*, ed. Thomas Hutchinson, revised by G. M. Matthews (Oxford University Press, 1970), p. 681. Chapman's more ponderous translation of the *Hymn to Hermes* is included in the *Whole Works of Homer* (1614–16). *Chapman's Homer* is published in a modern edition by Allardyce Nicoll, 2 vols. (London: Routledge & Kegan Paul, 1957).

23 Shelley, *Hymn to Mercury*, line 27. The fullest account of the Greek tortoise-lyre is by Martha Maas and Jane McIntosh Snyder, *Stringed Instruments of Ancient Greece* (New Haven, Conn. and London: Yale University Press, 1989), pp. 34–9, 79–112. See also Hortense Panum, *The Stringed Instruments of the Middle Ages: their Evolution and Development*, trans. Jeffrey Pulver (London: Reeves, 1940), pp. 23ff, and H. Roberts, 'Reconstructing the Greek Tortoise-Shell Lyre', *WA*, 12 (1981), 303–12.

24 'Iubal ... was the father of all that playe on the harpe and organes' (Gen. 4:21, *The Geneva Bible*, facsimile of the 1560 edn with an introduction by Lloyd E. Berry (Madison, Wis.: University of Wisconsin Press, 1969), fol. 3).

25 *The Divine Weeks and Works of Guillaume de Saluste Sieur Du Bartas*, trans. Joshua Sylvester, ed. Susan Snyder, 2 vols. (Oxford: Clarendon Press, 1979), I, 395.

26 *A Song for St Cecilia's Day, 1687*, lines 16–24, *The Works of John Dryden*, ed. H. T. Swedenborg Jr, 19 vols. (Berkeley and Los Angeles: California University Press, 1956–84), III (1969), 201.

27 'Shell' is an imitation of Latin *testudo*, meaning either tortoise or shell, or, figuratively, lyre. For examples of the latter usage see Virgil, *Georgics*, IV.464; Horace, *Odes*, III.xi.3, *Ars poetica*, 395; Propertius, *Elegies*, II.xxxiv.79. For a late-nineteenth-century example of the shell as a symbol of poetry see the pair of pastoral poems entitled *The Song of the Happy Shepherd* and *The Sad Shepherd* that introduce Yeats' *Crossways* (1889).

28 See Benjamin Boyce, 'Sounding Shells and Little Prattlers in the Mid-Eighteenth-Century Ode', *ECS*, 8 (1975), 245–64.

29 *The Works of William Collins*, ed. Richard Wendorf and Charles Ryskamp (Oxford: Clarendon Press, 1979), p. 27.

30 The dimensions of the Rose orpharion are given by Donald Gill in 'An Orpharion by John Rose', *LSJ*, 2 (1960), 34. Djilda Abbott and Ephraim Segerman argue that the tapering body of the instrument indicates that it was originally a cittern ('The Cittern in England before 1700', *LSJ*, 17 (1975), 37).

31 Pringle, 'The Founder of English Viol-Making', p. 506.
32 William Barley, *A New Booke of Tabliture for the Orpharion* (1596), ed. W. N. Newcomb as *Lute Music of Shakespeare's Time* (University Park, Pa.: Pennsylvania State University Press, 1966), p. 57.
33 The following writers have documented the use of the scallop in European art and literature: Mortimer Wheeler, 'A Symbol in Ancient Times' in *The Scallop: Studies of a Shell and its Influence on Humankind*, ed. Ian Cox (London: Shell, 1957), pp. 33–48; Christopher Hohler, 'The Badge of St James', in ibid., pp. 49–70; James Laver, 'The Cradle of Venus', in ibid., pp. 73–88; Wind, *Pagan Mysteries in the Renaissance*, revised edn (Harmondsworth: Penguin, 1967), appendix 5, 'Aphrodite's Shell', pp. 263–4; Marion Lawrence, 'The Birth of Venus in Roman Art', *Essays in the History of Art Presented to Rudolf Wittkower*, ed. Douglas Fraser, Howard Hibbard and Milton J. Lewine (London and New York: Phaidon, 1967), pp. 10–16. The most exhaustive iconographic study of the scallop in the Middle Ages is by Meg Twycross, *The Medieval Anadyomene: A Study in Chaucer's Mythography*, Medium Aevum Monographs, ns 1 (Oxford: Blackwell, 1972).
34 See Hohler, 'The Badge of St James', pp. 51–70.
35 See Wheeler, 'A Symbol in Ancient Times', pp. 35–48.
36 Ibid., pp. 36–7.
37 John Maplet, *The Diall of Destiny* (London, 1581), Sig. c4.
38 Twycross, *The Medieval Anadyomene*, pp. 21ff. The author of the fourteenth-century *Libellus de Imaginibus Deorum* writes: 'Venus was painted as a very fair maiden, naked and swimming in the sea, holding a shell in her right hand and accompanied by doves which fluttered round her' (quoted in E. H. Gombrich, 'Botticelli's Mythologies: A Study in the Neoplatonic Symbolism of his Circle', *JWCI*, 8 (1945), p. 30).
39 Gerald Legh, *Accedence of armory* (London, 1562), fol. 163.
40 *The Diall of Destiny*, Sig. c6.
41 Ibid., Sig. c3^v.
42 Quoted in Wind, *Pagan Mysteries* (1958), p. 82.
43 Quoted in ibid.
44 See S. K. Heninger, *Touches of Sweet Harmony: Pythagorean Cosmology and Renaissance Poetics* (San Marino: Huntington Library, 1974), pp. 146–200.
45 In the Middle Ages Boethius' *Consolation* was the *locus classicus* for the belief that it is love 'that governythe both the land and the sea, and likewyse comaundeth the heven, and kepyth the world in due order and good accorde' (*Consolation of Philosophy*, trans. George Colville (London, 1556); ed. Ernest Belfort Bax, The Tudor Library Series (London: Nutt, 1897), p. 52).
46 *The Diall of Destiny*, Sig. c4^v.
47 See Plato, *Symposium*, 180E. Bernard Silvestris gives a classic medieval (twelfth century) expression of the traditional distinction between the

two Venuses in his *Commentary on Six Books of Virgil's Aeneid*: 'We read that there are two Venuses, a legitimate goddess and a goddess of wantonness. We say that the legitimate Venus is the music of the world, that is, the equal proportion of things' (quoted by R. P. Miller, *Chaucer: Sources and Background* (New York: Oxford University Press, 1977), p. 343n).

48 *The Knight's Tale*, III.1920–3, *The Works of Geoffrey Chaucer*, ed. F. N. Robinson, 2nd edn (Oxford University Press, 1957), p. 36.

49   The statue of Venus, glorious for to se,
             Was naked, fletynge in the large see,
             And fro the navele doun al covered was
             With wawes grene, and bright as any glas.
             A citole in hir right hand hadde she.   (III.1955–9)

David Munrow writes, 'the generally accepted view is that the citole was the ancestor of the Renaissance cittern' (*Instruments of the Middle Ages*, p. 26). On Chaucer's citole, see J. M. Steadman, 'Venus' *Citole* in Chaucer's *Knight's Tale* and Berchorius', *Spec*, 34 (1959), 620–4, and Twycross, *The Medieval Anadyomene*, pp. 63–70.

50 See K. Meyer-Baer, *Music of the Spheres and the Dance of Death: Studies in Musical Iconology* (Princeton University Press, 1970), p. 97.

51 See chapter 8.

52 Legh, *Accedens of armory*, fol. 163.

53 Karl Lehman, 'The Dome of Heaven', in *Modern Perspectives in Western Art History*, ed. W. Eugene Kleinbauer (New York: Holt, Rinehart & Winston, 1971), pp. 228–70.

54 Walter C. Leedy, Jr, *Fan Vaulting: A Study of Form, Technology, and Meaning* (London: Scolar Press, 1980), p. 31.

55 *Orchestra*, stanza 19. It is, of course, that same 'heauens vault' that King Lear imagines cracking in his apocalyptic lament for the dead Cordelia (v.iii.261).

56 Titus Burckhardt, *Moorish Culture in Spain*, trans. Alisa Jaffa (London: Allen & Unwin, 1972), p. 14.

57 Lehman, 'The Dome of Heaven', p. 242.

58 Friedman, *Orpheus in the Middle Ages*, p. 84.

59 Bernard Silvestris, *Commentary on Virgil's Aeneid* (see above note 47).

60 *Trackers of Oxyrhynchus*, p. 55.

7 *ARS AMATORIA*: PHILIP ROSSETER AND THE TUDOR COURT LYRIC

1 Philip Rosseter, *A Booke of Ayres set foorth to be song to the Lute, Orpherian and Base Violl* (London, 1601), Sig. L2^v.

2 *To Mr Creech on his translation of Lucretius* (1682) *The Poems of Edmund Waller*, ed. G. Thorn Dury, 2 vols. (London: Routledge, 1893), II, 90.

3 Gary Waller, *English Poetry of the Sixteenth Century* (London: Longman, 1986), p. 47.

4 In the case of the lute song Barthes' comparison between the performance of musical scores and the 'active' reading of literary texts ('From Work to Text', *Image-Music-Text*, trans. Stephen Heath (New York: Hill & Wang, 1977), pp. 155–64) ceases to be analogy and becomes literal fact: the intelligent singer is both an interpreter of musical signs and a producer of poetic meaning.

5 For a musical analysis of Rosseter's songs see Nigel Fortune, 'Philip Rosseter and his Songs', *LSJ*, 7 (1965), 7–14.

6 Sig. A2ᵛ. As Fortune rightly says, 'If Campion did not actually write for Rosseter the ... address "To the Reader" then we can at least say it owes almost everything to Campion's teaching' ('Philip Rosseter and his Songs' p. 9).

7 For modern discussions of number symbolism in Elizabethan poetry see chapter 5, note 41.

8 *Opera omnia*, 1 (Basle, 1573), 10, quoted by Fowler, *Triumphal Forms: Structural Patterns in Elizabethan Poetry* (Cambridge University Press, 1970), p. 137 (Fowler's translation).

9 In the *De imagine mundi libri tres* (II.lix) Honorius of Autun says that with his seven voices (corresponding to the seven notes of the musical scale), man reproduces in facsimile the celestial music of the macrocosm (see Russell A. Peck, 'Number as Cosmic Language' in *By Things Seen: Reference and Recognition in Medieval Thought*, ed. David L. Jeffrey (University of Ottawa Press, 1979), p. 51).

10 Macrobius gives more attention to seven than to any other number; in the *Commentary on the Dream of Scipio* he writes: 'The number seven is distinguished for having so many functions, whether exercised in the combinations amounting to seven or by itself, that it is deservedly considered and called full' (trans. William Harris Stahl (New York: Columbia University Press, 1952), p. 117).

11 Sir William Ingpen, *The Secrets of Numbers* (London, 1624), p. 2.

12 *Orchestra*, line 714, *The Poems of Sir John Davies*, ed. Robert Krueger (Oxford: Clarendon Press, 1975), p. 117.

13 For a reading of Wyatt's lyrics as gambits in a social power game see Michael McCanles, 'Love and Power in the Poetry of Sir Thomas Wyatt', *MLQ*, 29 (1968), 145–60. See also Stephen Greenblatt, *Renaissance Self-Fashioning from More to Shakespeare* (University of Chicago Press, 1980), pp. 136–7, 141–2. No consideration of the element of play in Wyatt's lyrics can afford to ignore John Stevens' chapters on 'The "Game of Love"' and 'The Courtly Makers' in *Music and Poetry in the Early Tudor Court* (1961; repr. Cambridge University Press, 1979), pp. 154–229.

14 *Collected Poems of Sir Thomas Wyatt*, ed. Kenneth Muir (London: Routledge, 1949), p. 122.

15 Ivy L. Mumford, 'Musical Settings to the Poems of Sir Thomas Wyatt', *ML*, 37 (1956), 317–20.

16 *The Autobiography of Thomas Whythorne*, ed. James M. Osborn (Oxford: Clarendon Press, 1961), p. 40.

17 Ibid., p. 41.

18 Ibid., p. 54 (my italics).

19 Ibid., p. 55.

20 'Philip Rosseter and his Songs', p. 10.

21 Standard accounts of the medieval garden of love are Ernst Robert Curtius, *European Literature and the Latin Middle Ages*, trans. Willard R. Trask (London: Routledge & Kegan Paul, 1953), pp. 195–200; A. Bartlett Giamatti, *The Earthly Paradise and the Renaissance Epic* (Princeton University Press, 1966), pp. 48–67.

22 *The Poems of Sir Philip Sidney*, ed. William A. Ringler (Oxford: Clarendon Press, 1962), p. 165.

23 *Autobiography*, pp. 232–43.

24 *Of the Laws of Ecclesiastical Politie*, *The Works of Richard Hooker*, Folger Library edn, ed. W. Speed Hill, 4 vols. (Cambridge, Mass.: Harvard University Press, 1977–82), II (1977), 151.

25 *The Essays of Montaigne*, trans. John Florio (1603), 3 vols. (1910; repr. London: Dent, 1928), II, 184.

26 Ibid., 216–17.

27 Ibid., I, 256.

28 Ibid., III, 24.

29 M. M. Knappen, *Tudor Puritanism: A Chapter in the History of Idealism* (University of Chicago Press, 1939), p. 393.

30 Jean Calvin, *The Institution of Christian Religion*, trans. Thomas Norton (London, 1561), fol. 1.

31 Richard F. Jones shows that in this period, 'The idea that truth's appropriate dress is plainness and simplicity, that it needs no ornament but itself, and that a rude and base style which reveals the truth ... is more fitting than eloquent expression, occurs with almost monotonous regularity' ('The Moral Sense of Simplicity' in *Studies in Honour of Frederick W. Shipley*, (Washington University Press, 1942), p. 271.

32 *Hero and Leander*, 1.338, *The Complete Works of Christopher Marlowe*, ed. Fredson Bowers, 2nd edn, 2 vols. (Cambridge University Press, 1981), II, 440.

33 *Autobiography*, p. 65.

34 *Astrophil and Stella*, *The Poems*, ed. Ringler, p. 166.

35 *A Defence of Ryme*, ed. Arthur Colby Sprague (1930; repr. University of Chicago Press, 1965), p. 131.

36 *A Treatie of Humane Learning*, stanza 107, *Poems and Dramas of Fulke Greville*, ed. Geoffrey Bullough, 2 vols. (London: Oliver & Boyd, 1938), I, 180.

37 *I care not for these ladies*, Rosseter's *Booke of Ayres*, Sig. B2ᵛ.

38 *Jordan II*, *The Works of George Herbert*, ed. F. E. Hutchinson (Oxford: Clarendon Press, 1941), p. 102.

39 *The Author to the Critical Peruser, Centuries, Poems and Thanksgivings*, ed. H. M. Margoliouth, 2 vols. (Oxford: Clarendon Press, 1958), II, 2.

40 *The Works of John Dryden*, ed. H. T. Swedenberg Jr, 19 vols. (Berkeley, Los Angeles and London: University of California Press, 1956–84), II (1972), 109.

41 *Astrophil and Stella, The Poems*, ed. Ringler, p. 171.

42 *The Canonization, John Donne: The Elegies and the Songs and Sonnets*, ed. Helen Gardner (Oxford: Clarendon Press, 1965), p. 73.

43 For a conspectus of representative expressions of this view see Anne Ferry, *The 'Inward' Language: Sonnets of Wyatt, Sidney, Shakespeare, Donne* (University of Chicago Press, 1983), p. 259, n. 26.

44 George Puttenham, *The Arte of English Poesie*, ed. Gladys Doidge Willcock and Alice Walker (Cambridge University Press, 1936), p. 45.

45 Francis Meres, *Palladis Tamia* (1598), facsimile edn, with an introduction by Don Cameron Allen (New York: Scholars Facsimiles and Reprints, 1938), fol. 280.

46 Donald L. Guss, *John Donne, Petrarchist* (Detroit: Wayne State University Press, 1966), p. 15.

47 'An Homyly against excesse of Apparell', *The seconde Tome of Homelyes* (London, 1563), fol. 117ᵛ (my italics).

48 Baldassare Castiglione, *The Book of the Courtier*, trans. Sir Thomas Hoby, (London: Dent, 1928), p. 46.

49 *A Defence of Poetry, The Complete Works of Sir Philip Sidney*, ed. Albert Feuillerat, 4 vols. (Cambridge University Press, 1912–26), III (1923), p. 25.

50 *The Book of the Courtier*, p. 99.

51 Ibid., p. 20.

52 John Lyly, *Euphues Glasse for Europe, The Complete Works*, ed. R. Warwick Bond, 3 vols. (Oxford: Clarendon Press, 1902), II, 198.

53 For a discussion of Renaissance courtesy books as manuals of strategic social interaction see Frank Whigham, *Ambition and Privilege: The Social Tropes of Elizabethan Courtesy Theory* (Berkeley, Los Angeles and London: University of California Press, 1984). See also Daniel Javitch, *Poetry and Courtliness in Renaissance England* (Princeton University Press, 1978).

54 'The Metaphysical Poets', *Selected Essays 1917–1932* (London: Faber, 1932), p. 275.

55 *The Arte of Englishe Poesie*, p. 154.

8 DOWLAND, FICINO AND ELIZABETHAN MELANCHOLY

1 In *Englands Eliza* Nicols writes:

> No sooner did this Empires royall crowne
> Begirt the temples of her princelie hed;
> But that *Jove*-born *Astraea* straight came downe
> From highest heaven againe, to which in dread

Of earths unpietie before shee fled:
Well did shee know, *Elizaes* happie reigne
Would then renew the golden age againe.
(Richard Nicols, *Englands Eliza*, printed in *A Mirour for Magistrates*, ed. John Higgins (London, 1610), p. 784).

2 *The First Anniversarie*, lines 205–13, *The Epithalamions, Anniversaries and Epicedes*, ed. W. Milgate (Oxford: Clarendon Press, 1978), p. 27–8.

3 *The Anatomy of Melancholy*, I.ii.10, 3 vols., ed. Thomas C. Faulkner, Nicolas K. Kiessling and Rhonda L. Blair (Oxford: Clarendon Press, 1989–), I, 274.

4 See in particular George Williamson, 'Mutability, Decay, and Seventeenth-Century Melancholy', *ELH*, 2 (1935), 121–50; Lawrence Babb, *The Elizabethan Malady: A Study of Melancholia in English Literature from 1580–1642* (East Lansing: Michigan State University Press, 1951); Herschel Baker, *The Wars of Truth: Studies in the Decay of Christian Humanism in the Earlier Seventeenth Century* (1952; repr. Cambridge, Mass.: Harvard University Press, 1969); Victor Harris, *All Coherence Gone: A Study of the Seventeenth Century Controversy over Disorder and Decay in the Universe* (Chicago University Press, 1949); Raymond Klibansky, Erwin Panofsky and Fritz Saxl, *Saturn and Melancholy: Studies in the History of Natural Philosophy, Religion and Art* (London: Nelson, 1964); Bridget Gellert Lyons, *Voices of Melancholy: Studies in Literary Treatments of Melancholy in Renaissance England* (London: Routledge & Kegan Paul, 1971).

5 John Donne, *The Calme*, line 14, *The Satires, Epigrams and Verse Letters*, ed. W. Milgate (Oxford: Clarendon Press, 1967), p. 58.

6 *A gorgious Gallery of gallant Inuentions* (1578), facsimile edn (Menston: Scolar Press, 1972), Sig. Fi^v.

7 In *The Optick Glasse of Hvmors* (London, 1607) Thomas Walkington describes how the melancholiac will typically withdraw to 'grots, caues, and other hidden celles of the earth' (fol. 68). See also note 72 below.

8 For conventions of the Elizabethan funeral elegy see Dennis Kay, *Melodious Tears: The English Funeral Elegy from Spenser to Milton* (Oxford: Clarendon Press, 1990). See also G. W. Pigman, *Grief and English Renaissance Elegy* (Cambridge University Press, 1985).

9 Anthony Rooley, 'New Light on John Dowland's Songs of Darkness', *EM*, 11 (1983), 153–65.

10 D. P. Walker, *Spiritual and Demonic Magic from Ficino to Campanella* (London: Warburg Institute, 1958), pp. 3–29. See also Paul Oskar Kristeller, *The Philosophy of Marsilio Ficino*, trans. Virginia Conant (New York: Columbia University Press, 1943), p. 308; Walker, *The Ancient Theology: Studies in Christian Platonism from the Fifteenth to the Eighteenth Century* (London: Duckworth, 1972), pp. 24–5.

11 See D. P. Walker, 'Musical Humanism in the 16th and Early 17th Centuries', *MR*, 2 (1941), 1–13, 111–21, 220–7, 288–308; James

Hutton, 'Some English Poems in Praise of Music', *EngM*, 2 (1951), 1–63, repr. in *Essays on Renaissance Poetry*, ed. Rita Guerlac (Ithaca, NY and London: Cornell University Press, 1980), pp. 17–73; Gretchen Ludke Finney, *Musical Backgrounds for English Literature: 1580–1650* (New Brunswick: Rutgers University Press, 1961), pp. 47–68; John Hollander, *The Untuning of the Sky: Ideas of Music in English Poetry 1500–1700* (1961; repr. New York: Norton, 1970), pp. 36–43; 91–122; S. K. Henniger Jr, *Touches of Sweet Harmony: Pythagorean Cosmology and Renaissance Poetics* (San Marino: Huntington Library, 1974), pp. 103–4; Claude V. Palisca, *Humanism in Italian Renaissance Musical Thought* (New Haven, Conn. and London: Yale University Press, 1985), pp. 161–90, 407.

12 Marsilio Ficino, *In Plotinum commentaria, Opera Omnia* (Basle, 1576), p. 1746, quoted and trans. Walker, *Spiritual and Demonic Magic*, p. 23.

13 Ficino, *De viia coelitus comparanda, Opera*, p. 562, quoted and trans. Walker, *Spiritual and Demonic Magic*, p. 16.

14 Walker, *Spiritual and Demonic Magic*, p. 4.

15 A classical medieval view of Saturn is contained in the following lines (2456–69) from Chaucer's *Knight's Tale*:

> Myn is the drenchyng in the see so wan;
> Myn is the prison in the derke cote;
> Myn is the stranglyng and hangyng by the throte,
> The murmure and the cherles rebellyng,
> The groynyng, and the pryvee empoysonyng ...
>
> And myne be the maladyes colde,
> The derke tresons, and the castes olde;
> My lookyng is the fader of pestilence.
>
> (*The Works of Geoffrey Chaucer*, ed. F. N. Robinson, 2nd edn (London:
> Oxford University Press, 1957), p. 41).

16 Rooley, 'New Light on John Dowland's Songs of Darkness', p. 19.

17 On magic and occultism in the Renaissance in general see Lynn Thorndike, *A History of Magic and Experimental Science*, 8 vols. (New York: Columbia University Press, 1923–58) v (1941), 127–8, vi (1941), 390–465; D. P. Walker, *Spiritual and Demonic Magic and The Ancient Theology*; Wayne Shumaker, *The Occult Sciences in the Renaissance: A Study in Intellectual Patterns* (Berkeley, Los Angeles and London: University of California Press, 1972); Robert S. Westman, 'Magical Reform and Astronomical Reform: The Yates Thesis Reconsidered' in Robert S. Westman and J. E. McGuire, *Hermeticism and the Scientific Revolution* (Los Angeles: Clark Memorial Library, 1977), pp. 1–91.

On the currency of occult studies in Renaissance England see Don Cameron Allen, *The Star-Crossed Renaissance: The Quarrel about Astrology and its Influence in England* (Durham NC: Duke University Press, 1941); Frances A. Yates, *Giordano Bruno and the Hermetic Tradition* (London: Routledge & Kegan Paul, 1964), chaps. 12–13; Yates 'The Hermetic Tradition in Renaissance Science' in *Art, Science and History in the*

Renaissance, ed. Charles S. Singleton (Baltimore: Johns Hopkins University Press, 1967), pp. 255–74; Yates, *The Occult Philosophy in the Elizabethan Age* (London, Boston and Henley: Routledge & Kegan Paul, 1979); Keith Thomas, *Religion and the Decline of Magic: Studies in Popular Beliefs in Sixteenth and Seventeenth-Century England* (London: Weidenfeld & Nicolson, 1971), chaps. 9–12; Eluned Crawshaw, 'Hermetic Elements in Donne's Poetic Vision' in *John Donne: Essays in Celebration*, ed. A. J. Smith (London: Methuen, 1972), pp. 324–48; Peter J. French, *John Dee: The World of an Elizabethan Magus* (London: Routledge & Kegan Paul, 1972); Charles B. Schmitt, 'Philosophy and Science in Sixteenth-Century Universities' in *The Cultural Context of Medieval Learning*, ed. John Emery Murdoch and Edith Dudley Sylla (Dordrecht: Reidel, 1975), pp. 485–530; J. E. McGuire, 'Neoplatonism and Active Principles: Newton and the *Corpus Hermeticum*' in Westman and McGuire, *Hermeticism and the Scientific Revolution*, pp. 95–142; Mordechai Feingold, 'The Occult Tradition in the English Universities of the Renaissance' in *Occult and Scientific Mentalities in the Renaissance*, ed. Brian Vickers (Cambridge University Press, 1984), pp. 73–94; Brian Vickers, 'Analogy versus Identity: The Rejection of Occult Symbolism, 1580–1680', in *Occult and Scientific Mentalities*, pp. 95–163; G. J. R. Parry, *A Protestant Vision: William Harris and the Reformation of Elizabethan England* (Cambridge University Press, 1987), pp. 303–4.

18 Chapman's words are from the dedication to *Ovid's Banquet of Sence* (1595), *The Poems of George Chapman*, ed. Phyllis Brooks Bartlett (New York: Russell & Russell, 1962), p. 49.

19 For Millar MacLure, Chapman exemplifies 'the appalling eclectism and imprecision of the most unphilosophical of philosophical movements, which sought wisdom and became contented with rhetoric' (*George Chapman: A Critical Study* (University of Toronto Press, 1960), p. 32).

20 *The Occult Philosophy*, p. 144.

21 Ibid., p. 131.

22 James Hutton, 'Some English Poems in Praise of Music' in *Essays on Renaissance Poetry*, pp. 17–73.

23 *The Occult Philosophy*, p. 96.

24 Feingold, 'The Occult Tradition in the English Universities', pp. 73–94.

25 Parry, *A Protestant Vision*, pp. 303–4.

26 Ibid., p. 304.

27 *The Occult Sciences in the Renaissance*, p. 246.

28 Ibid., p. 236.

29 'New Light on John Dowland's Songs of Darkness', p. 9.

30 Ibid., pp. 12, 19.

31 Ibid., p. 13.

32 See M. C. Bradbrook, *The School of Night: A Study in the Literary*

Relationships of Sir Walter Ralegh (Cambridge University Press, 1936); see also Frances A. Yates, *A Study of 'Love's Labours Lost'* (Cambridge University Press, 1936).

33 Yates, *The Occult Philosophy*, p. 75.

34 According to Babb, the Elizabethan attitude towards melancholy was, in general, 'definitely one of respect' (*The Elizabethan Malady*, p. 180). However, negative representation of the melancholiac in expository physiological treatises and of the malcontent in satirical literature casts some doubt on this conclusion.

35 John Gower, *Confessio Amantis*, VII.404, *The Complete Works of John Gower*, ed. G. C. Macaulay, 4 vols. (Oxford: Clarendon Press, 1899–1902), III (1901), 244.

36 *The Diall of Destiny* (London, 1581), fols. 62–3.

37 *Spiritual and Demonic Magic*, p. 21; cf. Walker, *The Ancient Theology*, pp. 24–5.

38 Lyons notes that Elizabethan physiologists claim that black bile produces dreams and visions connected with death and evil spirits, with night and with graveyards, and with the animals and plants associated with these places, especially bats, owls, yews and cypresses (*Voices of Melancholy*, p. 44).

39 *Hvmor say what mak'st thou heere*, John Dowland, *Second Booke of Songs* (London, 1600), Sig. N.

40 Philip Brett, 'The English Consort Song 1570–1625', *PRMA*, 88 (1961–62), 73–88; Joseph Kerman, 'England: 1540–1610' in *Music from the Middle Ages to the Renaissance*, ed. F. W. Sternfeld (London: Weidenfeld & Nicolson, 1973), pp. 315–41.

41 Sir Thomas More, *Utopia*, trans. Raphe Robinson (1551) (1910; repr. London: Dent, 1918), p. 110.

42 Although rhetoric books underwent a radical transformation in the sixteenth century, utilitarian treatises continued to be produced until the end of the century, as the subtitle of Angel Day's *The English Secretary* (1599) indicates: *Methods of Writing Epistles and Letters with a Declaration of such Tropes, Figures, and Schemes, as either usually or for ornament sake are therein required.*

43 Richard Sherry, *A Treatise of Schemes and Tropes*, facsimile reproduction with an introduction by Herbert W. Hildebrandt (Gainesville, Fla.: Scholars Facsimiles & Reprints, 1961), p. 7.

44 See Introduction, note 14.

45 Henry Peacham the Elder, *The Garden of Eloquence*, facsimile reproduction of 1577 edn (Menston: Scolar Press, 1971), Sig. Aiii.

46 George Puttenham, *The Arte of English Poesie*, ed. Gladys Doidge Willcock and Alice Walker (Cambridge University Press, 1936), p. 4.

47 Ibid., p. 159.

48 Ibid., p. 154.

49 Ibid., p. 45.

50 Ibid., p. 45.

51 *Tamburlaine the Great*, Part I, Prol. 1, *The Complete Works of Christopher Marlowe*, ed. Fredson Bowers, 2nd edn, 2 vols. (Cambridge University Press, 1981), I, 79.

52 Thomas Morley, *A Plain and Easy Introduction to Practical Music* (London, 1597), p. 177.

53 A long and more or less continuous tradition of debate on the pleasures and dangers of melancholy stretches from the Middle English *Owl and the Nightingale* to Milton's *L'Allegro* and *Il Penseroso* and beyond. Defence of one position or another is not necessarily an indication of personal commitment on the poet's part. On the forensic element in English Renaissance drama see Joel B. Altman, *The Tudor Play of Mind: Rhetorical Inquiry and the Development of Elizabethan Drama* (Berkeley, Los Angeles and London: University of California Press, 1978).

54 Antony Easthope, *Poetry as Discourse*, Methuen New Accents (London: Methuen, 1983), p. 95 (see Introduction, p. 18).

55 Baldassare Castiglione, *The Book of the Courtier*, trans. Sir Thomas Hoby (London: Dent, 1928), p. 61.

56 *The Arte of English Poesie*, p. 47.

57 Dedication to *Lachrimae, or Seaven Teares Figures in Seaven Passionate Pavans* (London, 1604–5).

58 Bruce Pattison, *Music and Poetry of the English Renaissance*, 2nd edn (London: Methuen, 1970), pp. 109–10.

59 Ibid., p. 101.

60 Susan McClary, 'The Blasphemy of Talking Politics during the Bach Year' in *Music and Society: the Politics of Composition, Performance and Reception* ed. Richard Leppert and McClary, (Cambridge University Press, 1987), p. 19.

61 Ibid., p. 18.

62 *John Dowland*, 2nd edn (London: Faber, 1982), p. 319. Poulton draws attention to the parallels between *In darknesse let me dwell* and *Flow my teares* and *Mourne, day is with darkness fled* (p. 256).

63 Thomas Nashe, prefatory epistle to pirated edn of *Astrophil and Stella* (1591), *The Works of Thomas Nashe*, ed. Ronald B. McKerrow, 5 vols. (Oxford: Blackwell, 1958), III, 329.

64 Dedicatory sonnet by 'G.W.', *The Poetical Works*, ed. Smith and de Selincourt, p. 562.

65 *The Arte of English Poesie*, p. 138.

66 *Certayne notes of Instruction concerning the making of verse or ryme in English*, *The Complete Works of George Gascoigne*, ed. John W. Cunliffe, 2 vols. (Cambridge University Press, 1907–10), I (1907), 465.

67 *Sonnets from the Portuguese*, no. 30, *The Poetical Works of Elizabeth Barrett Browning* (London, Oxford University Press, 1908), p. 324.

68 *Certayne notes of Instruction*, pp. 465–6.

69 On the thematic relation between these two songs see Daniel Leech-

Wilkinson, 'My Lady's Tears: a Pair of Songs by John Dowland', *EM*, 19 (1991), 227–33.

70 Surrey's *Set Me Wheras the Sonne Dothe Perche the Grene* is a translation of Petrarch's *Pommi ore 'l sole occide i fiori e l'erbe* (*In Vita*, 145. Cf. Horace's *Integer vitae sclerisque purus* (*Odes*, 1.xxii) which contains the lines 'pone me pigris ubi nulla campis / arbor aestiva recreatur aura, / quod latus mundi nebulae malusque / Iuppiter urget'.

71 'New Light on John Dowland's Songs of Darkness', p. 17.

72 *Metamorphoses*, VI.431–2, ed. Frank Justus Miller, Loeb Classical Library, 2 vols. (London: Heinemann, 1916), I, 319.

73 Sir John Hawkins, *A General History of the Science and Practice of Music* (1776), with an introduction by Charles Cudworth, 2 vols. (New York: Dover, 1963), I, 62.

74 Henry Peacham the Elder, *The Garden of Eloquence*, facsimile reproduction of 1593 edn with an introduction by William G. Crane (Gainesvile, Fla.: Scholars' Facsimiles and Reprints, 1954), p. 144.

75 Richard Barnfield, *If Musique and sweet Poetrie agree, The Complete Poems*, ed. George Klawitter (Selinsgrove: Susquehanna University Press, 1990), p. 181.

76 Henry Peacham the Younger, *Peacham's Complete Gentleman* (1634), with an introduction by G. S. Gordon, Tudor and Stuart Library (Oxford: Clarendon Press, 1906), p. 103.

9 'YDLE SHALLOWE THINGS': LOVE AND SONG IN *TWELFTH NIGHT*

1 On the association of *Venus vulgaris* with the melody of the flesh see D. W. Robertson Jr, *A Preface to Chaucer: Studies in Medieval Perspectives* (1962; repr. London, 1967), pp. 96–8.

2 Howard R. Patch, *The Goddess Fortuna in Medieval Literature* (1927; repr. London: Cass, 1967), pp. 96–8.

3 On the conception, birth and character of Jocus see Alain de Lille, *The Plaint of Nature*, Prose 5, trans. and ed. James J. Sheridan (Toronto: Pontifical Institute of Medieval Studies, 1980), p. 164.

4 See chapter 6 note 47.

5 G. Wilson Knight, *The Shakespearean Tempest* (1932; 3rd edn London: Methuen, 1953), pp. 126–7.

6 John Hollander, *The Untuning of the Sky: Ideas of Music in English Poetry 1500–1700* (1961; repr. New York: Norton, 1970), p. 155.

7 Clifford Leech, *'Twelfth Night' and Shakespearean Comedy* (Toronto University Press, 1965), p. 55.

8 Leo Salingar, 'The Design of *Twelfth Night*', *SQ*, 9 (1958), 117–39, repr. in *Dramatic Form in Shakespeare and the Jacobeans* (Cambridge University Press, 1986), p. 72.

9 Nevill Coghill, 'The Basis of Shakespearian Comedy' *EStud*, 36 (1950), p. 13.

10 *The Secrets of Numbers* (London, 1624), p. 2.

11 See John Hollander, *The Untuning of the Sky*.

12 Edward E. Lowinsky, 'The Musical Avant-Garde of the Renaissance' in *Art, Science and History in the Renaissance*, ed. Charles S. Singleton (Baltimore: Johns Hopkins University Press, 1967), p. 116.

13 *Odyssey*, IV.561ff. Spenser gives an imaginary account of the music of Elysium in *The Ruines of Time*, 330ff.

14 Although critics of *Twelfth Night* are more or less evenly divided between those who believe that the characters 'learn nothing from their experience' (Herschel Baker, Introduction to Signet Classic edn of the play (New York: New American Library, 1963), p. xxx) and those who believe that the characters 'have learnt a new attitude to others and to themselves' (Harold Jenkins, 'Shakespeare's *Twelfth Night*', Rice Institute Pamphlet, 45 (1959), repr. in *Shakespeare: The Comedies*, ed. Kenneth Muir (Englewood Cliffs: Prentice-Hall, 1965), p. 73), there is general agreement that *Twelfth Night* is about deception and self-deception. Joseph H. Summers, for example, argues that most of the characters in the play 'know neither themselves, nor others, nor their social world' ('The Masks of *Twelfth Night*', *UR*, 22 (1955), repr. in *'Twelfth Night': A Casebook*, ed. D. J. Palmer (London: Macmillan, 1972), p. 87), while Ralph Berry claims that 'the main business of *Twelfth Night* is illusion, error, and deceit' (*Shakespeare's Comedies: Explorations in Form* (Princeton University Press, 1972), p. 199).

15 *The Works of Geoffrey Chaucer*, ed. F. N. Robinson, 2nd edn (Oxford University Press, 1957), p. 401.

16 Quotations from the *Roman de la Rose* are from Chaucer's translation, ed. Robinson.

17 *The Poems of Sir Philip Sidney*, edited by William A. Ringler, Jr (Oxford: Clarendon Press, 1962), p. 237.

18 *The Poems and Letters of Andrew Marvell*, 2 vols., ed H. M. Margoliouth, 3rd edn rev. Pierre Legouis and E. E. Duncan-Jones (Oxford: Clarendon Press, 1971), I, 39.

19 See, for example, Boccaccio's gloss on the Temple of Venus in the *Teseida*, VII.50–66, extracted and trans. Robert P. Miller, *Chaucer: Sources and Backgrounds* (New York: Oxford University Press, 1977), pp. 336–43.

20 In Chaucer's *Parlement of Foulys* 'Richesse' is Venus' porter.

21 Describing the social world of the Elizabethan great house, Lawrence Stone writes: 'Here, and here alone, well-born young persons of both sexes were thrown together away from parental supervision and in a situation of considerable freedom … They also had a great deal of leisure, and in the enclosed hot-house atmosphere of these great houses, love intrigues flourished as nowhere else' (*The Family, Sex and Marriage in England: 1500–1800* (New York: Harper & Row, 1977), pp. 103–4).

22 W. H. Auden writes: 'Beside [Orsino] sits the disguised Viola, for whom

the Duke is not a playful fancy, but a serious passion. It would be painful enough for her if the man she loved really loved another, but it is much worse to be made to see that he only loves himself, and it is this insight which at this point Viola has to endure' ('Music in Shakespeare' in *The Dyer's Hand* (1948; repr. London: Faber, 1963), p. 522).

23 Gloss to *Teseida*, VII, in Miller, *Chaucer: Sources and Backgrounds*, p. 340.

24 *Romaunt of the Rose*, ed. Robinson, 2258–9.

25 Robert Jones, *The First Booke of Songes and Ayres* (London, 1600), Sigs. D4ᵛ–EI.

26 Elizabeth M. Yearling, 'Language, Theme and Character in *Twelfth Night*', *ShS*, 35 (1982), 84.

27 John Robert Moore, 'The Function of Songs in Shakespeare's Plays' in *Shakespeare Studies by the Members of the Department of English at the University of Wisconsin* (Madison, Wis.: University of Wisconsin Press, 1916), p. 85.

28 *The Poems of Thomas Carew*, edited by Arthur Vincent (London: Lawrence & Bullen, 1899), p. 3.

29 John Donne, *The Calme, The Satires, Epigrams and Verse Letters*, ed. W. Milgate (Oxford: Clarendon Press, 1967), p. 58.

30 *Andreas Capellanus on Love*, trans. and ed. P. G. Walsh (London: Duckworth, 1982), p. 233.

31 *The Arte of English Poesie*, ed. Gladys Doidge Willcock and Alice Walker (Cambridge University Press, 1936), p. 91.

32 *The Owl and the Nightingale*, edited by Eric Gerald Stanley (London: Nelson, 1960), p. 91.

CODA: *FLOREAT ORPHEUS*

1 George Puttenham, *The Arte of English Poesie*, ed. Gladys Doidge Willcock and Alice Walker (Cambridge University Press, 1936), p. 3.

2 Ibid.

3 Ibid., pp. 8–9.

4 Ibid., p. 3. Puttenham argues that the poet 'is both a maker and a counterfaitor: and Poesie an art not only of making, but also of imitation' (p. 3).

5 On essentialism, atomism and human nature see Scott Meikle, *Essentialism in the Thought of Karl Marx* (London; Duckworth, 1985), pp. 154ff.

6 *The Rambler, The Works of Samuel Johnson*, Yale edn, 15 vols. (New Haven, Conn. and London: Yale University Press and Oxford University Press, 1958–   ), IV (ed. W. J. Bate and Albrecht B. Strauss, 1969), 120.

7 *Critical Practice* (London and New York: Methuen, 1980), pp. 144–5.

8 *Meaning by Shakespeare* (London and New York: Methuen, 1992), pp. 1–10.

9 Raymond Williams, 'Base and Superstructure in Marxist Cultural

Theory', *NLR* 82 (1973); repr. in *Problems in Materialism and Culture* (London: Verso, 1980), p. 44.

10 Introduction to *Political Shakespeare: New Essays in Cultural Materialism*, ed. Jonathan Dollimore and Alan Sinfield (Manchester University Press, 1985), p. 4.

11 Louis Montrose, 'Renaissance Literary Studies and the Subject of History', *ELR*, 16 (1986), 6.

12 James Winny, *The Frame of Order* (London: Allen & Unwin, 1957), p. 9.

13 Catherine Belsey, 'Tragedy, Justice and the Subject' in *1642: Literature and Power in the Seventeenth Century*, ed. Francis Barker *et al.* (Colchester: University of Essex Press, 1981), p. 169.

14 Leonard Tennenhouse, *Power on Display: the Politics of Shakespeare's Genres* (New York and London: Methuen, 1986), pp. 14–15.

15 Jean E. Howard, 'The New Historicism in Renaissance Studies', *ELR*, 16 (1986), 42.

16 John R. Searle, 'The World Turned Upside Down', review article, *NYRB*, 27 October 1983, p. 78.

17 Recent discussions of the philosophical questions involved in the post-structuralist critique of 'literature' include Raymond Tallis, *Not Saussure: A Critique of Post-Saussurean Literary Theory* (Houndmills: Macmillan, 1988) and Richard Freadman and Seumas Miller, *Re-Thinking Theory: A Critique of Contemporary Literary Theory and an Alternative Account* (Cambridge University Press, 1992).

18 Jonathan Dollimore, Introduction to *Political Shakespeare*, p. 5.

19 *The Counter-Renaissance* (1950; repr. New York: Grove Press, 1960), p. 4.

20 *The Business of Criticism* (Oxford: Clarendon Press, 1959), p. 34.

21 'The New Historicism in Renaissance Studies', p. 43.

22 *The Business of Criticism*, p. 32.

23 'The New Historicism in Renaissance Studies', p. 43.

24 *The Business of Criticism*, p. 51.

25 'The New Historicism in Renaissance Studies', p. 43.

26 *The History of Rasselas, Prince of Abyssinia* (1930; repr. London: Dent, 1961), p. 57.

27 *The Counter-Renaissance*, p. 7.

28 Stephen Greenblatt, *Shakespearean Negotiations: The Circulation of Social Energy in Renaissance England* (Oxford: Clarendon Press, 1988), p. 4.

29 In *From Divine Cosmos to Sovereign State* Collins argues that in the early seventeenth century thinkers were becoming increasingly conscious of the role played by ideology in the construction of ideas of social order: 'Order was coming to be understood not as natural, but as artificial, created by man, and manifestly political and social' (p. 28).

Index